TOO MANY MEN ON THE ICE

Women's Hockey In North America

JOANNA AVERY & JULIE STEVENS

POLESTAR
BOOK PUBLISHERS

Polestar Book Publishers acknowledges the ongoing support of The Canada Council,
the British Columbia Ministry of Small Business, Tourism and Culture, and the
Department of Canadian Heritage.

Edited by Suzanne Bastedo
Cover design by Jim Brennan
Cover photo by Mike Reynolds/Freestyle Photography
Printed and bound in Canada

Canadian Cataloguing in Publication Data
Stevens, Julie Anne, 1966-
      Too many men on the ice
      ISBN 1-896095-33-X

      1. Hockey for women — History. 2. Women hockey players — Biography. I.
Avery, Joanna. II. Title.
GV848.6.W6S73 1997   796.962'.082 C97-910813-6

Library of Congress Card Catalog Number: 97-80432

If your team or organization is interested in using this or another Polestar book as a
fundraiser, contact the promotions office in Vancouver (see back page).

Polestar Book Publishers
P.O. Box 5238, Station B
Victoria, British Columbia
Canada   V8R 6N4
http://mypage.direct.ca/p/polestar/

In the United States:
Polestar Book Publishers
P.O. Box 468
Custer, WA
USA   98240-0468

For TD, whose unconditional love and support I cherish; DRM and PFM, for allowing me the time to do this project; and all the women and girls who play the great sport of hockey.

— JLA

For Ron, whose passion for hockey encouraged me to write this book, and whose love and support helped me finish it.

— JAS

CONTENTS

FOREWORD

In 1991, women's hockey appeared on the program of the Canada Winter Games for the first time. I had just started a new job at the Canadian Hockey Association (CHA) and these games were my first event. During the week of the games, I toured the length and breadth of Prince Edward Island, witnessing a frenzy of support for women's hockey. Nowhere was this support more fervent than at the hockey rinks. For the first time, I saw the potential of the Canadian women's National Team to inspire girls to dream of playing hockey. I recall one rally of the 10 provincial teams in a local school auditorium. After the introductory speeches, we showed a video of the 1990 World Championship. Then, with the noise level already rising, we introduced members of that National Team. The auditorium erupted into thunderous applause, cheers and whistles. France St. Louis, assistant coach for Team Quebec, asked the group: "Who would like to play for Canada one day?" And 200 teenage girls screamed at the top of their lungs, "Me! I would!"

While we were in PEI, the CHA taped television interviews with some of the original Charlottetown Abbie Sisters, one of whom, at the age of 84, declared, "I would rather skate than eat!" In the same clip, a very young member of the Quebec team (who was later called to try out for Canada's Olympic team) burst out with youthful bravado: "I am going to skate until the day I die!" *Too Many Men on the Ice* fills the gap between the generations, giving us a practical overview of the development of the game, but never straying far from the passion shared by these two women — and an ever increasing number of women hockey players.

Women's hockey is one of sport's best kept secrets. Women have played the game for well over 100 years in almost total obscurity. Much of this rich history has already been lost. Today, as women's hockey experiences a tumultous, critical period in its evolution, a book like *Too Many Men on the Ice* becomes all the more important. Julie Stevens and Joanna Avery have taken on the daunting tasks of sharing the rich history of women's hockey in North America, and navigating the exciting new world of women's hockey — a world that has expanded rapidly over the last decade with the advent of high-performance programs. They remind us that we must chronicle our history and today's new period of growth, knowing that we are at a watershed in the game. And we must bequeath our history and our experience to our daughters.

It has often been said that women's hockey has developed in the shape of an "upsidedown pyramid" — that there are many skilled older players, and relatively few young ones. Over the last 10 years this has certainly been true, but our history — and the history of individual players — tells a more complex story. The authors of this book look closely at the lives of several National Team players from both Canada and the United States, showing their very different routes towards hockey careers. As readers, we are forced to ask ourselves: How has women's hockey really grown? Research by Avery and Stevens shows that it has evolved in a very ad hoc fashion indeed. They conclude that our challenge today is to shape this game in a way that preserves its unique character and captivating soul.

I have the privilege of being part of the development of women's hockey from day to day. I ask myself many of the questions posed by the authors and players in *Too Many Men on the Ice* and I often long for a crystal ball to reveal the shape of women's hockey in the future. Across North America, those of us who are involved at all levels of the game would do well to read these pages and reflect upon their rich treasure trove of information, looking for help with policy making, promotion, and development initiatives.

It is clear that the decisions we make now will determine the face of women's hockey in the next millenium. As I write this, I glance toward the bookshelf in my office and see row upon row of books on hockey — men's hockey. Someday soon, I will need a reference and will stroll to the shelves, still stacked with books on hockey — but this time, women's hockey. One of the first among them will be *Too Many Men on the Ice*.

Glynis Peters
Manager, Women's Programs
Canadian Hockey Association

PREFACE

They are out there. They can be heard cheering on their favourite players, debating some of the finer points of the game with the coach and suggesting that referees invest in a pair of corrective lenses. They are the female spectators at hockey games, and they constitute 41 percent of the paying and viewing audience. Some may arrive at the rink only to admire Brett Hull or Geraldine Heaney, but most leave the rink awed by the fluid skating, superb stickhandling and acrobatic saves many of the players demonstrated. Indeed, an increasing number of women want to learn those skills, skate stride for stride in pursuit of a loose puck, stickhandle their way through traffic and pop one in on the top shelf, or deflect the puck with the blocker to save the game.

Too Many Men on the Ice: Women's Hockey in North America is about these women who love the game for its competitiveness, its gracefulness, its speed and its action. It will explore the women's game of yesterday and today, including the opportunities available for women on and off the ice, and profile some of the women who play and support hockey.

Although the authors of this book come from distinctively different backgrounds, they share a common love for hockey. Joanna Avery's involvement with women's hockey began only a few years ago. Always a fan of the game, she grew up in a small town in New Hampshire in front of the television set watching the Big Bad Boston Bruins. She admired the skill and speed of the players in the National Hockey League and dismissed nearly every other type of hockey as inferior. It was not until January 1997 that she witnessed a US women's varsity college game and a Canadian women's senior AA game. These games reaffirmed a commitment she had made in 1994 to let it be known that women can play hockey — an exciting, clean and fun brand of hockey that would make anyone want to lace up the skates, grab a stick and join them on the ice.

Avery graduated from the University of Massachusetts at Amherst in 1990 with a degree in journalism and continued to stay close to the game of hockey by writing freelance articles for *Hat Trick* magazine, covering the Boston Bruins. In 1993 she graduated from broadcasting school and landed a job at a talk radio station in Worcester, Massachusetts. The next year the American Hockey League added a franchise in Worcester, the Worcester Ice Cats, and Avery became the beat reporter of the team for the radio station. By interviewing players, she heard stories about junior and semi-professional hockey and within a few months she had a new-found respect for all levels of the game.

In 1994, while reading an article in the subway about Manon Rhéaume (the first woman to play in the NHL), Avery realized that women could play hockey on more than a recreational level. Her interest was piqued and she wanted to learn more. With a little research she uncovered a whole network of girls and women playing hockey, from grassroots community clubs to women's national teams to three women playing in professional men's leagues. It was then she realized the story had to be told. She volunteered with the local girls' youth hockey program, helping to teach squirts (the beginners in girls' hockey) how to play the game, and continued to learn about and talk with interesting women who loved to play the game. While researching at the Hockey Hall of Fame in Toronto, Avery discovered a master's thesis on women's hockey written by Julie Stevens in 1992. Realizing that writing about hockey history and players from two countries was a formidable task, Avery contacted Stevens and asked if she wanted to collaborate on telling the story of US and Canadian women's hockey. A partnership was born.

Julie Stevens has been a hockey nut for as long as she can remember. She grew up in rural Ontario in Erin and Belfountain, two small towns about six miles apart. She first learned to play hockey by going to the open learn-to-play sessions every Saturday morning at the old Erin arena. Every night, she would head down the street to join the neighbourhood road-hockey game. She first started playing organized hockey with peewee boys and then moved into girls' hockey with a bantam team in Orangeville. From there she played in the Brampton Canadettes organization and then went into womens' senior hockey with the Caledon Queens. Stevens finished her competitive hockey years playing on the varsity team at Queen's University in Kingston, Ontario, where she won all-star, most valuable player, top scorer and Queen's University athletic honours. She now coaches girls at midget level and plays recreational hockey in Edmonton, Alberta.

Stevens has two vivid hockey memories. The first was in 1972. She was in her Grade One classroom watching the final Canada-Russia game when Paul Henderson scored the winning goal to give Canada the edge over the Russians.

She can remember the excitement as all the children came running out of the school yelling and cheering. Then, 18 years later, she was at the Ottawa Civic Centre to see Canada come from behind to win the gold medal over the United States at the first Women's World Ice Hockey Championship. When Geraldine Heaney scored the goal that clinched the gold medal for Canada, Stevens felt the same excitement she had experienced when she jumped out of her seat to cheer in 1972.

These two special moments show the two sides of Stevens' love for hockey — she has enjoyed watching the National Hockey League and Canada Cup games, but women's hockey has always been her true love and interest. Once Stevens began university, she transferred this interest in women's hockey towards her scholarly work. She completed a Bachelor of Physical and Health Education and a Master of Arts in Sport Sociology at Queen's University. She is currently enrolled in a doctoral program in Organizational Analysis and Sport Studies in the Faculty of Physical Education and Recreation at the University of Alberta in Edmonton. Her research focuses on the history, development and structure of women's and men's hockey in Canada and abroad.

For Stevens, this book represents the culmination of a process that began as a youngster when she first learned the game and enjoyed every moment that skates were on her feet. Her academic studies, however, have given her a new perspective on the sport of hockey — one that is more critical and less reminiscent. As a player, she experiences the camaraderie, fair play and enjoyment of the game. As an academic, she realizes these benefits are not available to every girl and woman in North America.

ACKNOWLEDGEMENTS

The task of writing a book cannot be truly understood until one spends endless hours researching, interviewing, writing and obtaining a publisher. We are grateful to all those whose expertise and experiences in women's hockey have turned the idea of a book into a reality.

We would like to thank Polestar Book Publishers — specifically, our publisher, Michelle Benjamin, and our marketing and promotions manager, Emiko Morita, for believing in us and our project. We also greatly appreciate the interest and effort of our editor, Suzanne Bastedo.

Joanna Avery would like to thank Kelly Dyer for sharing her time and stories, and the many men and women who have contributed to women's hockey, including Kris Pleimann at USA Hockey, Julie Andeberhan, Julia Ashmun, Joe Bertagna, Karyn Bye, Peggy Cunha, Maria Dennis, Tony Dennis, Shirley Fischler, Cammi Granato, Carl Gray, Zoe Harris and Cindy Daley, Laura Halldorson, Hudson Nighthawks girls' hockey, Jackie Isaacs, Karen Kay, Tony Marmo, Fred Miller, Lynn Olson, Ben Smith, Syrilyn Tong, Ellen Weinberg and Mitzi Witchger.

Julie Stevens would like to thank each of the women who took the time to share their thoughts and ideas with her: Shirley Cameron, Danielle Dubé, Judy Diduck, Angela James, Karen Kost, Dawn MacGuire, Glynis Peters and Jane Robinson. She would also like to thank John MacKinnon, Communications Director at the Canadian Hockey Association, for his help obtaining information and Jan Harris for transcribing all the colourful stories.

Since writing is such a personal business, we also thank the many friends and relatives who have supported and assisted us along the way.

Joanna Avery would like to thank Bill Keevan for believing in her in the beginning, when the task seemed insurmountable, Marie Caci for lending a hand at the last minute, and everyone who was willing — and sometimes eager — to read and critique the many chapter drafts.

Julie Stevens would like to thank her family for their support as she embarked on this exciting project. Specifically, she is grateful to her mother, Sharon, father, Ron, and sisters, Robyn and Suzanne, for their support in everthing she does — whether in hockey or academics.

INTRODUCTION

In *Too Many Men On The Ice: Women's Hockey in North America*, we analyze the people, organizations and circumstances that have increased awareness of, and participation in, women's hockey to record levels. We detail various components of the women's game, including the history and development of women's hockey in the US and Canada. Focusing on these two countries allows us to conduct a comparative review of the social, legal and historical factors which have influenced female hockey within each country and how these factors have resulted in different forms of development.

The distinction between men's hockey and women's hockey, and the effects of this distinction on women's hockey, is a common theme throughout this book. Through interviews, we look at the women who play on women's national teams and at the recreational level. We also take a critical view of the growth and development of female hockey in order to reflect upon the impact of various differences and similarities in the US and Canada.

We begin this book with a look at the state of women's hockey at the international level, and include lists of Canadian and US national team rosters. These rosters form the first compilation of its kind in one book, and provide a much-needed first step in building a historical reference for women in hockey.

Next, we chronicle the history of women's hockey in Canada and the US. We show that although women have been playing hockey for over 100 years, they have endured many hardships and struggles and still must overcome obstacles today. Legal challenges have faced female hockey players from the 1950s to today. Girls had been denied access to boy's hockey in schools for decades until, in 1972, Title IX legislation in the US opened the doors for equal athletics for girls and women in that country. In Canada, lawsuits in the 1970s and 1980s allowed girls to legally skate alongside the boys. In addition, we study organized hockey systems, particularly at the grassroots level, to identify women's roles and opportunities within the amateur hockey structure.

Next, in order to illustrate the difference in women's hockey structures in Canada and the US, we look at the Canadian and US national teams — their development, their current structures and their courses of action for the future —

and we recount the careers of two national team players, Kelly Dyer and Angela James. There are so many outstanding female players in the US and Canada, it was difficult to pick just two for the detailed profiles. We have chosen players who have experienced as many different facets and levels of women's hockey as possible. At the same time, we wanted to clearly depict the differences in grass-roots structures and opportunities between the two countries. Kelly Dyer tended goal for the US women's national team in the 1990, 1992 and 1994 World Championships and in two Pacific Rim Tournaments. She grew up playing hockey on an all-girls team in an all-girls league. She backstopped her women's varsity college team to two conference titles. She then switched to the men's team because the level of competition among senior women's teams was not high enough, and played semi-professional men's hockey in two leagues. Angela James, a Canadian women's national team centre since 1990, began her career on a boys' team. James excelled and became a top player on her team, but switched over to girls' hockey at age 10 to play in a Catholic church house league. After a few years with the house league she moved on to a senior C women's team. A year later she was playing with a senior AA team, the top level in women's hockey at the time, and continued in that league through college and beyond.

In the final chapter of this book, we discuss how the women's game is distinct from the men's and whether a women's professional league can survive. We also explore other opportunities available to women in hockey, such as coaching, refereeing and administrative positions.

The use of quotes throughout the book reflects a conscious decision by the authors to let the women involved in hockey tell their own stories. Unless otherwise noted, Avery and Stevens conducted all the interviews in this book. Stevens conducted the Canadian interviews in person, and Avery conducted the US interviews either in person or by telephone. Certain standard questions were asked of each interviewee — for example, Where did you play? How old were you when you first started playing? and How did you first get involved? Once the basic information was established, and the interviewees had related their stories, we asked for their opinions on specific topics covered in the book — such as how the women's game is distinct and whether a women's professional league is viable. Questions pertained closely to the interviewee's experiences with hockey and did not cover any aspect of their personal lives unless it had a significant bearing on their hockey experiences.

When the research process began, Avery's experience with women's hockey was limited, as was her list of contacts. She volunteered with a girls' squirt team in 1995, and began talking with the coaches, who were former girls' hockey players themselves. They suggested the names of people involved with women's hockey, who in turn provided more names, and every interview ended with a list of more people to contact. Stevens, on the other hand, had grown up playing hockey and now coaches a midget girls' team. Her personal contacts within the hockey community, developed over years of research in women's hockey, led her to a wide variety of female players, coaches, officials, volunteer administrators, and professional managers. This book also includes information gathered during the past eight years of Stevens' academic career. During this time she has studied the history, structure and development of women's hockey in Canada. Her work involves ongoing interaction with many staff and professionals involved in women's hockey at the national and provincial levels.

Overall, the players we interviewed for this book had different grassroots experiences and played on different national teams at the 1990, 1992, 1994 and 1997 Women's World Championships. Stevens conducted interviews in 1996 and 1997 with the following people: Shirley Cameron, Judy Diduck, Danielle Dubé, Angela James, Dawn MacGuire, Glynis Peters, Ron Robison and Jane Robinson. From 1995 to 1997, Avery inverviewed Julie Andeberhan, Karyn Bye, Maria Dennis, Tony Dennis, Kelly Dyer, Shirley Fischler, Cammi Granato, Carl Gray, Laura Halldorson, Karen Kay, Tony Marmo, Fred Miller, Lynn Olson, Ben Smith and Ellen Weinberg.

Interviews were not the only source of information used in this book. Brian McFarlane's *Proud Past, Bright Future* and information from provincial and city archives provided a base of information for the Canadian history chapter. Some Canadian information was obtained from Elizabeth Etue and Megan Williams' book *On The Edge: Women Making Hockey History*, and some from Stevens' own insights. Hockey Hall of Fame archives were used to research the Canadian legal cases that changed the rules of the game, and US law libraries were used to research Title IX and other information about legal matters. Other books were used for the history of women and sports in the US history chapter, including Helen Lenskyj's *Out of Bounds: Women, Sport & Sexuality*, Allen Guttmann's *Women's Sports: A History*, and Mariah Nelson Burton's *Are We Winning Yet?* Newspaper articles from *The Boston Globe, The Boston Herald, Canadian Hockey*

Magazine, The Globe and Mail (Toronto), *Edmonton Journal, Maclean's, New York Times, Telegram & Gazette* (Worcester, Massachusetts), *The Toronto Star, The Toronto Telegram, USA Today, Winnipeg Free Press, The Vancouver Sun* and others, provided additional information and ideas throughout the book. In this age of technology, the Internet also proved to be a useful tool, particularly Andria Hunter's website on women's hockey, subscribers to the women-in-hockey mailing list, the Canadian Hockey Association website and USA Hockey's website.

For readers wanting more information about women's and girls' hockey, there is a reference section at the end of the book. It includes an index, lists of several books and a magazine on girls' and women's hockey, internet and print sources of information, and addresses of major hockey organizations in North America.

Although we have addressed a wide range of topics, this book is not exhaustive. Any of the chapters could be expanded to become books themselves. We hope that this book will inspire others to study and write about girls' and women's hockey in Canada and the United States.

AGHA (American Girls Hockey Association)

AHAUS (Amateur Hockey Association of the United States)

AIAW (Association for Intercollegiate Athletics for Women)

AWHA (American Women's Hockey Association)

CAAWS (Canadian Association for the Advancement of Women and Sport)

CAHA (Canadian Amateur Hockey Association)

CCWIHA (Central Collegiate Women's Ice Hockey Association)

CHA (Canadian Hockey Association)

CIAU (Canadian Interuniversity Athletic Union)

CNN (Cable News Network)

COWHL (Central Ontario Women's Hockey League)

DWAHA (Dominion Women's Amateur Hockey Association)

ECAC (Eastern College Athletic Conference)

ECHL (East Coast Hockey League)

EGHA (Eastern Girls' Hockey Association)

GREAT (Girls Really Expect a Team)

HEW (Department of Health, Education and Welfare)

IIHF (International Ice Hockey Federation)

IOC (International Olympic Committee)

LMFHL (Lower Mainland Female Hockey League)

LOHA (Ladies Ontario Hockey Association)

MCWHA (Midwestern Collegiate Women's Hockey Alliance)

MSSPA (Massachusetts Secondary Schools Principal's Association)

MTHL (Metropolitan Toronto Hockey League)

NAAF (National Amateur Athletic Federation)

NCAA (National Collegiate Athletic Association)

NHL (National Hockey League)

OCAA (Ontario Colleges Athletic Association)

OHA (Ontario Hockey Association)

OMHA (Ontario Minor Hockey Association)

OWHA (Ontario Women's Hockey Association)

OWIAA (Ontario Women's Interuniversity Athletic Association)

QIHF (Quebec Ice Hockey Federation)

SJHA (Seattle Junior Hockey Association)

UNH (University of New Hampshire)

USOC (United States Olympic Committee)

1 / TAKING ON THE WORLD
Women's Hockey Today

Fast skating. Adept stickhandling. Swift passing. Solid defence. Pinpoint shooting. Quick goaltending. Aggressive forechecking. Strong puck protection. It's women's hockey. Exciting, emotional and pure.

Women from the United States and Canada to China and Australia, and many European countries in between, have learned to love the sport. These elite-level athletes need competition to improve, and the growth of women's hockey depends upon their involvement to attract new players to the game.

During the past 10 years, an international circuit has developed in women's hockey. There have been World Championships, Pacific Rim Tournaments, Three Nations Cups, European Championships and numerous exhibitions involving different countries. International play will reach its peak in 1998 with the debut of women's ice hockey at the Winter Olympics.

One of the earliest recorded women's international hockey tournaments took place in Cleveland, Ohio, in 1916 and featured teams from Canada and the

19

United States. In the 1930s, other games took place between American and Canadian squads (the Canadians were usually from Ontario or Quebec) and some were held at Madison Square Garden in New York City. In the 1970s, the international scene began to boom outside North America, with Sweden, Finland, Japan, China, Korea, Norway, Germany and Switzerland forming women's teams.

In 1979, the Mississauga Indians from Ontario travelled to Finland to play a series of exhibition games. Five years later, the Finnish women's national team returned the favour with a tour of Canada. The Finnish team, which consisted of 15- to 23-year-olds, played six games against women's second-level teams in Ontario. The Finns finished with a record of two wins, three losses and one tie.

In the United States, Carl Gray, founder of the Assabet Valley Girls' Hockey Association, has always tried to provide his players with the best hockey experience he can, and sometimes that means international play. Gray took a peewee team (ages 12 and 13) to Switzerland in 1985 with Karen Kay as the coach, and two years later another team went to France. In August 1996, Gray and 14 players, aged 13 to 16, toured Australia, playing five exhibition games in two weeks. The team faced off against teams in Sydney, Canberra, Adelaide and Perth and met the first-ever Australian national team. Three years earlier, the trip Down Under would not have been possible, since there were no women's teams there. By the time Assabet Valley made their trek to Australia, however, there were 15 teams! The trip to Australia had started out as just an information exchange between Gray and the organizers in Australia. By April 1996, the conversations had shifted to a US team visiting Australia. The entire trip cost the American team

The Assabet Valley girls' peewee team toured Australia for two weeks in August 1996. Assabet faced five Australian teams, including the first-ever Australian National Team.

about $40,000. The players were responsible for their transportation — nearly $1,600 each — and the rest was paid by Gray and Assabet Valley.

Vail, Colorado, has had a women's team since 1977 and has claimed the Colorado title seven times. They also hold the distinction of being the first North American women's ice hockey team to compete in China. The Vail team embarked on a five-game, 17-day trip on September 17, 1996. They met teams in Harbin and Hong Kong and faced off against the Chinese women's national team.

Recently, tours between national teams have become the trend as countries try to gain more international experience. USA Hockey is very active in organizing international exchanges. In August 1995, the US women's select team travelled to Finland where they skated to a four-game sweep over the Finnish women's national team. One year later, the US women's select team went to Sweden and claimed a similar record against the Swedish Women's national team. Team Canada travelled to Finland in the fall of 1997 for an exhibition series against the Finnish and Swedish women's national team and other women's club teams.

In January 1997, the US women's national team travelled to China for an exhibition series. The tour was added to the team schedule in order to develop competition for the players and help them prepare for the World Championship in March 1997. Although the Canadians were invited, they did not attend the China series and instead opted to host a 25-player national camp in January 1997. This decision was based primarily on cost-effectiveness and the need for Team Canada to play together. The Americans had been together for months and the China trip was part of their training schedule.

The Europeans have also arranged exchanges and competitions amongst themselves. The Swiss team travelled to France late in November 1995 for two games against Team France, then returned to host the Netherlands for two matches. The 1995 Christmas Cup was held in Germany and included Germany, Denmark, Switzerland and Russia. The Swiss beat Russia in the final. In February 1996, Sweden, Finland and Norway played each other twice in an exhibition exchange.

MOVING TOWARDS THE WORLDS

The first official Women's World Championship, held in 1990 in Ottawa, Ontario, was the first opportunity for the US, Canada, Japan, Finland, Sweden, Switzerland, West Germany and Norway to claim a recognized international title. The

Championship was possible mainly because of the impact of two very important tournaments: the international division in the 1985 Brampton Canadettes Dominion Ladies Hockey Tournament and the 1987 Women's World Hockey Tournament.

The Brampton Canadettes Girls' Hockey Association first held the Dominion Ladies Hockey Tournament (known as the Dominion Tournament) in 1967. It was a rare opportunity for women's teams throughout Ontario to compete against each other. Its popularity soon led to an increase in divisions and teams, including teams from other provinces and from the United States. Some 30 years later, the Dominion Tournament — sometimes called the Brampton Tournament — is the largest women's and girls' hockey tournament in the world and the highlight of the season for many teams. In 1985, Dominion Tournament officials decided to host a special international division, including two Canadian clubs — the Milverton Cal's Gals from Ontario and St. Hyacinthe from Quebec; two American teams — the Ironbound Bandits from Waldwick, New Jersey, and the Stoneham Unicorns from Stoneham, Massachusetts; and two European teams — the HOKIJ Devils from Holland and the North Rhine Westphalia, an all-star team from Dusseldorf, West Germany. The Devils and Westphalia represented the first overseas entries in the tournament's history. St. Hyacinthe won the division.

Riding the wave of international enthusiasm, the Ontario Women's Hockey Association (OWHA) organized a Women's World Hockey Tournament two years later in North York, Ontario. The event was endorsed by the International Ice Hockey Federation (IIHF) as an invitational tournament, not as a world championship. Despite this formality, the 1987 tournament was heralded as the "unofficial world championship" and became the springboard for the official 1990 inaugural event.

The Amateur Hockey Association of the United States (AHAUS) sanctioned a select US team to participate in the 1987 tournament. The selection process involved various mini-camps in Massachusetts, New York, Michigan and Minnesota to assemble a team within two months. Team Canada was represented by the reigning women's national champions at the time, the Hamilton Golden Hawks. Five players from other parts of the country were added to the roster: Shirley Cameron and Dawn McGuire from Alberta, France St. Louis from Quebec, Margot Verlaan from Ontario and Donna Levasseur from Saskatchewan. Another Canadian team — from the host province of Ontario — also participated. Overall, seven teams competed: the United States, Holland, Japan, Switzerland, Sweden and the two teams from Canada — Team Canada and Team Ontario.

Joe Benedetto, then vice-president of the AHAUS and chair of the youth council, noted in *American Hockey Magazine* that AHAUS would be closely watching the level of competition and noting how such a tournament might encourage enrolment of more players and teams, and lead to the establishment of "national calibre teams" on a yearly basis.

WORLD CHAMPIONSHIP

The summer of 1989 was an active time for women's international hockey. The IIHF president at the time, Dr. Gunther Sabetzki, attended the 1989 European Championship to judge the calibre of play. He was impressed enough to support the Canadian contingent pushing for a women's world championship at the IIHF Congress later that month. Canada was named the host country for the 1990 Women's World Championship and in August 1989, Ottawa, Ontario was selected as the host city. The following month at the IIHF Fall Congress, the entries for the 1990 World Championship were finalized. The top five teams from the 1989 European Championship qualified: Finland, Sweden, Norway, Switzerland and West Germany. The remaining entries were Canada, the United States and Japan representing Asia.

At the IIHF Fall Congress, a motion was put forth to include intentional bodychecking at this first World Championship. The motion was supported by the European countries, but opposed by the North Americans, who no longer allowed full bodychecking in women's and girls' hockey. In the end, bodychecking was allowed in the tournament. Despite their opposition to bodychecking, and even though they normally did not play that style, the Canadians and Americans dominated the physical play. Canada defeated the United States to win the gold medal, while Finland took the bronze from Sweden. Table 1-1 summarizes the final standings from the 1990 Women's World Championship.

Unlike the Men's World Championship, which is held annually, the women's event is currently held every other year. The 1992 Women's World Championship was hosted by Tampere, Finland. Two new teams participated — Denmark, who by virtue of their bronze-medal win at the 1991 European Championship had replaced Germany, and China, the Asian representative replacing Japan. Once again, Canada reigned supreme by extending its undefeated streak to 10 games in Worlds competitions. The Canadians dominated the gold medal game and soundly defeated the Americans by a score of 8-0. Finland once again claimed bronze over Sweden. Table 1-2 summarizes the final standings at the 1992 Women's World Championship.

The 1994 Women's World Championship moved back to North America, with eight teams competing in Lake Placid, New York. Top European teams from Finland, Sweden, Norway, Switzerland and Germany (who returned to world competition by taking their spot back from Denmark) joined the United States, Canada and China. Competition at the third Worlds showed strong improvement over the play of four years earlier. The scores were much closer and China surprised many nations by finishing fourth. Table 1-3 summarizes the final standings at the 1994 Women's World Championship.

The 1997 Women's World Championship, held in Kitchener, Ontario, was a success by all accounts. Attendance was at a record high with 6,247 fans attending the final gold-medal match between Canada and the United States — the largest crowd ever to watch a hockey game in the Kitchener Auditorium (even though

---

Table 1-1

1990 Women's World Hockey Championship — Final Standings

Ottawa, Ontario, Canada

Playoffs	Places Five to Eight	
Semi-finals	7th and 8th Place	5th and 6th Place
SUI - JPN 5-4	GER - JPN 9-2	SUI - NOR 7-6
NOR - GER 6-3		

Playoffs	Places One to Four	
Semi-finals	Bronze - 4th Place	Final: Gold - Silver
CAN - FIN 5-4	FIN - SWE 6-3	CAN - USA 5-2
USA - SWE 10-3		

CAN: Canada / FIN: Finland / GER: Germany / JPN: Japan / NOR: Norway / SUI: Switzerland / SWE: Sweden / USA: United States

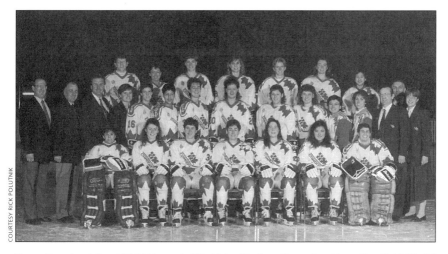

Team Canada at the 1990 Women's World Ice Hockey Championship — the Gold Medal winners. *Front (from left)*: Denise Caron, Geraldine Heaney, Teresa Hutchinson, Sue Scherer, Laura Schuler, Vicki Sunohara, Cathy Phillips. *Middle (from left)*: Rick Polutnik (Assistant Coach), Frank Libera (Chairman, Female Hockey), Pat Reid (Director of Operations), Kathy Joy (Team Coordinator), Heather Ginzel, Angela James, France St. Louis, Brenda Richard, France Montour, Judy Diduck, Marcella Donoto (Athletic Therapist), Gwen Prillo (Athletic Therapist), Dave McMaster (Head Coach), Jimmy Jackson (Equipment Manager), Lucie Valois (Assistant Coach). *Back (from left)*: Diane Michaud, Shirley Cameron, Margot Verlaan, Stacey Wilson, Dawn McGuire, Kim Ratushny, Susana Yuen.

it was a sell-out crowd, attendance was still less than at the inaugural 1990 Women's World Championship gold-medal game in the Ottawa Civic Centre). TSN, a Canadian sports network, reported 400,000 viewers per minute during its coverage of the final, with a peak of 700,000 per minute during the final half-hour of airtime. On the ice, the Canadian and American squads had never played such a close game at a World Championship. Canada outshot the US 35-27, but the Americans answered every Canadian goal to end regulation time with a 3-3 tie. Canada prevailed in overtime to defeat the United States and claim a fourth straight gold medal. Finland defeated China to take bronze. Table 1-4 summarizes the final standings at the 1997 Women's World Championship.

There were three main issues raised by media and team officials during the 1997 Worlds. First, there was some discussion about re-introducing

Table 1-2

1992 Women's World Hockey Championship — Final Standings

Tampere, Finland

Playoffs	Places Five to Eight			
Semi-finals	7th and 8th Place		5th and 6th Place	
PRC - SUI 2-1	DEN - SUI	4-3	PRC - NOR	2-1
NOR - DEN 2-0				

Playoffs	Places One to Four			
Semi-finals	Bronze - 4th Place		Final: Gold - Silver	
CAN - FIN 6-2	FIN - SWE	5-4	CAN - USA	8-0
USA - SWE 6-4				

CAN: Canada / DEN: Denmark / FIN: Finland / NOR: Norway / PRC: China / SUI: Switzerland / SWE: Sweden / USA: United States

intentional bodychecking into the World Championship. Bodychecking was allowed at the 1990 World Championship, but was disallowed for the three subsequent Worlds. Bodychecking is not allowed in Canada and the US in order to allow players of different ages and sizes to play together. In Europe, however, there are still some countries who allow bodychecking in women's hockey, mainly to differentiate it from another popular ice game, Bandy, which is similar to ringette in North America. During the Worlds, Swiss and Norwegian players were noted in the media as favouring bodychecking. They believed it would help them slow down the speedier US and Canadian players. At this time, international women's hockey competitions, including the 1998 Winter Olympics, will continue the no-intentional-bodychecking rule.

Some argue that there is too much disparity in women's hockey at the international level and that it is too soon for the sport to be an Olympic event. There will be six teams at the 1998 Olympics and eight teams four years later in Salt Lake City. This leads to the second issue: Does women's hockey have the depth to handle this rapid growth? When there are only a few strong teams, one or two

Table 1-3

1994 Women's World Hockey Championship — Final Standings

Lake Placid, New York, United States

Playoffs		Places Five to Eight		
Semi-finals		7th and 8th Place		5th and 6th Place
SWE - GER 7-1		SUI - GER	4-3	SWE - NOR 6-3
NOR - SUI 7-4				

Playoffs		Places One to Four		
Semi-finals		Bronze - 4th Place		Final: Gold - Silver
CAN - FIN 4-1		FIN - PRC	8-1	CAN - USA 6-3
USA - PRC 14-3				

CAN: Canada / FIN: Finland / GER: Germany / NOR: Norway / PRC: China / SUI: Switzerland / SWE: Sweden / USA: United States

countries can dominate international play for a number of years. But, as Bengt Ohlson, coach for the Swedish women's team at the 1997 World Championship, stated in a *Globe and Mail* story on April 8, 1997: "We have to start somewhere."

Norway and Russia, countries which did not qualify for the 1997 World Championship, have very small player pools, as does China, which did qualify for the event. In order for the overall level of women's international hockey to improve, these nations need to develop their women's hockey systems, not just their national teams. Canada and the United States will play an active role in this development. Bob Nicholson, Vice-President of Hockey Operations with the Canadian Hockey Association, commented in the *Globe and Mail* on April 4, 1997: "The sport needs equal competition. We [Canada] want to stay on top but it's also in our interest to grow the game internationally." The IIHF has decided to cancel the Pacific Rim Tournament and the European Championships, and will host two pools (or tiers) at the 1999 Women's World Championship. This will help some national teams gain funding since the second pool will be an official qualifying event to enable teams to move up and qualify for the first pool. Only time will

Table 1-4

1997 Women's World Hockey Championship — Final Standings

Kitchener, Ontario, Canada

Playoffs	Places Five to Eight	
Semi-finals	7th and 8th Place	5th and 6th Place
SWE - SUI 7-1	SUI - NOR 1-0	SWE - RUS 3-1
RUS - NOR 2-1		

Playoffs	Places One to Four	
Semi-finals	Bronze - 4th Place	Final: Gold - Silver
CAN - FIN 2-1	FIN - PRC 3-0	CAN - USA 4-3 (OT)
USA - PRC 6-0		

CAN: Canada / FIN: Finland / NOR: Norway / PRC: China / RUS: Russia / SUI: Switzerland / SWE: Sweden / USA: United States

tell whether the level of play will even itself out. In the meantime, the gap may widen before it narrows.

The third issue debated at the 1997 Worlds involved talent depth for officiating, since there are not enough high calibre female officials qualified to officiate at international games. The IIHF struck new ground at the 1997 World Championship by having only female officials fill the 19 positions at the event. This group included four Canadians: Marina Zenk and Laurie Taylor-Bolton as referees, and Sue Cassidy and Isabelle Giguere as linespersons. The United States was represented by three officials: Vicki Kale as a referee, and Debora Parece and Evonne Young as linespersons. Marina Zenk commented in the *Edmonton Journal* on April 2, 1997: "This is a huge step for female officials. Women have a lot of appreciation for the game. It's a different mentality. The sportsmanship is really unique." Sandra Dombrowski from Switzerland refereed the gold medal match between the United States and Canada and was noticeably overwhelmed by the calibre of play. She had a difficult time managing the game and keeping up with its pace. The officials who have the most experience in competitive games are

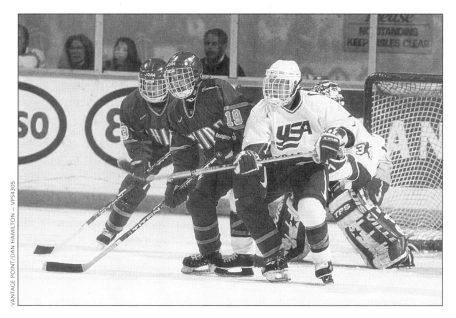

VANTAGE POINT/DAN HAMILTON — VP54305

Chinese player Jingping Ma powers the American defender and American goaltender Erin Whitten during 1997 World Championship play.

from Canada and the US, but they are not able to officiate in games in which their own country competes. The IIHF has not decided whether the all-female officials policy will apply for the 1998 Olympics or if the policy will suggest that only officials working female hockey games will be considered for the Olympics. The all-female policy was in place for the Worlds in order to prevent male officials ranked too low for male international competitions from being assigned to the women's events. It is an important policy for developing international-level female officials.

The 1997 Women's World Championship showcased the incredible calibre of play that has developed in women's hockey. Countries may vary in their views of the rules of the game and the development of the game, but they certainly agree in two key areas — a love of the game and a desire to excel.

INTERNATIONAL EVENTS ON THE RISE

As the calibre of national women's teams has increased, so has the number of international events for the teams to showcase their talents. In order to provide some competition beyond the world championships, new inter-national events have been hosted by different countries. In 1993, for example, Team Canada was invited by USA Hockey to participate in its annual US Olympic Festival in San Antonio, Texas. This was the first time women's hockey was included in the festival. The festival usually involves only American athletes, but in preparation for the 1994 World Championship, an exhibition series was organized between Canada and the US. Team USA's defeat of Canada in a two-game series represented Team USA's first victory over Canada in international tournament play.

In 1995 the IIHF endorsed an international event called the Pacific Women's Hockey Championship or the Pacific Rim Tournament. Teams from Canada, the United States, Japan and China participated in San Jose, California. Although the United States beat Canada by a score of 5-2 in one of the round-robin games, Canada defeated the US in an overtime shootout for the gold medal. In 1996, a second Pacific Rim Tournament was held in Richmond, British Columbia. China defeated Japan 4-1 for the bronze medal while Canada claimed its second Pacific gold, topping Team USA by a score of 4-1.

Another international event established by Canada in 1996, the Three Nations Cup, engaged Canada, Finland and the United States in play. After defeating Finland in round-robin play, Team USA and Team Canada battled for gold, with Canada edging out a 1-0 victory to claim the first Three Nations Cup. At this event, the Americans claimed an overtime round-robin victory over Canada to raise their total number of wins against their northern neighbours in international competition to three.

INTERNATIONAL COMPETITION

China is fast becoming a contender on the women's international hockey scene. China has won the last three Asian championships. In 1996, the Asian Championship was a very popular event, with over nine thousand fans attending the gold-medal game between China and Japan. The 1996 title qualified China for the 1997 World Championship as the Asian representative. China finished a distant fourth (8-1) in the 1994 Worlds, but closed the margin significantly to lose 3-0 to Finland in the bronze-medal game at the 1997 Worlds. Kelly Dyer, former Team USA goalie, commented on the improvement of Team China: "We beat China the first time we played them a couple of years back, maybe 9-0. This year [1996]

COURTESY GAETAN BOURBONNAIS

Team USA at the 1996 Three Nations Cup.

we beat them 3-2. Very scary. They're big girls, they're very strong, they're very hard to knock off the puck."

China's neighbour, Japan, has faltered slightly in international competition. After participating in the 1990 World Championship, they have yet to return to the Worlds and have finished last at the two Pacific Rim Tournaments. Japan will participate in the 1998 Olympic Games by virtue of being the host team. In preparation for the games they have invested tremendous resources in the women's national hockey team program. Former Canadian men's National Team head coach, Dave King, is a program advisor.

There is no doubt that the European teams are starting to improve and may one day challenge the North Americans for the top medals at the World Championships. European teams qualify for the World Championships by placing in the top five at the European A championships. This event was first held in 1989 when eight teams competed for the inaugural title. Two years later, the event grew to include 10 teams. The expansion led to the development of two European championships, with A and B titles. In 1996, eight teams competed in the B championship and six teams battled for the A championship title. The A and B championships differ in calibre — the A championship is the strongest event and by having the last-place team relegated to the B championship, the best six teams always compete together.

Team Canada at the 1996 Three Nations Cup.

In the past five European A championships, the most successful country by far has been Finland, which has collected four gold medals and one bronze. Finland will be challenged by Sweden for the title of top European contender at the Olympics. Sweden has also fared well in the medal standings, collecting four silvers and finally gaining its first gold in 1996. Other countries have battled for the final medal spot and the bronze has changed hands among Norway, Germany, Denmark and Switzerland. Table 1-5 summarizes the top five placings in the European A championships between 1989 and 1996.

Finland has been the most consistent and dominant performer of all the European countries. There is a fairly active women's league program within Finland, with eight teams in the National Women's League and 12 teams in Division I.

Although a few of the European women's leagues help to develop their players, the growth of the game has been a slow process. Lack of ice time — and lack of rinks — is the biggest cause of slow growth. In a presentation at the World Hockey Summit in Boston in July 1996, Rauno Korpi, head coach of Team Finland, stated that the European women who do play are very focused and motivated, but lack the commitment to conditioning which exists in the US and Canada. According to Korpi, Finnish players' understanding of the game is also poorer than that of North American players — most of the women are active only when they have the puck. They don't understand the many other aspects of the game beyond puckhandling, and because of their lack of technical shooting, Team Finland finds scoring difficult. Korpi felt that in order to increase participation in women's hockey and improve the calibre of its women's national team, Finland needed better media relations, more cooperation between national team coaches and club team coaches, and a good program sponsored by the Finnish Olympic Committee.

Before 1996, Sweden was the quiet player on the international scene. Team Sweden placed fourth or fifth in the first three World Championships and was always runner-up to Finland in the European A championships. Finally, in 1996, Sweden broke through to claim its first gold medal at the European Championship and, in 1997, finished fifth at the Women's World Championship to qualify for the Olympic Games. Riding the wave of that success, the team is primed and ready for the 1998 Olympics, hoping to finish in the medals for the first time in a worldwide women's hockey event.

Sweden's improvement is the result of a long process of growth and expansion. MoDo AIK, the first women's team in the country, was formed in 1969. Regular competition among women's teams began in 1981 and women's hockey officially joined the Swedish Hockey Federation in 1984. Today, registration includes approximately one thousand girls and women. Girls learning the game generally begin playing with boys until the girls reach the age of 10 to 14 years. Bodychecking is not allowed for the junior, or under 15 years of age, category, but it is allowed in women's play. This poses problems when girls under 15 play on a senior women's team. There are three main women's leagues in Sweden: the Northern League with six teams, including MoDo; the Dalecarlia League, which also has six teams; and the Stockholm League, with three divisions and a total of 18 teams. Nacka HK, the strongest women's team in the country, plays in the Stockholm Division I league.

Team Sweden's climb further up the international ladder can be attributed to this growth process and its efforts to attract younger players to the game. Canadian official Karen Kost refereed at the 1996 European A Championship in Russia. "They [Sweden] are all young and they ended up winning the European Championship," remarked Kost. "They are fast skaters and the girls are beginning to think. They are saving their skating energies and putting them into the mental [aspect] and into being at the right place at the right time. You could see that from the time they started their first game in that tournament until the end."

Table 1-5

European Women's Hockey A Championships — Top-Five Placings, 1989-1997

	Gold	Silver	Bronze	Fourth	Fifth
1989 — Germany:	FIN	SWE	GER	NOR	SUI
1991 — Frydek-Mistek and Havirov, Czechoslovakia:	FIN	SWE	DEN	NOR	SUI
1993 — Esbjerg, Denmark:	FIN	SWE	NOR	GER	SUI
1995 — Riga, Latvia:	FIN	SWE	SUI	NOR	GER
1996 — Yaroslavl, Russia:	SWE	RUS	FIN	NOR	SUI

DEN: Denmark / FIN: Finland / GER: Germany / NOR: Norway / RUS: Russia / SUI: Switzerland / SWE: Sweden

Switzerland is another country with active women's leagues. A few years ago the league format was reorganized and currently there are three levels of play. The Women's national A and B leagues involve six teams in each division. Teams within the A League compete for the Swiss national championship and the players on these teams are the main candidates for the national women's team roster. The national team is coached by France Montour, a former Canadian women's national team player. A third league, simply referred to as Group C, has three levels of play and involves about 17 teams. Team Switzerland often travels to other European countries for exhibition play. In 1995, they participated in the Christmas Cup in Germany where they won the gold medal by beating Russia 3-2. Although the Swiss team has qualified for the European A and World Championships, its performance at these events has not been consistent.

Norway is also struggling to win medals in European and World championships. Although Norway has won one medal in the European Championship — a bronze in 1993 — and qualified for all four World Championships, Team Norway's performance at the Worlds has been lacklustre: a consistent sixth place in the first three and an eighth-place finish in 1997. Unless they step up their efforts, Norway may have a difficult time qualifying for future World Championships.

Germany, another rather low performer, is the only other European country

VANTAGE POINT/DAN HAMILTON — VPS4180

At the 1997 World Championship, American goalie Erin Whitten battles a Finnish forward in front of the net.

to have competed in the World Championships. There are five women's leagues in the country: Division I North and South, Bavaria, Hessen and North Rhine Westphalia. Fifty-one teams were registered during the 1994-95 season. The highest calibre of play is in the Division I league, which has 17 teams. The top four teams from this league compete at the German national championship. Internationally, Germany's only medal performance came at the 1989 European Championship where it won a bronze medal. From that point, Team Germany has slowly fallen in the ranks. Karen Kost saw Germany at the 1996 A European Championship where they finished sixth and therefore did not qualify for the 1997 Worlds. "I think they [Team Germany] have been somewhat disappointing," commented Kost. "I heard their last game was their best game in the tournament. They finally decided to play with some heart."

One country that quickly charged onto the scene in 1996 was Russia, which finished second in its first European A Championship. Team Russia first appeared in European competition when it won the 1995 European B Championship. With that victory, they moved into the A Championship for 1996. Russia aggressively developed its women's national team in an attempt to peak for the 1997 World

Championship. Unfortunately, Team Russia lost to Sweden for fifth place and did not qualify for the 1998 Olympics. The women's national team was started in February 1994 and is based full-time out of St. Petersburg. In 1993 and 1994, a Russian women's select team, the forerunner to the formal women's national team, travelled to Canada and the United States respectively. These were the first Russian women's teams to compete in North America. Since 1992, the White Nights Hockey Tournament, held in St. Petersburg, has had an international flavour, with other countries participating. The Russian Ice Hockey Federation officially sanctioned the tournament in 1994 and it was renamed the Women's Open Ice Hockey Cup of Russia. In October 1996, Concordia University women's hockey team from Montreal, Quebec travelled to Russia to play in a tournament against Russian and Swedish national teams and a Finnish junior development team.

Women's hockey is also played in many other countries around the world. Several European countries compete in the B championships, including Latvia, Slovakia, France, Great Britain, Denmark, the Czech Republic, the Netherlands and Kazakhstan. Australia is also expanding its women's hockey program with developmental leagues formed in 1994 for under-14, under-16, under-18, and under-21 divisions. The Australian Ice Hockey federation has a national women's development director to oversee these programs as well as the women's national championships. This event was held for the third time in 1996 when four states competed for the Joan McKowen Memorial Trophy, the symbol of Australian women's hockey supremacy. In August 1996, an elite players' camp was held. With this kind of effort and commitment, Australia may blast onto the women's international hockey scene just as Russia did.

OLYMPIC GLORY

On November 17, 1992, the International Olympic Committee (IOC) announced that women's hockey would be a part of the 1998 Winter Olympic Games in Nagano, Japan. The decision was not won without a battle. Japanese organizers were reluctant to pay for hosting another event, particularly one in which they were not overly skilled. An arrangement was made, however, between the IIHF and the Canadian Hockey Association (CHA) where Canada would provide organization and coaching skills to the Japanese team to aid them in becoming competitive on the Olympic level. The 1998 Winter Olympics will see Canada,

VANTAGE POINT/DAN HAMILTON – VP54305

Swedish player Camilla Kempf powers by Russian Svetlana Gavrilova during the 1997 World Championship. Sweden won the game to claim the last qualifying spot for the 1998 Winter Olympics in Nagano, Japan.

the United States, Finland, China, Sweden and Japan compete for the first gold medal in women's hockey.

The announcement came after 20 years of efforts by women's ice hockey enthusiasts to have the sport included on the Olympic agenda. One of the goals of the American Girls Hockey Association, organized by Tony Marmo in 1971, was to have women's hockey recognized as an Olympic sport. By 1975 an application had been filed with the IOC for the addition of women's hockey to the program by the Amateur Hockey Association of the United States, the organization that can put forth such a request from a petitioning group in the US. The application was even accepted in June of that year by AHAUS. One requirement of establishing an Olympic sport is proving the existence of at least nine organized teams in each of five countries. Toward that end, Marmo scheduled trips to Sweden, Norway, Finland, Russia and Czechoslovakia in 1974. When the energy shortage hit Europe, one of the first sacrifices each country made was to close the ice rinks and discontinue their hockey programs. The tour was cancelled.

Marmo petitioned again for women's hockey to be included in the 1980

Olympics, but when he received an acknowledgment letter back from the US Olympic Committee (USOC) notifying him that his requested sport had been accepted, the letter read "field hockey" instead of ice hockey. The USOC had assumed he was referring to field hockey, and Marmo was too embarrassed to tell the USOC they had made a mistake. The USOC's oversight shows the lack of interest in women's hockey within the sports community at the time. After that, Marmo became less active with girls' ice hockey and his hopes for women's Olympic hockey were left to the efforts of other US female hockey enthusiasts.

In Canada, all the international efforts were focused on the same goal — getting women's hockey into the Olympics. For the OWHA, who played a major role in organizing the international tournaments, the addition of women's hockey to the Olympics was never in question — it was simply a matter of time. After the 1985 Easter weekend when the Brampton Canadettes Dominion Tournament hosted the first international division, Fran Rider, president of the OWHA and a Dominion Tournament organizer, was quoted in the *Toronto Sun*: "I know we'll one day build to the level where we can hold world championships in the sport and have it part of the Olympics." It was only five years later when the first part of her dream — the Women's World Hockey Championship — became a reality.

Now the Olympics are a reality as well, and organizers are trying to make the world's first glimpse at women's hockey memorable. As Kelly Dyer explains, "They [Olympic organizers] want to keep the cream on the top. And from there, they're going to expand women's hockey. They figure that more countries will have more time to improve their program. But they just want to make sure from the viewing and the marketing angles that they have good games."

Olympic women's hockey organizers in the US hope that the 1998 Winter Olympics give as much exposure to women athletes as did the 1996 Summer Olympics. The 1996 Summer Olympics in Atlanta, Georgia, were often referred to by the press as the "Women's Games." Of the 44 gold medals won by the United States, 19 were placed around the necks of women, an impressive feat indeed considering the US male:female athlete ratio was 382:280. Of course, women's ice hockey was not included in Atlanta, but the achievements of the other women's teams, particularly the basketball team, will have an impact on women's ice hockey in the 1998 Winter Olympic Games. The support and attention showered on the women's basketball team showed television networks that women athletes play the purest form of sport, and that viewers were interested in that.

With the 1998 Olympics, viewers will have the same chance to see women excel in hockey.

For women's hockey in the US, the debut of the Olympic Dream Team in men's ice hockey will also be a benefit. It will be the first Olympics in which members of the National Hockey League (NHL) will be able to represent their country in the quest for an Olympic gold medal. Suddenly, the US Olympic team will have a legitimate chance of repeating the 1980 "Miracle On Ice." Interest and coverage will be at an all-time high.

The same excitement about representing one's country exists for the Canadian players. Because of their track record, the women's team in Canada is expected to win a gold medal. The Canadian media will definitely focus on the men's national team, supplemented by such NHL players as Wayne Gretzky and Eric Lindros, but stories of the women's Team Canada may also reach newspapers and magazines that have never carried news of women's hockey before. On the other hand, the premiere of the NHL Dream Teams may overshadow the incredible accomplishment of women's hockey reaching the Olympic Games.

The Olympics could be the single most important event to promote the growth of women's hockey in Canada and the United States. Female participation in hockey has already skyrocketed over the past 10 years, but a medal for the US and/or Canadian women's team could do for women's hockey in North America what Wayne Gretzky and Bobby Orr have done for the sport in general. Whoever wins the medals, the 1998 Olympics will give the girls entering the game today something far more important than a Wayne Gretzky or a Bobby Orr — it will give them a female role model.

Table 1-6

1997 Canadian Women's National Team (World Championship)

No.	Player	Position	Birthdate	Hometown	Last Team
35	Dubé, Danielle	G	10/03/76	Vancouver, BC	Central Texas Stampede
30	Reddon, Leslie	G	15/11/70	Fredericton, NB	Calgary-Olympic Oval
6	Brisson, Terèse	D	05/10/66	Fredericton, NB	Maritime Sports Blades
77	Campbell, Cassie	D	22/11/73	Brampton, ON	Toronto Aeros
21	Diduck, Judy	D	21/04/66	Sherwood Park, AB	Edmonton Chimos
5	Fahey, Rebecca	D	31/01/75	Sackville, NB	Calgary-Olympic Oval
91	Heaney, Geraldine	D	01/10/67	Weston, ON	Toronto Aeros
9	Smith, Fiona	D	31/10/73	Edmonton, AB	Edmonton Chimos
18	Drolet, Nancy	F	02/08/73	Drummondville, PQ	Jofa-Titan
12	Dupuis, Lori	F	14/11/72	Williamstown, ON	Newtonbrook Panthers
15	Goyette, Danielle	F	30/01/66	St. Nazaire, PQ	Calgary-Olympic Oval
16	Hefford, Jayna	F	14/05/77	Kingston, ON	University of Toronto Blues
8	James, Angela	F	22/12/64	Thornhill, ON	Newtonbrook Panthers
20	Letendre, Luce	F	19/04/71	Brossard, PQ	Ferlands 4-Glaces
97	Nystrom, Karen	F	17/06/69	Scarborough, ON	Newtonbrook Panthers
3	St. Louis, France	F	17/10/58	St. Hubert, PQ	Ferland 4-Glaces
27	Schuler, Laura	F	03/12/70	Scarborough, ON	University of Toronto Blues
61	Sunohara, Vicki	F	18/05/70	Scarborough, ON	Newtonbrook Panthers
22	Wickenheiser, Hayley	F	12/08/78	Calgary, AB	Calgary-Olympic Oval
17	Wilson, Stacey	F	12/05/65	Moncton, NB	Calgary-Olympic Oval

Head Coach: Shannon Miller (Calgary, AB)

Assistant Coach: Danielle Sauvageau (St-Eustache, PQ)

Assistant Coach: Ray Bennett (Red Deer, AB)

Table 1-7

1997 United States Women's National Team (World Championship)

No.	Player	Position	Birthdate	Hometown	1996-1997 Team
29	Tueting, Sarah	G	04/26/76	Winnetka, IL	US Women's Training Pgm
30	Whitten, Erin	G	10/26/71	Glens Falls, NY	US Women's Training Pgm
24	Bailey, Christina	D	02/05/72	Marietta, NY	US Women's Training Pgm
5	Coyne, Colleen	D	9/19/71	Falmouth, MA	US Women's Training Pgm
8	Mounsey, Tara	D	3/12/78	Concord, NH	Brown University
14	Movsessian, Vicki	D	11/6/72	Lexington, MA	US Women's Training Pgm
27	O'Leary, Kelly	D	1/19/68	Auburn, MA	US Women's Training Pgm
4	Ruggiero, Angela	D	1/3/80	Harrison Twp, MI	Choate Rosemary Hall
28	Baker, Laurie	F	11/6/76	Concord, MA	Providence College
18	Blahoski, Alana	F	4/29/74	St. Paul, MN	US Women's Training Pgm
3	Brown-Miller, Lisa	F	11/16/66	Union Lake, MI	US Women's Training Pgm
6	Bye, Karyn	F	5/18/71	River Falls, WI	US Women's Training Pgm
25	Dunn, Tricia	F	4/25/74	Derry, NH	US Women's Training Pgm
21	Granato, Cammi	F	3/25/71	Downers Grove, IL	Concordia University
20	King, Katie	F	5/24/75	Salem, NH	Brown University
15	Looney, Shelley	F	1/21/72	Trenton, MI	US Women's Training Pgm
11	Mleczko, A.J.	F	6/14/75	Nantucket, MA	US Women's Training Pgm
19	O'Sullivan, Stephanie	F	7/31/71	Dorchester, MA	US Women's Training Pgm
22	Ulion, Gretchen	F	5/4/72	Marlborough, CT	US Women's Training Pgm
9	Whyte, Sandra	F	8/24/70	Saugus, MA	US Women's Training Pgm

Head Coach: Ben Smith (Gloucester, MA)

Assistant Coach: Peter Haberl (Brookline, MA)

Assistant Coach: Tom Mutch (Newton, MA)

Table 1-8

1996 Canadian Women's National Team (Three Nations Cup)

No.	Player	Position	Birthdate	Hometown
35	Dubé, Danielle	G	10/03/76	Vancouver, BC
30	Reddon, Leslie	G	15/11/70	Fredericton, NB
1	Rhéaume, Manon	G	24/02/72	Lac Beauport, PQ
6	Brisson, Terèse	D	05/10/66	Fredericton, NB
77	Campbell, Cassie	D	22/11/73	Brampton, ON
7	Chartrand, Isabelle	D	20/04/78	Anjou, PQ
21	Diduck, Judy	D	21/04/66	Sherwood Park, AB
5	Fahey, Rebecca	D	31/01/75	Sackville, NB
91	Heaney, Geraldine	D	01/10/67	Weston, ON
11	Pounder, Cheryl	D	21/06/76	Mississauga, ON
10	Scheibel, Carol	D	04/04/77	Wilcox, SK
9	Smith, Fiona	D	31/10/73	Edmonton, AB
39	Benoit, Amanda	F	22/01/76	Welland, ON
13	Deschamps, Nancy	F	06/11/72	Montreal, PQ
18	Drolet, Nancy	F	02/08/73	Drummondville, PQ
12	Dupuis, Lori	F	14/11/72	Williamstown, ON
15	Goyette, Danielle	F	30/01/66	St. Nazaire, PQ
24	Haz, Melanie	F	26/11/75	Edmonton, AB
8	James, Angela	F	22/12/64	Thornhill, ON
20	Letendre, Luce	F	19/04/71	Brossard, PQ
32	Luhowy, Tracey	F	17/06/71	Calgary, AB
96	Nystrom, Karen	F	17/06/69	Scarborough, ON
3	St. Louis, France	F	17/10/58	St. Hubert, PQ
27	Schuler, Laura	F	03/12/70	Scarborough, ON
61	Sunohara, Vicki	F	18/05/70	Scarborough, ON
22	Wickenheiser, Hayley	F	12/08/78	Calgary, AB
17	Wilson, Stacey	F	12/05/65	Moncton, NB

Head Coach: Shannon Miller (Calgary, AB)

Assistant Coach: Danielle Sauvageau (St-Eustache, PQ)

Table 1-9

1996 United States Women's National Team (Three Nations Cup)

No.	Player	Position	Birthdate	Hometown
1	Tueting, Sarah	G	4/26/76	Winnetka, IL
30	Whitten, Erin	G	10/26/71	Glens Falls, NY
24	Bailey, Christina	D	2/5/72	Marietta, NY
16	Cofran, Wendy	D	4/20/72	Holliston, MA
5	Coyne, Colleen	D	9/19/71	Falmouth, MA
2	Johansson, Michelle	D	8/10/71	Walnut Creek, CA
7	Merz, Suzanne	D	4/10/72	Greenwich, CT
14	Movsessian, Vicki	D	11/6/72	Lexington, MA
23	O'Leary, Kelly	D	1/19/68	Auburn, MA
26	Amidon, Michele	F	6/7/72	Harpswell, ME
18	Blahoski, Alana	F	4/29/74	St. Paul, MN
3	Brown-Miller, Lisa	F	11/16/66	Union Lake, MI
6	Bye, Karyn	F	5/18/71	River Falls, WI
25	Dunn, Tricia	F	4/25/74	Derry, NH
21	Granato, Cammi	F	3/25/71	Downers Grove, IL
19	Kilbourne, Andrea	F	4/19/80	Saranac Lake, NY
15	Looney, Shelley	F	1/21/72	Trenton, MI
11	Mleczko, Allison	F	6/14/75	Nantucket, MA
19	O'Sullivan, Stephanie	F	7/31/71	Dorchester, MA
17	Sobek, Jeanine	F	2/22/72	Coon Rapids, MN
22	Ulion, Gretchen	F	5/4/72	Marlborough, CT
9	Whyte, Sandra	F	8/24/70	Saugus, MA

Head Coach: Ben Smith (Gloucester, MA)

Assistant Coach: Margaret Degidio-Murphy (Brown University)

Assistant Coach: Tom Mutch (Boston, MA)

Table 1-10

1996 Canadian Women's National Team (Pacific Rim Tournament)

Player	Position	Birthdate	Hometown	Last Team
Dubé, Danielle	G	10/03/76	Vancouver, BC	Bakersfield Fog
Rhéaume, Manon	G	24/02/72	Charlesbourg, PQ	Charlotte Checkers
Brisson, Terèse	D	05/10/66	Fredericton, NB	Maritime Sports Blades
Campbell, Cassie	D	22/11/73	Brampton, ON	University of Guelph
Diduck, Judy	D	21/04/66	Sherwood Park, AB	Edmonton Chimos
Fahey, Rebecca	D	31/01/75	Sackville, NB	Calgary-Olympic Oval
Heaney, Geraldine	D	01/10/67	Weston, ON	Toronto Aeros
Smith, Fiona	D	31/10/73	Edam, SK	Edmonton Chimos
Deschamps, Nancy	F	06/11/72	Hawkesbury, ON	Concordia University
Drolet, Nancy	F	02/08/73	Drummondville, PQ	Jofa-Titan
Dupuis, Lori	F	14/11/72	Cornwall, ON	University of Toronto
Goyette, Danielle	F	30/01/66	Ste-Foy, PQ	Jofa-Titan
Grnak, Marianne	F	01/09/67	Richmond Hill, ON	Toronto Aeros
James, Angela	F	22/12/64	Thornhill, ON	Toronto Red Wings
Letendre, Luce	F	19/04/71	Brossard, PQ	Ferland 4-Glaces
Nystrom. Karen	F	17/06/69	Scarborough, ON	Toronto Red Wings
St. Louis, France	F	17/10/58	St. Hubert, PQ	Ferland 4-Glaces
Schuler, Laura	F	12/03/70	Scarborough, ON	University of Toronto
Wickenheiser, Hayley	F	12/08/78	Calgary, AB	Calgary-Olympic Oval
Wilson, Stacey	F	12/05/65	Moncton, NB	Maritime Sports Blades

Head Coach: Shannon Miller (Calgary, AB)

Assistant Coach: Melody Davidson (Castor, AB)

Assistant Coach: Karen Hughes (Agincourt, ON)

Table 1-11

1996 United States Women's National Team (Pacific Rim Tournament)

No.	Player	Position	Birthdate	Hometown	1994-1995 Team
1	DeCosta, Sara	G	05/13/77	Warwick, RI	Toll Gate High School
30	Whitten, Erin	G	10/26/71	Glens Falls, NY	Flint Generals
24	Bailey, Christina	D	02/05/72	Marietta, NY	Eastern Selects
5	Coyne, Colleen	D	09/19/71	Falmouth, MA	Hobomock Hawks
8	Mounsey, Tara	D	03/12/78	Concord, NH	Concord High School
14	Movsessian, Vicki	D	11/06/72	Lexington, MA	Assabet Valley Senior A
23	O'Leary, Kelly	D	01/19/68	Auburn, MA	St. Gallen
4	Ruggiero, Angela	D	01/03/80	Simi Valley, CA	Choate Rosemary Hall
20	Beagan, Beth	F	10/20/70	Falmouth, MA	Concordia University
18	Blahoski, Alana	F	04/29/74	St. Paul, MN	Providence College
3	Brown-Miller, Lisa	F	11/16/66	Union Lake, MI	Princeton University
6	Bye, Karyn	F	05/18/71	River Falls, WI	Concordia University
21	Granato, Cammi	F	03/25/71	Downers Grove, IL	Concordia University
15	Looney, Shelley	F	01/21/72	Trenton, MI	Hobomock Hawks
7	Merz, Suzanne	F/D	04/10/72	Greenwich, CT	SC Lyss
11	Mleczko, Allison	F	06/14/75	New Canaan, CT	Harvard University
28	O'Sullivan, Stephanie	F	07/31/71	Dorchester, MA	Eastern Selects
16	Sittler, Meaghan	F	02/22/72	East Amherst, NY	Colby College
17	Sobek, Jeanine	F	02/22/72	Coon Rapids, MN	Toronto Red Wings
9	Whyte, Sandra	F	08/24/70	Saugus, MA	Canton Senior A

Head Coach: Julie Andeberhan (Cornell University)

Assistant Coach: Tim Gerrish (Saranac Lake, NY)

Assistant Coach: Jack Kirrane (Brookline, MA)

Table 1-12

1995 Canadian Women's National Team (Pacific Rim Tournament)

No.	Player	Position	Birthdate	Hometown
31	Dubé, Danielle	G	10/03/76	Vancouver, BC
1	Reddon, Leslie	G	05/11/70	Fredericton, NB
7	Campbell, Cassie	D	22/11/73	Brampton, ON
3	Judy Diduck	D	21/04/66	Sherwood Park, AB
4	Fahey, Rebecca	D	31/01/75	Sackville, NB
5	Francouer, Cindy	D	n/a	Shaunavon, SK
6	Leclair, Chantal	D	03/04/71	Montreal, PQ
2	Smith, Fiona	D	31/10/73	Edmonton, AB
8	Auger, Bobbi	F	11/03/74	Ponoka, AB
11	Berube, Martine	F	02/11/71	Montreal, PQ
10	Deschamps, Nancy	F	06/11/72	Montreal, PQ
9	Drolet, Nancy	F	02/08/73	Drummondville, PQ
12	Dupuis, Lori	F	14/11/72	Williamstown, ON
14	Grnak, Marianne	F	01/09/67	Richmond Hill, ON
15	Haz, Melanie	F	26/11/75	Edmonton, AB
16	Letendre, Luce	F	19/04/71	Brossard, PQ
20	Rodrigue, Anne	F	25/10/73	St-Georges, PQ
18	Schuler, Laura	F	03/12/70	Scarborough, ON
19	Wickenheiser, Hayley	F	08/12/78	Calgary, AB
17	Wilson, Stacey	F	12/05/65	Moncton, NB

Head Coach: Shannon Miller (Calgary, AB)

Assistant Coach: Julie Healy (Montreal, PQ)

Assistant Coach: Danielle Sauvageau (St-Eustache, PQ)

Table 1-13

1995 United States Women's National Team (Pacific Rim Tournament)

No.	Player	Position	Birthdate	Hometown	1994-1995 Team
1	Dyer, Kelly	G	03/01/66	Acton, MA	West Palm Beach Blaze
30	Whitten, Erin	G	10/26/71	Glens Falls, NY	Utica Blizzard
24	Bailey, Christina	D	02/05/72	Marietta, NY	Providence College
5	Coyne, Colleen	D	09/19/71	Falmouth, MA	Hobomock Hawks
4	Davidson, Shawna	D	06/23/70	Duluth, MN	Minnesota Senior
11	Movsessian, Vicki	D	11/06/72	Lexington, MA	Northeastern University
27	O'Leary, Kelly	D	01/19/68	Auburn, MA	Switzerland Women's Lg.
22	Boyd, Stephanie	F	12/11/72	Kilworthy, Ont.	Toronto Red Wings
3	Brown, Lisa	F	11/16/66	Skillman, NJ	Princeton University
6	Bye, Karyn	F	05/18/71	River Falls, WI	Concordia University
10	Curley, Cindy	F	11/12/63	Hudson, MA	Assabet Valley
21	Granato, Cammi	F	03/25/71	Downers Grove, IL	Concordia University
15	Looney, Shelley	F	01/21/72	Trenton, MI	Northeastern University
7	Merz, Suzanne	F	04/10/72	Greenwich, CT	Switzerland Women's Lg.
12	Mleczko, Allison	F	06/14/75	New Canaan, CT	Harvard University
28	O'Sullivan, Stephanie	F	07/31/71	Dorchester, MA	Providence College
17	Sobek, Jeanine	F	02/22/72	Coon Rapids, MN	Northeastern University
20	Tatarouns, Wendy	F	11/20/72	Billerica, MA	Univ. of New Hampshire
8	Ulion, Gretchen	F	05/04/72	Marlborough, CT	Assabet Valley
9	Whyte, Sandra	F	08/24/70	Saugus, MA	Canton Senior

Head Coach: Karen Kay (University of New Hampshire)

Assistant Coach: Paul Donato (Arlington, MA)

Table 1-14

1994 Canadian Women's National Team (World Championship)

No.	Player	Position	Birthdate	Hometown	Last Team
30	Reddon, Leslie	G	15/11/70	Mississauga, ON	Maritime Blades
1	Rhéaume, Manon	G	24/02/72	Lac Beauport, PQ	Nashville Knights
6	Brisson, Terèse	D	05/10/66	Montreal, PQ	Ferland 4-Glaces
7	Campbell, Cassie	D	22/11/73	Brampton, ON	U of Guelph
21	Diduck, Judy	D	21/04/66	Sherwood Park, ON	Edmonton Chimos
91	Heaney, Geraldine	D	01/10/67	Weston, ON	Toronto Aeros
27	Picard, Nathalie	D	12/09/64	Mont St-Hilaire, PQ	St. Michel Sports
4	Pounder, Cheryl	D	21/06/76	Mississauga, ON	Toronto Jr. Aeros
18	Drolet, Nancy	F	02/08/73	Drummondville, PQ	Jofa-Titan
15	Goyette, Danielle	F	30/01/66	Ste-Foy, PQ	Jofa-Titan
33	Grnak, Marianne	F	01/09/67	North York, ON	Toronto Aeros
55	Hunter, Andria	F	22/12/67	Peterborough, ON	Scarborough Firefighters
8	James, Angela	F	22/12/64	Thornhill, ON	Toronto Aeros
19	Leslie, Laura	F	17/05/69	Beaconsfield, PQ	Concordia University
94	Nystrom, Karen	F	17/06/69	Scarborough, ON	Scarborough Firefighters
18	Page, Margot	F	27/06/64	Kitchener, ON	Toronto Aeros
16	Robinson, Jane	F	29/07/63	Edmonton, AB	Edmonton Chimos
3	St. Louis, France	F	17/10/58	St. Hubert, PQ	Ferland 4-Glaces
22	Wickenheiser, Hayley	F	12/08/78	Calgary, AB	Northwest Bantam AA
17	Wilson, Stacey	F	12/05/65	Moncton, ON	Maritime Blades

Head Coach: Les Lawton (Dorval, PQ)

Assistant Coach: Melody Davidson (Castor, AB)

Assistant Coach: Shannon Miller (Calgary, AB)

Table 1-15

1994 United States Women's National Team (World Championship)

No.	Player	Position	Birthdate	Hometown	1993-1994 Team
1	Dyer, Kelly	G	03/01/66	Acton, MA	Daytona
30	Whitten, Erin	G	10/26/71	Glens Falls, NY	Dallas Freeze
	Hanley, Jennifer*	G	3/10/73	Bloomington, MN	St. Thomas University
24	Bailey, Christina	D	02/05/72	Marietta, NY	Providence College
5	Coyne, Colleen	D	09/19/71	Falmouth, MA	Univ. of New Hampshire
4	Davidson, Shawna	D	06/23/70	Duluth, MN	Univ. of Minnesota-Duluth
11	DiFronzo, Michelle	D	02/17/67	Chelmsford, MA	Hudson Nighthawks
2	Movsessian, Vicki	D	11/06/72	Lexington, MA	Providence College
27	O'Leary, Kelly	D	01/19/68	Auburn, MA	Switzerland
20	Beagan, Beth	F	10/20/70	Falmouth, MA	Hobomock Hawks
12	Boyd, Stephanie	F	12/11/72	Kilworthy, Ont.	University of Toronto
3	Brown, Lisa	F	11/16/66	Skillman, NJ	Princeton University
6	Bye, Karyn	F	05/18/71	River Falls, WI	Concordia University
10	Curley, Cindy	F	11/12/63	Hudson, MA	Assabet Valley
21	Granato, Cammi	F	03/25/71	Downers Grove, IL	Concordia University
15	Looney, Shelley	F	01/21/72	Trenton, MI	Northeastern University
7	Merz, Suzanne	F	04/10/72	Greenwich, CT	Univ. of New Hampshire
28	O'Sullivan, Stephanie	F	07/31/71	Dorchester, MA	Providence College
10	Sobek, Jeanine	F	02/22/72	Coon Rapids, MN	Northeastern University
8	Ulion, Gretchen	F	05/04/72	Marlborough, CT	Dartmouth College
9	Whyte, Sandra	F	08/24/70	Saugus, MA	Switzerland

*alternate goaltender

Head Coach: Karen Kay (University of New Hampshire)

Assistant Coach: John Marchetti (Providence College)

Table 1-16

1992 Canadian Women's National Team (World Championship)

No.	Player	Position	Birthdate	Hometown	Last Team
1	Rhéaume, Manon	G	24/02/72	Lac Beauport, PQ	Les Jaguars de Louisville
31	Roy, Marie-Claude	G	03/04/70	Montreal, PQ	Ladies Stingers
21	Diduck, Judy	D	21/04/66	Sherwood Park, AB	Edmonton, Chimos
01	Heaney, Geraldine	D	01/10/67	Weston, ON	Toronto Aeros
4	McGuire, Dawn	D	26/03/60	Edmonton, AB	Edmonton Chimos
17	Michaud, Diane	D	01/03/62	Ste. Foy, PQ	Sherbrooke
77	Picard, Nathalie	D	12/09/64	Saint-Hilaire, PQ	Sherbrooke
24	Rivard, Nathalie	D	21/01/72	Cumberland, ON	Toronto Aeros
9	Drolet, Nancy	F	02/08/73	Drummondville, PQ	Sherbrooke
16	Ginzel, Heather	F	14/08/62	Brampton, ON	Toronto Aeros
14	Goyette, Danielle	F	30/01/66	Ste. Foy, PQ	Sherbrooke
55	Hunter, Andria	F	22/12/67	Peterborough, ON	Scarborough Firefighters
8	James, Angela	F	22/12/64	Thornhill, ON	Toronto Aeros
5	Montour, France	F	17/12/65	Edmonton, AB	Edmonton Chimos
15	Nystrom, Karen	F	17/06/69	Scarborough, ON	Scarborough Firefighters
3	St. Louis, France	F	17/10/58	St. Hubert, PQ	Ferland 4-Glaces
22	Schuler, Laura	F	03/12/70	Scarborough, ON	Northeastern University
11	Scherer, Sue	F	22/08/56	Brampton, ON	Guelph Eagles
18	Verlaan, Margot	F	27/06/64	Kitchener, ON	Toronto Aeros
13	Wilson, Stacey	F	12/05/65	Salisbury, NB	T and R Sports

Head Coach: Rick Polutnik (Red Deer, AB)

Assistant Coach: Pierre Charette (Laval, PQ)

Assistant Coach: Shannon Miller (Calgary, AB)

Table 1-17

1992 United States Women's National Team (World Championship)

No.	Player	Pos.	Birthdate	Hometown	1990 Team
29	Dyer, Kelly	G	03/01/66	Acton, MA	Assabet Valley
1	Hanley, Jennifer	G	03/10/73	Edina, MN	Hamline University
30	Whitten, Erin	G	10/26/71	Glens Falls, NY	Univ. of New Hampshire
2	Apollo, Lauren	D	06/17/63	Scituate, MA	Assabet Valley
10	Curley, Cindy	D	11/12/63	Leominster, MA	Assabet Valley
4	Davidson, Shawna	D	06/23/70	Duluth, MN	Univ. of New Hampshire
27	O'Leary, Kelly	D	01/19/68	Auburn, MA	Providence College
17	Sobek, Jeanine	D	02/22/72	Coon Rapids, MN	Northeastern University
5	Weinberg, Ellen	D	07/08/68	Dallas, TX	Univ. of New Hampshire
8	Amidon, Michele	F	06/07/72	Portland, CT	St. Lawrence University
20	Beagan, Beth	F	10/20/70	Falmouth, MA	Providence College
3	Brown, Lisa	F	11/16/66	Skillman, NJ	Princeton University
6	Bye, Karyn	F	05/18/71	River Falls, WI	Univ. of New Hampshire
14	Cardinale, Tina	F	10/20/66	Hudson, MA	Nighthawks
7	Coyne, Colleen	F	09/19/71	East Falmouth, MA	Univ. of New Hampshire
21	Granato, Cammi	F	03/25/71	Downers Grove, IL	Providence College
19	Haman, Kim	F	06/28/73	Fairbanks, AK	Northeastern University
11	Issel, Kathy	F	10/05/73	Ann Arbor, MI	Princeton University
12	Looney, Shelley	F	01/21/72	Trenton, MI	Northeastern University
7	Merz, Suzanne	F	04/10/72	Greenwich, CT	Connecticut Polar Bears
18	Tatarouns, Wendy	F	11/20/72	Billerica, MA	Assabet Valley
9	Whyte, Sandra	F	08/24/70	Saugus, MA	Harvard University

Head Coach: Russ McCurdy (University of New Hampshire)

Assistant Coach: Margaret Degidio-Murphy (Brown University)

Table 1-18

1990 Canadian Women's National Team (World Championship)

No.	Player	Position	Birthdate	Hometown	Last Team
30	Caron, Denise	G	31/12/60	Terrebonne, PQ	Repentigny
31	Patry, Michelle	G	07/07/64	Edmonton, AB	Edmonton Chimos
1	Phillips, Cathy	G	07/08/60	Hamilton, ON	Hamilton Golden Hawks
21	Diduck, Judy	D	21/04/66	Sherwood Park, AB	Edmonton Chimos
91	Heaney, Geraldine	D	01/10/67	Weston, ON	Toronto Aeros
36	Hutchinson, Terese	D	21/10/66	Mississauga, ON	Mississauga Warriors
4	McGuire, Dawn	D	26/03/60	Edmonton, AB	Brampton Canadettes
17	Michaud, Diane	D	01/03/62	Ste. Foy, PQ	Sherbrooke
20	Richards, Brenda	D	10/05/68	Don Mills, ON	Toronto Aeros
7	Cameron, Shirley	F	08/12/52	Edmonton, AB	Edmonton Chimos
16	Ginzel, Heather	F	14/08/62	Brampton, ON	Hamilton Golden Hawks
8	James, Angela	F	22/12/64	Thornhill, ON	Mississauga Warriors
5	Montour, France	F	17/12/65	Edmonton, AB	Sherbrooke
9	Ratushny, Kim	F	24/06/69	Ottawa, ON	Cornell University
3	St. Louis, France	F	17/10/58	St. Hubert, PQ	Repentigny
11	Scherer, Sue	F	22/08/56	Kitchener, ON	Hamilton Golden Hawks
22	Schuler, Laura	F	03/12/70	Scarborough, ON	Northeastern University
6	Sunohara, Vicki	F	18/05/70	Scarborough, ON	Northeastern University
32	Yuen, Susana	F	02/08/66	Winnipeg, MB	University of Manitoba
18	Verlaan, Margot	F	27/06/64	Kitchener, ON	Toronto Aeros
19	Wilson, Stacey	F	12/05/65	Moncton, NB	Moncton Right Spot

Head Coach: Dave McMaster (Toronto, ON)

Assistant Coach: Rick Polutnik (Red Deer, AB)

Assistant Coach: Lucie Valois (Montreal, PQ)

Table 1-19

1990 United States Women's National Team (World Championship)

No.	Player	Pos.	Birthdate	Hometown	1990 Team
1	Dyer, Kelly	G	03/01/66	Acton, MA	Assabet Valley
29	Jones, Mary	G	03/14/60	Madison, WI	University of Madison
2	Apollo, Lauren	D	06/17/63	Scituate, MA	Assabet Valley
27	O'Leary, Kelly	D	01/19/68	Auburn, MA	Providence College
16	Owen, Kelley	D	05/19/62	Golden Valley, MN	Bobcats
24	Parish, Judy	D	02/24/69	Hanover, NH	Dartmouth College
9	Percy, Yvonne	D	05/23/64	South Hadley, MA	Assabet Valley
13	Stidsen, Sharon	D	01/30/64	Waltham, MA	Nighthawks
15	Andeberhan, Julie	F	01/03/66	Boston, MA	Assabet Valley
20	Beagan, Beth	F	10/20/70	Falmouth, MA	Providence College
3	Brown, Lisa	F	11/16/66	Skillman, NJ	Princeton University
14	Cardinale, Tina	F	10/20/66	Hudson, MA	Nighthawks
12	Chalupnik, Heidi	F	09/21/68	Fairbanks, AK	Univ. of New Hampshire
10	Curley, Cindy	F	11/12/63	Hudson, MA	Assabet Valley
4	Davidson, Shawna	F	06/23/70	Duluth, MN	Univ. of New Hampshire
8	Denis, Maria	F	02/08/66	South Windsor, CT	Georgetown University
11	Eisenreid, Kimberly	F	11/14/66	West Seneca, NY	Cheektowaga
21	Granato, Cammi	F	03/25/71	Downers Grove, IL	Concordia University
7	Merz, Suzanne	F	04/10/72	Greenwich, CT	Connecticut Polar Bears
15	Sasner, Julie	F	01/03/66	Cambridge, MA	Assabet Valley
10	Sobek, Jeanine	F	02/22/72	Coon Rapids, MN	Northeastern University

Head Coach: Don Macleod (Northeastern University)

Assistant Coach: Karen Kay (Assabet Valley)

Table 1-20

1987 Team Canada — World Tournament

No.	Name	Position	Home Province	Last Team
30	Levasseur, Donna	G	Saskatchewan	Saskatchewan Saskies
1	Phillips, Cathy	G	Ontario	Hamilton Golden Hawks
24	Landry, Norma	D	Ontario	Hamilton Golden Hawks
25	Lickers, Helen	D	Ontario	Hamilton Golden Hawks
22	McGuire, Dawn	D	Alberta	Edmonton Chimos
5	Repei, Joanne	D	Ontario	Hamilton Golden Hawks
7	Sanderson, Sharon	D	Ontario	Hamilton Golden Hawks
16	Van de Ven, Mo	D	Ontario	Hamilton Golden Hawks
9	Boyd, Sandi	F	Ontario	Hamilton Golden Hawks
2	Cameron, Shirley	F	Alberta	Edmonton Chimos
19	Cole, Lois	F	Ontario	Hamilton Golden Hawks
3	Coveny, Marion	F	Ontario	Hamilton Golden Hawks
20	Dann, Dayna	F	Ontario	Hamilton Golden Hawks
17	Eatough, Tracy	F	Ontario	Hamilton Golden Hawks
8	Fowley, Diana	F	Ontario	Hamilton Golden Hawks
11	Ginzell, Heather	F	Ontario	Hamilton Golden Hawks
15	Kohen, Colleen	F	Ontario	Hamilton Golden Hawks
12	Reid, Jodi	F	Ontario	Hamilton Golden Hawks
18	St. Louis, France	F	Quebec	Ferland 4-Glaces
14	Stone, Janet	F	Ontario	Hamilton Golden Hawks
4	Verlaan, Margot	F	Ontario	Ontario Ladies AAA
10	Weaver, Kelly	F	Ontario	Hamilton Golden Hawks
21	White, Pat	F	Ontario	Hamilton Golden Hawks

Head Coach: Dave McMaster (Toronto, ON)

Assistant Coach: Jane Gilhuly (Ontario)

Manager: Jackie Hughes (Agincourt, ON)

Manager: Pat Krusto (Ontario)

Table 1-21

1987 United States Select Women's Team — World Tournament

No.	Player	Pos.	Hometown
33	Haggerty, Jackie	G	Southgate, MI
30	Weston, Joan	G	Medford, MA
35	Whitcomb, Lisa	G	Woburn, MA
2	Apollo, Lauren	D	Quincy, MA
20	Lori Bivans	D	Minneapolis, MN
21	Brown, Mary	D	Minneapolis, MN
6	Hill, Tracy	D	Berlin, MA
3	Kelly, Stephanie	D	N. Falmouth, MA
15	Beverly Lathigee	D	Woburn, MA
18	Weisse, Bonnie	D	Stoneham, MA
9	Ahrens, Deb	F	Minneapolis, MN
10	Curley, Cindy	F	Stow, MA
17	Eisenried, Kim	F	West Seneca, NY
7	Halldorson, Laura	F	Plymouth, MN
14	Marrone, JoAnn	F	Stoneham, MA
19	Pomphrett, Donna	F	Burlington, MA
5	Thompson, Cindy	F	Minneapolis, MN
22	Ticknor, Estey	F	Concord, MA
11	Titcomb, Cheryl	F	Stoneham, MA
23	Voichick, Jennifer	F	Madison, WI
4	Wood, Kimberley	F	Massena, NY

Head Coach: Chris Hartung (Stoneham, MA)

Assistant Coach: Carl Gray (Concord, MA)

Assistant Coach: Eric Gray (Hudson, MA)

2 / WOOLEN SKIRTS, FIGURE SKATES AND HOCKEY STICKS
The History of Women's Hockey in Canada

THE EARLY YEARS

Ice hockey is the heart and soul of Canada. Canadians have been playing their beloved sport since its birth in the 1880s. And while New Englanders claim to have played early versions of hockey in 1853, one fact remains uncontested — the women have been there from the start.

Since there are conflicting reports of when and where the first "real" hockey game took place, it is no surprise that the first-ever women's match in Canada is shrouded in controversy as well. Most believe the first recorded women's game was played in Barrie, Ontario in 1892. But women were competing against each other in Ottawa a year earlier, as noted by a newspaper account in the *Ottawa Citizen*, dated February 11, 1891. Newspaper clippings in Ottawa also reported that in the 1880s, women were playing alongside the men on the Rideau Hall rink at the invitation of Lord and Lady Stanley. The Stanleys regularly held mixed skating parties which often broke into games of shinny, or pick-up games.

Lord Stanley, Canada's sixth governor general, is best known for the Stanley Cup, his contribution to professional men's hockey. During his term, he developed a great passion for the game, and at the urging of his family donated a silver bowl worth about $50 which would be awarded each year to the amateur men's hockey champions of Canada. Originally, the Stanley Cup competition was open to both amateur and professional players, and teams from different regions of Canada could challenge for the championship. In 1903, the trustees of the Cup decided to allow the champions of the Canadian Amateur Hockey Association (CAHA) to defend the trophy against a challenger. By 1914, there was no longer a challenge for the Cup; rather, it was awarded to the interleague champion between the Pacific Coast Hockey League and the National Hockey Association. Since that time, the Stanley Cup has been the property of professional hockey and is now the symbol of excellence among National Hockey League teams.

WILLIAM JAMES TOPLEY/NATIONAL ARCHIVES OF CANADA – PA42256

Ottawa Ladies College group preparing for a face-off (1906).

But Stanley's contributions went beyond those of just the men's game. He was responsible in part for the early interest, development and success of women's hockey in Canada. So how did an Englishman acquire such a passion for hockey? The Stanleys first arrived in Ottawa in 1888 from London. They attended the annual Winter Carnival games in Montreal where they saw the Montreal Vics battle the Montreal Amateur Athletic Association. Upon his return to Ottawa, Lord Stanley was eager to strap on a pair of skates and pick up a stick himself. He encouraged his wife, eight sons and two daughters to join him and soon they were all tearing up the rink, moving in for a shot on goal. His daughter Isobel developed a liking for the game and became one of the first women hockey players in Canada. She played for a Government House team, and while there is no substantial documentation, a match against the Rideau Ladies could have occurred as early as 1889, although the 1891 account in the Ottawa newspaper is the first public report of a women's game. A photograph of the match was published and once young women saw the noble Isobel and her sophisticated friends out-sticking each other for the puck, many wanted to join in the fun.

Fortunately for women's hockey, the social and economic trends in Canada were shifting by the turn of the century and people were more accepting of women's interest in the new sport. An increase in the population created larger urban centres and urban settlement, and there were new jobs across Canada. The amateur ideals of colonial Canada shifted with the upswing tempo of

WILLIAM JAMES COLLECTION/CITY OF TORONTO ARCHIVES – SC244-475

Women playing hockey in Toronto (c. 1912).

industrialism which resulted in the organization of schools, colleges and clubs focusing on social and sports activities. Women experienced new freedom in education and athletics within this changing social context. In 1901 the University of Toronto in Ontario offered a degree in physical education for women and McGill University in Montreal offered a similar program in 1908. While the graduates' opportunities were limited to teaching, it was progress. In the clubs and universities, women took up the same sports as men and were just as competitive. Where women were banned from competing against the men, they organized their own clubs and teams.

In western Canada, women did not experience the same benefits as their metropolitan eastern sisters, but living on the frontiers had its advantages. In Saskatchewan, for example, women were often accepted as hockey players. When there were not enough men available for a good game of shinny, the women were a necessary substitute and their skills were often equal or superior to the men's. One woman, Annie McIntyre, was one of the fastest skaters in the province and in 1896 helped organize a women's hockey team.

The growth of women's hockey continued throughout much of Canada. Hockey reached Alberta in the 1890s, first with the men, but soon the women took to the ice. A report in *The Medicine Hat Times* from March 11, 1897, described a match between two ladies' teams. Edmonton women were also playing the game before the turn of the century at the Strathcona Ladies Hockey Club. Calgary, Banff, Medicine Hat, Red Deer and Vancouver produced women's teams in the west, and by 1898, women were playing in such eastern locations as Kingston, Toronto, Ottawa, Montreal, Quebec City, Fredericton, Saint John and Moncton. Despite the formation of women's teams in New Brunswick, women were not welcomed everywhere in eastern Canada. In Prince Edward Island and Cape Breton women were discouraged from playing hockey and only after great persistence did they form their own teams.

The boom also reached the far northern stretches of the country, including Dawson City in the Yukon. The Klondike gold rush brought thousands of young men and women to Dawson City at the turn of the century and the hockey fever that followed led to the construction of an indoor arena in the bustling mining town.

With new teams popping up all over Canada, hockey became more organized. The first professional men's league — the Trolley League — was created in 1908 with teams from Toronto, Waterloo, Brantford, Guelph, Galt and Kitchener, but a women's league preceded it by eight years. In 1900 three women's teams from Montreal and one each from Trois-Rivières and Quebec City formed a league in Quebec.

The first revenue-producing women's game was held in 1900 when the Quebec Society, a women's group, charged admission for an exhibition hockey game, giving the proceeds to the Soldiers' Wives League. According to a *Toronto Star* report, the event was well attended, with many people wanting to watch the game and others simply curious about women playing hockey. The *Star* reported: "A most agreeable surprise they got, for the game was well-played and the match was an exciting one." The *Star* went on to report that the game was played in "three halves, or rather thirds, of about a quarter of an hour each," a forefather, or perhaps foremother, to today's three-period game.

Uniforms and equipment for hockey-playing women began to emerge in the early 1900s as well. One story about the use of team sweaters involved teams from Saint John, Moncton and Fredericton. The women often competed against one another and travelled among their respective cities. As the number of teams grew, these women began stitching emblems or large letters across their sweaters, primarily to serve as identification for the referees and perhaps the players themselves. Soon the members of every team were wearing coordinating

ALUMNI COLLECTION/QUEEN'S UNIVERSITY ARCHIVES

Queen's University women's hockey team was the intercollegiate champion in 1925-1926. These players were the first women athletes at Queen's to receive their athletic letters.

sweaters. Another important part of the women's uniform at the turn of the century was the long woolen skirt. Although the skirts were cumbersome, it was unheard of that women would wear pants. As most games were still held on outdoor rinks, the skirts provided warmth against the bitter temperatures and biting winds. Goaltenders soon found the skirts had another advantage — stopping the puck. Some women goalies even sewed buckshot pellets into the hem of their skirts, providing additional weight to keep the skirts at ice level.

Most women hockey players were eager to learn the skills of the game and did not shy away from aggressive play. Publicity about women's games was almost nonexistent and most of the newspapers of the day were only a few pages long, leaving little space for sports articles. Many of the games and practices were not accessible to the public, including reporters, as the outdoor rinks often had no enclosure to protect against wind and snowfall. When the games were eventually opened to the public, they were not well promoted or attended. It was not until leagues were formed and the women began competing for trophies that public

B.L. McGREGOR/KOOTENAY MUSEUM & HISTORICAL ASSOCIATION – NO. 94.85

The 1909-1910 Nelson Ladies Hockey Club — the Sterlings and Wanderers — played teams from surrounding towns in southeastern British Columbia. The team included members of professional hockey's famous Patrick family: Lester Patrick, NHL player and entrepreneur, (at left) was the coach and general trainer. His sisters Dora (1911 team captain) and Cynda were strong players. Note the position names, including rover, point and cover point, used in the early years of hockey.

Front (from left): Hazel Gore (Treasurer, Centre), Dora Patrick (Rover), Winifred Ellis (Centre), Louise Gilchrest (R. Wing). *Middle (from left)*: Jane McLauchlan (L. Wing), Mabel Manhart (Goal), Minnie Grant (Secretary, R. Wing), Isobel Goodwin (Cover Point), Cynda Patrick (Manager, Point), Ida Elliot (Captain, Goal), Minerva Turner (Rover), Leda Henders (Cover Point), Winifred Foote (Point), Helen Gigot (L. Wing). *Back (from left)*: Mrs. A.L. McCullogh (President), Mrs. Wm. Waldie (Honourary President), Mrs. W. Rutherford (Vice President), Ola Cavanah (Captain, Rover; missing).

awareness and press coverage increased. As early as 1908, a women's team from Banff, Alberta shut out the Calgary Barracks Club 2-0 during the Banff Winter Carnival to claim the Rocky Mountain Park Trophy.

By 1910, Northern Ontario had produced a competitive and popular brand of women's hockey which included a fierce rivalry amongst teams. A four-game series held in 1911 between the women's teams of Cobalt and Haileybury was well attended, and marked by examples of tight checking and defence. The *Cobalt*

Daily Nugget reported: "Those who saw the game were well pleased with the class of hockey played, because hockey played by the girls has attained a standing in estimation of fans never before held. The game has passed the comedy stage, and lovers of the sport take as much interest in the game played by the fair ones as they do when two men's teams are engaged in battle. The crowds at the girls' games are proof of this."

Over one thousand fans attended the 1911 series. The first game was played in Cobalt, and was won by the Haileybury team by a score of 2-0. After game two ended with no score, the tournament shifted to Haileybury where, two nights later, the third game ended in another scoreless tie. The series returned to Cobalt for a fourth and deciding game. The match ended with each team scoring twice. The Cobalt players demanded an overtime to decide the winner, but Haileybury refused, skating off the ice. The tied games posed a problem, as nobody was certain how a champion should be determined under such circumstances. Haileybury, having outscored the Cobalt women four goals to two, lobbied for the total number of goals to determine the winner. Cobalt preferred the total number of wins to decide the championship. On March 11, the trustees ruled that the total number of goals would outweigh the total number of wins and the Haileybury team was declared the champion.

With the continued formation of new teams and leagues around the country, more tournaments were organized. A team from Picton won the first women's Ontario provincial hockey championship, which was held in 1914. Two years later an international tournament was organized in Cleveland, Ohio, and featured both American and Canadian teams.

WOMEN'S HOCKEY BOOMS IN THE TWENTIES

World War I changed the lives and attitudes of most Canadians. While thousands of men fought on the frontlines in Europe, many women found themselves taking jobs as well as maintaining the homefront. After the war, hockey found new life with women who rediscovered the sport and the thousands more who were enjoying it for the first time.

In the 1920s, travel became easier and less time-consuming, allowing teams to expand their range of competition. Leagues continued to grow and women strived to claim titles and trophies all across Canada — the Lady Meredith Trophy, for example, was awarded to the champion of the Quebec Ladies

Amateur Hockey Association. As a result, the games became more competitive and somewhat more aggressive and some of the players were tagged as the roughest and toughest women around.

At that time, the Patterson Pats of Toronto were the dominant team in Ontario. The Pats, led by Bobbie Rosenfeld, an outstanding softball and hockey player who was described as the "superwoman of ladies' hockey" by reporters, won the 1924 Ladies Ontario Hockey Association (LOHA) finals. The Patterson Pats also led the Toronto Hockey League in 1927, behind the incredible play of goaltender Annie Miller, who allowed only two goals the entire season. Bobbie Rosenfeld continued to dominate, along with Casey McLean and Winnie Simpson. One *Toronto Star* reporter remarked: "In Bobbie Rosenfeld and Casey McLean, the Pats have two players who could earn a place on any Ontario Hockey Association [men's] junior team."

The Pats continued to tear up the league and won the LOHA title in 1929. Later that year, over 12,000 spectators witnessed the Pats defeat the Quebec champions, Northern Electric Verdun, 2-0 at the Montreal Forum during the annual Winter Carnival. The next night the Pats squared off against the Ottawa Alerts in a game that ended in a 2-2 tie. Alexandrine Gibb, a reporter for the *Toronto Star*, noted that despite its success, women's hockey was still not being taken seriously by some referees: "The time has come when the LOHA executives had better step in and inform the male hockey officials who get paid for officiating at the ladies' hockey games that it isn't a joke. In an Ontario final with all the tussle and anxiety to win, there is bound to be reason for calling some penalties. But there weren't any called in the Ottawa hockey final for girls at Ottawa Saturday afternoon — and there should have been plenty for illegal body checking and slashing. That will kill the game quicker than anything else."

One year later the much anticipated rematch between the Pats and the Alerts was cancelled when the Alerts were disqualified for failing to send in players' certificates on time. The LOHA declared that Chalk River would represent Ottawa in the provincial finals to be played at the Montreal Forum during Winter Carnival. Toronto soundly defeated the team from Chalk River 4-0. A large crowd turned out to see the afternoon match, including several members of the Montreal Canadiens and the Boston Bruins, who would meet for a Stanley Cup game at the Forum that same night.

Women's hockey was also thriving outside of Ontario and Quebec. In the

Maritimes and western Canada, telephone company employees, usually operators, formed leagues and teams to compete against one another. Teams formed
from Sydney and Halifax in Nova Scotia to Sherbrooke in Manitoba. In between,
there were teams in Main-Garry, St. John and Fort Rouge. One star who emerged
in the west was Genevra "Ginger" Catherwood. Ginger Catherwood skated with
the University of Saskatchewan of the Western Inter-Varsity Athletic Union, and
on a road trip to Manitoba in 1921, scored 20 goals in just two games.

By the late 1920s women's participation had boomed to the point that one
league in Toronto had graduated from outdoor rinks to artificial-ice arenas complete with paying spectators. The changes in the game and in attitudes throughout the 1920s produced a change in uniform as well. As the game moved to indoor
rinks, the heavy long skirts were replaced by shorter skirts or knee-length bloom-
ers. Later in the decade, hockey pants were introduced, a thinner, narrower version of those worn today. Shin pads were also borrowed from the men's game, or
if they were not available, newspaper-stuffed stockings provided protection.
Leather gloves completed the outfit and the women were equipped for a faster,
more exciting style of play, inspiring even more women to pick up sticks and
join the action.

What about protection for the players' faces? Men's hockey was slow to adopt
face protection. In 1930, an early version of a face mask was introduced to the
NHL by Clint Benedict when he wore a protective leather mask to cover a broken nose. The idea of a mask didn't take root, however, and Benedict discarded
his when his nose healed. Most historians credit Montreal goaltender Jacques
Plante with being the first goaltender to wear a face shield when he sported a
mask for a game on November 1, 1959. In fact, Elizabeth Graham, a player on
the Queen's University women's hockey team, had donned a wire fencing mask
to protect her face during intercollegiate games more than three decades before.
Her appearance in goal wearing the protective device prompted this report from
the *Montreal Star* in 1927: "The Queen's goalie gave the fans a surprise when
she stepped into the nets and then donned a fencing mask. It was safety first
with her and even at that she can't be blamed for her precautionary methods."

While Canadian women made impressive progress in the 1920s, old sexist attitudes were not easily changed. Doctors still warned of the dangers of athletic
exertion for women. Star athlete Bobbie Rosenfeld argued a different position in
a *Chatelaine* story in 1933: "The modern girl is a better worker and a happier

woman by reason of the healthy pleasure she takes in tennis, hockey, lacrosse, swimming, running, jumping and other sports." Whatever the attitude, women's sports events were increasingly covered in newspapers as sports journalists, some of them women and many of them ex-athletes, were hired in major cities. In fact, women's events received more coverage in the 1920s and 1930s than in the four decades that followed.

Too Much Hockey for a Woman?

The aggressive play demonstrated by the teams of the 1920s continued into the 1930s. Bodychecking, hooking, slashing, scrapes, cuts and stitches were all part of the women's game. Many male spectators encouraged the pushing and shoving the women displayed. Other men disapproved of the roughness and forbade their wives and girlfriends to participate. Such was the case of Mrs. Fran (Crooks) Westman, the star of the 1932 University of Toronto team. Mrs. Westman scored all her team goals in 1932. When she helped form a team called the Vagabonds in 1933, she became a major drawing card. However, the number of games the newly married goal scorer played began to decline, and back-to-back games were out of the question. It seems her husband felt that two games in two days was "too much hockey for a woman." Eventually, at the urging of her husband, Mrs. Westman stopped coming to the rink altogether.

THE RISE OF THE RIVULETTES

The success of the Preston Rivulettes from Preston, Ontario (now called Cambridge) shows how popular women's hockey became in the 1930s. In their 10-year history, the Rivulettes tallied 350 victories, three ties and two losses. The team's origin was in another sport — softball. In the early 1930s, members of the Preston Rivulettes softball team held a meeting at what was then the very old Lowther Street arena to discuss the team's future. One member suggested they form a hockey team. An onlooker scoffed at the idea and challenged them to follow through, and the Preston Rivulettes hockey team was formed. Nine players attended the first practice, including Hilda Ranscombe, Nellie Ranscombe and Marm Schmuck. These three players became the backbone of the team as Hilda and Marm developed into the top forwards in the country, and Nellie established herself as one of the strongest netminders in women's hockey.

As the team became more of a force in women's hockey, it acquired a coach, manager, secretary-treasurer and the inevitable chaperone. By 1932, the Preston Rivulettes were tearing up the intermediate league in Ontario. Always looking for a challenge, the Preston team invited the University of Toronto varsity women's team to an exhibition game. The game was fast-paced and the Rivulettes out-checked their opponents. With a strong third-period rally, they defeated the varsity team 4-0. The victory gained them the respect of the LOHA and the Rivulettes successfully petitioned for membership within the senior division for the 1933 season.

Moving up a division did not slow the Rivulettes down. In front of one thousand fans, they defeated the North Toronto women's team (which included Bobbie Rosenfeld) in an eastern Ontario playoff game. In 1933, the Rivulettes challenged the western Canadian champions, the Edmonton Rustlers, for the first Dominion Women's Hockey Championship national title. The series was held in Edmonton. Preston arrived with little time for preparation and, due to the cost of the trip, with few alternate players. The Rustlers were too strong for the Rivulettes, beating the Ontario squad twice by a 3-2 score and claiming the first Dominion title. These losses were the only two in the Rivulettes' history.

In the spring of 1935, the Rivulettes defeated the Crystal Sisters of Summerside, Prince Edward Island to claim the eastern Canadian title. In the meantime, the powerful Winnipeg Eatons captured the western title and travelled to Galt for a national showdown. Two thousand fans filled the Galt arena to watch the first game, which featured rough play by both sides. Although numerous penalties were handed out to both teams, the Rivulettes won by a 7-1 score. After hearing about the shenanigans of the first game, three thousand fans attended the second and saw the Rivulettes pull out a 3-1 victory to win their first Dominion title.

By the end of 1935, the Rivulettes had completed their fifth year in the Ontario league — two in intermediate and three in senior. They had claimed five Ontario championships, three eastern Canadian titles, and one Canadian championship. In 1936, their strongest rivals were the Montreal Maroons. The Maroons had won the 1935 Lady Meredith Trophy, which symbolized supremacy in Quebec women's hockey. During that season, the Maroons had a 34-1 goals for-and-

CITY OF CAMBRIDGE ARCHIVES — PH3468

The Preston Rivulettes, the Dynasty Team of the 1930s from southern Ontario. *(From left)* [?] Reed, Hilda Ranscombe, Marm Schmuck, Myrtle Parr, Nellie Ranscombe, Helen Sault, Gladys Hawkins Pitcher, Marie Bielstein.

against record. That lasted until they met the Rivulettes in Preston for the Eastern Canadian Championship. The Rivulettes buried more pucks in the Maroons net than had been scored during the previous three seasons combined and won the 1936 championship.

Even though many women's hockey teams were charging admission at the gates, funding for travel and championship play was hard to come by. The 1936 Eastern Championship game netted only about $250, forcing the Rivulettes to pay the Maroons $150 for travel expenses out of their own pockets. After this experience, Rivulettes manager M.J. Dykeman said there was little hope of a Dominion final against the Winnipeg Olympics, the Western champions. The Olympics team would travel to Preston only with an $800 guarantee for travel and the Rivulettes could not afford to risk that financial burden. As a result, there wasn't a 1936 Dominion final.

By 1937, the Rivulettes had cruised to their seventh consecutive Ontario title by sweeping the Stratford Maids 10-1 and 3-2. The Calgary Grills had won the Alberta and western Canada titles in a tournament at Banff and were eager to battle the Rivulettes for the Dominion title. The Grills announced they had received an offer from Maple Leaf Gardens of a cash guarantee which would cover the expenses of a trip east. But the championship series was not so easily scheduled. The Grills manager, Tommy Kolt, received a telegram from the Dominion Women's Amateur Hockey Association (DWAHA), which was formed to establish regulations for the Dominion championship series. Myrtle Cook McGowan, president of the DWAHA, notified Kolt that there would be a $10 registration flat-fee to compete in the Dominion playoffs. McGowan also informed Kolt that the western winners must raise their own money for expenses, which would be charged against gate receipts. Kolt replied that he had not heard of the DWAHA nor Mrs. McGowan and insisted his expenses were guaranteed by a Mr. Norris at Maple Leaf Gardens. Mrs. McGowan reiterated the new rule requiring the western team to raise its own expenses. The team would be reimbursed 70 percent of the gate receipts with additional expenses, if any, subsidized by the Dominion Association. The Rivulettes management guaranteed a flat sum of $400 to bring the Grills east, but Kolt refused, requesting an investigation of the legitimacy of the Dominion Association. A reporter investigated Kolt's claim of guaranteed expense money and use of the Maple Leaf Gardens and discovered that no one at the Gardens had ever heard of Kolt. Finally, Kolt cancelled all travel plans and the Grills did not compete for the Dominion title.

As the time for the final championship approached, the DWAHA continued to demand funds from the Calgary Grills. The Grills refused to pay. The difficulties in organizing the championship prompted the DWAHA to change its playoff format. For future Dominion championships, teams were required to pay their own travel costs and also pay registration fees to the DWAHA. Changing the format changed the nature of the championship. The Lady Bessborough Trophy, the prize for the best women's hockey team in Canada, would no longer be awarded to the most skilled squad but to the best among the teams that could afford to compete.

Time and ice were running out to declare a 1937 Dominion champion. Bobbie Rosenfeld, then president of the LOHA, intervened and in April arranged a series between the Winnipeg Olympics and the Rivulettes at an arena in Galt, Ontario. The Rivulettes defeated the Olympics 3-1 and 4-2 to retain the national title; the second game of the series was played before 3,126 spectators, the largest crowd ever to watch a hockey game at the Galt Arena. The gate receipts not only covered Winnipeg's travel expenses, but also gave a profit to each team and to the DWAHA.

The Rivulettes and the Winnipeg Olympics (often referred to as the "Ollies" by *Winnipeg Free Press* journalist Lillian Coo) met again in 1938 for the Dominion title. It looked as though the Olympics had an upset in the making when the opening game ended in a scoreless tie. But the Rivulettes dominated the second game and managed a 2-0 shutout in what Alexandrine Gibb, journalist for the *Toronto Daily Star*, called "the greatest battle I have ever seen for a Canadian women's hockey title."

Dominion playoff rules were changed in 1939 in favour of a more organized and cost-efficient schedule. The first playoff series matched the eastern champions, the Rivulettes, against their longtime foes the Winnipeg Olympics. The winner, finances permitting, would play the Maritime champions for the Dominion title. The Rivulettes won the first match against the Olympics 3-2 and finished the second game in a scoreless tie, then played the Charlottetown Islanders for the Dominion title. Preston breezed past the Islanders 5-2 and 7-1 to end the season undefeated with 13 wins, and close the decade as Canadian champions.

The success of the Rivulettes paralleled the growing talents of its players. Hilda Ranscombe and Marm Schmuck led the team in every championship series and were offered contracts with the Montreal Maroons Ladies Hockey Club. They decided to stay with the Rivulettes. The reputation of the team as a whole reached across the Atlantic Ocean to Europe and the Rivulettes were invited to demonstrate their skill in a European Tour in the late 1930s. The outbreak of World War II forced the cancellation of the trip.

In the spring of 1940, the Rivulettes were still the team to beat in Ontario, claiming their tenth provincial title with a 6-1 win over the Toronto Ladies. Although the Dominion title series between Preston and Winnipeg was cancelled, the Rivulettes and the Toronto Ladies finished up their season with an exhibition game, to cheers from a capacity crowd in St. Catharines, Ontario. Once the war was underway, financial resources were scarce and it was difficult for the Rivulettes to find funding and to travel, especially with the rationing of gasoline. In 1941, the Preston Rivulettes women's hockey team disbanded. The Dominion Championship event disappeared until 1982, when it was reinstated as the Senior

Women's National Championship. In 1963, the Preston Rivulettes were inducted into the Canadian Hockey Hall of Fame in recognition of their incredible record. The Rivulettes played every game intensely yet maintained a level of fun and friendship with their opponents. Almost singlehandedly, they brought credibility, respect and admiration to women's hockey.

THE RISE OF THE AMAZONS

Women's hockey in western Canada was just as active as in the east. Although there were not as many formal leagues, teams were formed in many communities and great effort was put into arranging games against neighbouring towns. One town which enthusiastically supported women's hockey was Red Deer, Alberta, where, during the 1930s, the Red Deer Amazons became a dominant force.

Red Deer was one of the first active areas for women's hockey in western Canada. A women's hockey team played in Red Deer in 1908, one year after the town's first covered ice rink was built. Many of the women involved were also members of the Alexandra Club, a young women's organization which provided assistance to the town's hospital. The partnership with the hospital was the main reason why the women became involved in hockey — their games were charitable events to raise money for the facility. From this group of women, two teams were formed — a senior squad, named the Stars, and a younger group, the Skookems.

Other western towns also supported women's teams and, in 1908, the Ladies Hockey League was formed in Calgary. The first provincial championship was held during the Banff Winter Carnival late in 1908. Red Deer later joined this league and had very heated matches against the Calgary squad. At one Calgary game, Red Deer defeated the Calgary Crescents by a score of 1-0 in front of eight hundred spectators.

The enthusiasm in Red Deer for its women's hockey teams was illustrated in the efforts of one town jeweller. In 1909, Mr. H.H. Humber produced a commemorative plate with a picture of the women's hockey team. Instead of giving out calendars that Christmas, he gave out the commemorative plates.

During the 1920s, women's hockey expanded in Alberta with teams sprouting up in every region. Not only did larger centres such as Edmonton and Calgary have teams, but smaller towns such as Olds, Vulcan and Claresholm also iced teams. A women's hockey team at the University of Alberta in Edmonton often

Members of the Edmonton Monarchs, who held the Western Canadian title in the early 1930s, with their spoils from the Banff Winter Carnival.

faced off against teams from towns such as Olds and Red Deer, and in 1925 Mount Royal College in Calgary formed a team.

During the 1933 season, the Amazons, as the Red Deer team was now called, travelled to Lethbridge to play the Kiwanettes in the first women's hockey game there in over eight years. The Amazons won the 1933 Coffey Memorial Trophy, emblematic of the Alberta Women's Intermediate Championship. The following year, they repeated as champions.

The Amazons fared well against senior women's teams, even though they started out as intermediates. In an exhibition game in 1934, the Amazons defeated the Winnipeg Eatons, who were Manitoba champions at that time. In three years the Amazons lost only once, to the Edmonton Rustlers, who were 1933 Dominion champions.

The Banff Winter Carnival continued to be a popular venue for women's hockey teams during the 1930s and the competition in Banff often determined the Alberta champion. In 1935, the Amazons won Banff's Alpine Cup and in 1938 they finished second, losing to the Calgary Chinooks. Through the 1930s, teams from different cities became more and more competitive. Like their eastern

Formal team picture of the Red Deer Amazons, 1933-34 Alberta Intermediate Champions. Shown are the Alpine Cup (Banff Winter Carnival), the Twin City Trophy (Edmonton - Red Deer Tournament) and the Coffey Trophy (Alberta Intemediate Championship).

counterparts the Rivulettes, however, the Red Deer Amazons were forced to disband after the outbreak of World War II.

WHEN THE LIGHTS WENT OUT

Women's hockey had made great strides by the 1930s, as exemplified by the immense popularity of the Rivulettes and the Amazons, but the men's game still took precedence. Even at the height of women's hockey popularity, ice time for women, whether for a game or a practice, could not be scheduled until after the men's teams were accommodated. By the end of the 1930s, however, World War II had forced many hockey teams, both women's and men's, to suspend play. The future of women's hockey was as uncertain as the outcome of the war. While women's leagues disbanded because of lack of interest and/or support, the men's National Hockey League (NHL) and senior men's community teams continued to be active even though many players traded in their team uniforms for fatigues.

THE ALBERTA AMATEUR
WOMEN'S HOCKEY ASSOCIATION

EDMONTON, ALBERTA

February 29, 1932

PRESIDENT
   MISS EDNA SAKEWELL
   EDMONTON
VICE-PRESIDENT
   MRS. R. J. FOSTER
   EDMONTON
SECRETARY-TREASURER
   J. A. McNEIL
   McLEOD BLDG.
   EDMONTON
1st HON. PRESIDENT
   MRS. W. L. WALSH
   EDMONTON
2nd HON. PRESIDENT
   MRS. ARTHUR MURPHY
   EDMONTON
3rd HON. PRESIDENT
   DR. GENEVA MISENER
   EDMONTON
DIRECTORS
   MRS. W. G. HARVEY
   EDMONTON
   MR. C. R. TUFFORD
   EDMONTON
   MR. LLOYD FRITH
   EDMONTON
   MR. E. R. WELLS
   RED DEER
   MR. R. HOWLETT
   DRUMHELLER

E. R. Wells, Esq.,
Red Deer, Alberta.

Dear Mr. Wells:

           Congratulations! You have
a real team. You are now drawn with Drumheller for the Provincial Championship.

           Would it be possible
to meet Drumheller in Calgary. Each
Team paying their own expenses. We will
try and secure ice.

           Kindly notify us by
return mail what you think of this
arrangement and submit any other
proposition that you may be able to
figure out.

           Yours truly,

           J. A. McNeil,
           Sec'y Treas.

JAM/SL

A letter from the Secretary Treasurer of the Alberta Amateur Women's Hockey Association to Mr. Wells of the Red Deer Amazons. The 11-member executive of the AAWHA was very active in the 1930s when Alberta staged senior and intermediate provincial championships.

According to papers of the day, it was important to support the men's game to keep up morale and give citizens something to cheer for while the world witnessed the atrocities in Europe.

During the 1940s and 1950s, the priorities of Canadians shifted from recreation and play to work and family. Many women took factory jobs to support the war effort while men travelled to Europe to fight. As for hockey, the public focused its attention on men's professional hockey and the farm systems the NHL was building. Support for women's hockey became increasingly difficult to find.

FERNIE AND DISTRICT HISTORICAL SOCIETY – PH#972

The Fernie Swastikas from British Columbia were a popular team during the 1920s, long before the swastika symbol took on its negative connotations in World War II. In 1923, the team won the Alpine Cup at the Banff Winter Carnival by defeating the Calgary Regents and the Vancouver Amazons, the 1922 champions. After the Carnival ended, Fernie travelled to Calgary to play a fundraising exhibition game with the Regents. On their return to Fernie, the team received a gala welcome from the townspeople. The celebration included the RCMP marching detachment and a decorated sled for the team. Speeches were held at City Hall, and team captain Dahlia Schagel thanked everyone for their financial support and encouragement.

How the Fernie team came to be called the Swastikas is unknown. The interesting point, however, is the meaning of "swastika." The word originates from the Sanskrit and, until the 1930s, was a synonym for good fortune, goodwill and well-being. The women most likely were thinking of these uses of the word when they named their hockey team.

With a shortage of indoor ice facilities, women's ice time became even more limited, with the result that only a handful of games were possible during the season and these games were usually played at "off-peak" hours. Drawing spectators during these undesirable hours was nearly impossible. Sponsors quickly realized that money was to be made from the public's growing interest in the men's game and most abandoned the women's teams. Newspaper coverage of women's games dropped off dramatically as well, as reporters turned to the professionals. Many journalists were wooed by the perks the big leagues had to offer — free meals, trips and gifts.

A few women's hockey teams managed to stay afloat. In the spring of 1939 a women's hockey tour of the United States drew 22,000 fans. In Montreal a three-team league survived the war and produced a few talented players, among them Hazel McCallion, who later served as mayor of Mississauga, Ontario. McCallion played in the league in 1942 and 1943 and was one of the first "professional" women hockey players, collecting five dollars per game. In 1951 and 1952, the Moose Jaw Wildcats captured the senior Canadian title with wins over the Port Arthur Bearcats and Winnipeg Canadianettes, respectively. By the end of the decade, however, the Wildcats were competing against men's teams because of the lack of female opponents.

Women continued to work on improving their equipment as best they could. Women's teams had been using equipment designed for men, and not all parts of the female anatomy could be covered with men's padding. While gloves and shin pads could be borrowed from the men, chest protectors did not exist. Ingenious hockey moms devised their own remedies for the situation. Marie Hiscock, writing in the *Charlottetown Journal Pioneer* in 1948, described how Maritime mothers protected their goalie daughters by fashioning homemade chest pads. First they sewed together layers of unbleached cotton. Several long pockets with open tops were attached to the front, packed with sawdust until they were an inch or two thick, then sewn tight to keep the pads as firm as possible.

While women's hockey equipment may have been improving slightly, the opportunities for using it were not. School athletic programs took a turn for the worse as far as women's participation was concerned, beginning in the late 1930s and climaxing in the 1950s. Athletic funds were drastically cut during the war years and the women's programs were the first to be sacrificed.

CRAWLING OUT OF THE DARK

Women's hockey finally started to revive in the 1960s. One driving force behind this resurgence was the growth of women's university teams. Since the beginning, varsity teams had been a part of women's hockey. Varsity women hockey players not only adopted the rules from the men's game, but the physical style as well. In 1894, for example, a women's team from Queen's University in Kingston, Ontario, called themselves the Love-Me-Littles after the school archbishop disapproved of their hard-hitting behaviour and forbade them to play — an order which they ignored.

After a lull in activity at the turn of the century, women's university hockey returned with a vengeance. In 1922, the Canadian Intercollegiate Women's Ice Hockey League was formed. In 1926, Queen's defeated the University of Toronto to claim the championship and the members of that team were the first women at the university to be given their university letter, an award recognizing participation in a varsity sport. In 1933, the varsity league became one of the casualties of the Depression and was disbanded while men's teams continued to compete.

University women's teams did not begin to return to the ice until the 1960s. Squads in Ontario included those at Queen's University in Kingston, the University of Western Ontario in London, the University of Toronto, and the Ontario Agricultural College in Guelph. The appearance of women's teams at universities in Ontario was due to the active efforts of students at Queen's University. In particular, Kay "Cookie" Cartwright lobbied for support from the Queen's women's athletic director of the time, Marion Ross, who agreed to include a women's hockey team in the women's varsity program. She believed a hockey team would attract new athletes to the program and serve the interests of a different group of women. The Ontario league had an all-time high of eight teams in the 1960s, but by 1977 the number of teams had dropped to five.

As of 1997, six university women's hockey teams compete in the Ontario university league, and several women's varsity teams competing in other regions of Canada. In Quebec, McGill University supports a women's team which competes in a formal league and the University of Concordia Stingers are a successful team that travels to Ontario and the northeast United States to play exhibition games. In western Canada and the Maritimes, women's hockey clubs are sponsored by the university recreation departments and are not considered to be competitive varsity teams. Women's hockey has continued to develop steadily, however. In January 1997, the University of Alberta hosted an invitational tournament for women's university clubs in western Canada. This event was held in order to begin to develop a league in the Canadian Interuniversity Athletic Union (CIAU) Canada West conference. In 1998, the first CIAU Women's Hockey Championship will be held at Concordia University in Montreal, Quebec. Table 2-1 summarizes the Canadian universities that offered varsity and club women's hockey in 1997.

COMMUNITY TEAMS

The return of women's hockey in the early 1960s was due not only to university teams but also to the growth of community teams. Invitational tournament play began again in Ontario, led by the Picton Provincial Women's Hockey Tournament, the Kingston Invitational, and the Jaycees Tourney in Wallaceburg. Most of the tournaments were well supported and some even drew the attention of NHL brass. In *Proud Past, Bright Future*, Brian McFarlane writes that at the first edition of the North American Girls Hockey Championship, Detroit Red Wings general manager Jack Adams commented that the girls "were using a lot more brains in this tournament than a lot of the players I've managed over the years."

Youth tournaments were also held, and in 1964 the Brampton Canadettes Girls' Hockey Association, under Roy Morris, organized the first youth house league for girls in Ontario. Three other teams skated in the league and players were matched against each other according to age and ability. In 1967, Morris also established an invitational tournament, the Dominion Ladies Hockey Tournament in Brampton, Ontario, which featured 22 teams in three divisions. Aside from promoting and developing the players' skills, the first hockey tournaments provided supporters of women's hockey a breeding ground for sharing stories and stimulating ideas.

Two major supporters were Harold and Lila Ribson. In 1958, Harold organized the Lucan Leprechauns, a peewee team in Lucan, Ontario. Seeking publicity for the girls, the Ribsons wrote to Ed Sullivan about the team and, incredibly, Sullivan responded with an invitation for the girls to appear on his television show. The Ribsons managed to raise the $600 in travel expenses and appeared with the team on *The Ed Sullivan Show* on St. Patrick's Day, 1958. The Leprechauns were also invited guests of the famed St. Patrick's Day Parade in New York

Table 2-1

Canadian Universities Offering Women's Varsity or Club Ice Hockey, 1997

University Varsity Teams*

Bishop's University Polar Bears

Concordia University Stingers

Dalhousie University

Laurier University Golden Hawks

McGill University Martlets

Queen's University Golden Gaels

St. Laurent - CÉGEP à Montréal

University of Guelph Gryphons

University of Toronto Blues

Université de Quebec à Trois-Rivières

University of Windsor Lancers

York University Yeowomen

University Clubs**

Acadia University

Dalhousie University

Lakehead University

McMaster University

St. Francis Xavier

St. Mary's University

University of Alberta

University of British Columbia

University of Calgary

University of Lethbridge

University of Manitoba

University of New Brunswick

University of Saskatchewan

* varsity teams include full-time students and are part of the university varsity athletic program

**may include student and non-student players, but are not part of the varsity athletic program

City. While they were the toast of New York, back in Lucan they were banned from competing in the provincial championships, as the "no girls allowed" rule prevailed.

The Ribsons' support and enthusiasm for women's hockey didn't stop at the peewee level. Harold was confident that women had the ability to play at any level, including the professional. A pending NHL strike prompted Harold to contact NHL president Clarence Campbell and offer the services of the Cobalt Silver Belles, whom Ribson supervised. Ribson suggested his team played better positional hockey than the men's team. As it turned out, the strike was averted and Ribson never had the chance to prove his theory. Still confident of women's abilities, the Ribsons organized a tournament in their home town of Wallaceburg, Ontario, to showcase and develop women's hockey talents. The Lipstick Tournament was attended by four hundred players over three days in 1967, its inaugural year.

While the Ribsons were organizing their Lipstick Tournament in Ontario, women's hockey in Montreal was also regaining popularity. Two leagues formed and they competed so fiercely that there were accusations that some teams were stealing players from others. The Aces Hockey League was formed in 1967 in the east end, with teams named Spades, Hearts, Clubs and Diamonds. When many of its players began crossing over to a new league playing out of the Paul Sauvé Arena, the Aces League began to ask its players to sign contracts and get player cards from the Quebec Amateur Hockey Association. Player cards register a player to a specific team and a release is needed to move to another team. The Aces League was well organized, with all of its teams fully sponsored and equipped. Trophies were awarded in several categories at the end of the season, including top scorer, best goalie, top defender and most valuable player, in addition to the regular season and playoff champions. Two of the league's teams journeyed to Manchester, New Hampshire, to play in exhibition games and to promote interest in women's hockey.

During the 1960s, Ontario began to re-establish itself as the stronghold of women's hockey. Toronto, Burlington, Barrie, Oshawa, Guelph and Pembroke fielded teams, and in 1969 the Picton League was formed with member teams in Kingston, Picton, Belleville, Peterborough, Napanee and Cobourg. The league boasted some exceptional talent, including Annabell Twiddy who scored 52 goals in 13 games.

While intercollegiate play adopted a no-intentional-bodychecking rule during the 1960s, the senior A league retained the rules it had followed for years, which closely resembled those in the men's game. The senior women's game remained rough and, as a result, its players began wearing more protective equipment. By 1965, players were beginning to resemble the players of today, sporting full protective gear.

In the 1970s, women's hockey in Canada became more structured as provinces like Ontario, Alberta, Prince Edward Island and British Columbia established organizations to govern women's hockey. Women officials were elected to head up the programs, and Rhonda Leeman became the first full-time director of a women's provincial hockey association in Ontario. The CAHA registered its first female players in 1977, when the Prince Edward Island Amateur Hockey Association forwarded applications for its female hockey players.

The Ontario Women's Hockey Association (OWHA) — one of the most successful administrations to support and advance the sport of women's hockey — was formed on September 6, 1975. According to the current OWHA executive director, Fran Rider, the main objective of the OWHA is "to provide meaningful opportunities for all female citizens in Ontario, [and] to provide an elite system for our highly competitive athletes." Its complete dedication to women's hockey makes the OWHA the only organization of its kind in the world. The OWHA promotes fun and fair play, but is also active in seeking new regulations for women's inclusion on all levels of competitive play. Ontario women enjoy strong house leagues and programs for all ages and skill levels, due largely to the OWHA's efforts. But the association goes far beyond the support of women's hockey in Ontario. It has effectively lobbied for women's hockey to be included in the Ontario Winter Games, the Canada Winter Games, the national championships, the World Championships and the Winter Olympics. (Other lobbying for inclusion of women's hockey in the Olympics came in 1974 from Kay Cartwright, the 1960s star of the Queen's University team. In a letter addressed to the American Hockey Association, Cartwright presented her recommendation that women's hockey be added to the Olympic slate. The Olympic Committee was not receptive then, but 20 years later Cartwright would see her concept become reality.)

The OWHA was incorporated in 1978, and in 1979 was recognized as part of the Ontario Hockey Council. The OWHA became a full-fledged member of the Ontario Hockey Association in 1980 and the association continues to be supported by the Ottawa District Hockey Association and the Thunder Bay Amateur Hockey Association in its efforts to establish and maintain women's hockey in the province.

Some corporations noticed the strides the women's game was making. In 1975, for instance, Lange, the ski and skate manufacturer, sponsored a women's tournament organized by the Montreal Cougars. And in the 1970s equipment manufacturers finally addressed women's needs and introduced jill straps and chest protectors specifically designed for women.

To understand how far women's hockey has come, it is important to note that when the CAHA first organized hockey nationally in 1914, women were not included in its mandate. At the same time, women were banned by the Amateur Athletic Union of Canada from participating in sports it controlled. The Canadian Hockey Association (CHA), the national sports organization which governs hockey in Canada, didn't even recognize female hockey until 1982 when the National Female Council was formed. The Council has been instrumental in developing women's hockey in Canada. It not only determines women's hockey policy, it directs championships such as the senior women's nationals, the under-18 nationals, and the Western Shield. All of this is a far cry from 1914.

3 / MAKING THE GRADE

The History of Women's Hockey
in the United States

THE EARLY YEARS

To understand the constraints put on women's hockey throughout its short history, one need look no further than the culture and society of the United States at the turn of the century. By the late 1800s, male doctors were directing athletic programs in a large number of colleges and universities. As a result, the female population of the schools was discouraged from most sports. There was nothing wrong with women exerting themselves to perform household chores — it was exercise outside of the home that was frowned upon. Some non-strenuous and carefully supervised activities were deemed worthwhile. Gymnastics and rowing, for example, were thought to be beneficial to a woman's general well-being and academic achievement. Although ice hockey was said to be out of the question for women, some American women became interested in the sport nonetheless. Photos dating back to 1892 portray women hockey players in Alaska engaging in friendship games with other women's teams. In 1899, the *Ottawa Citizen* reported that a game had been played at the Ice Palace in Philadelphia between two women's teams.

In the early 1900s, most women limited their physical activity in an American society which dictated that, in order for a woman to fulfill her destiny as a mother, it was her duty to monitor all activities which might endanger her ability to reproduce. Failure to use caution would mean a failure to uphold the country's religious, moral and patriotic beliefs. Private girls' schools and colleges continued to encourage young women to do just enough calisthenics to remain healthy and improve on their skills for survival — that is, to increase their chances of capturing a husband. Light exercise allowed females to develop skills and tone muscles needed to perform matronly functions. Sports, on the other hand, were still thought to ruin feminine charm and appearance and severely limit a woman's chances for marriage. Competitive sports were particularly to be avoided so that no unladylike rivalries could develop. Some women, however, wanted more than light exercise. They were not easily convinced of the widely accepted belief that while heavy work was safe, heavy play was dangerous and could possibly cause uterus displacement. Eventually there was a change in attitude on the displacement issue, led by business and industrial leaders who did not want to risk having to pay compensation to female workers claiming heavy labour had displaced their uteri. In fact, in the US, women's team sports were sponsored by industrial leagues or the Amateur Athletic Union rather than the prep schools and universities. As early as 1908, women at the University of Alaska played pick-up games against any willing opponent, but a university-sponsored team was not organized. In 1916, an American women's ice hockey team battled their Canadian sisters in an international tournament in Cleveland, Ohio.

After World War I, the War Department organized the National Amateur Athletic Federation (NAAF) to help develop a healthier and more physically fit nation. The Women's Division of the NAAF was created to promote exercise for girls. But the NAAF expressly warned that as sports became more competitive and people came to see women play, the women could be exploited and the game could lose its pureness. It might even become "commercialized," with promoters' and sponsors' promises of money motivating the women instead of love for the game. Organizers also warned that acclaim for highly talented female athletes would discourage the less talented ones. The purpose of the Women's Division was clear — it was not to encourage girls to become athletes, but rather to use athletics to promote good health, physical efficiency and good citizenship.

The women's movement of the 1920s, which eventually led to women's suffrage and the right to vote in 1926, led to challenges by women on limitations in education, work and play. Many doctors still claimed that women's unique anatomy and special moral obligations (childbearing) prohibited them from vigorous physical activity, but large numbers of women continued to compete in sports despite what doctors and educators preached. Swimming, track and field, and bicycle riding became popular among women in the late 1920s and early 1930s. Women continued to play ice hockey, too, and competitions were introduced on the intercollegiate, regional and national levels.

According to University of Minnesota yearbooks, women first played organized hockey at that school in 1916. In 1918, the following paragraph described the freshman team, under the heading "Ice Hockey":

"But girls can't play hockey," protested everyone when they heard that the girls at Minnesota intended to indulge in this strenuous sport. Just to prove that they could, and could do it well, the girls organized four strong class teams, with subs for each one. They didn't need to learn how to skate, for they were already experts, so they devoted arduous hours of practice under skilled coaches to developing teamwork. This resulted in a tournament of fast games which called forth an unusual amount of interest, and convinced people that girls really could play hockey. The first game was between the Freshmen and the Juniors, and the newly entered girls succeeded in winning from the upper classmen 5-0. The Sophomores lived up to their reputation as a fast team by defeating the Seniors 2-0. On February 27 the Sophomores and Freshmen fought for the class championship. Both teams displayed remarkable teamwork and the Sophomores only succeeded in carrying off the title by the narrow margin of 1-0.

The University of Minnesota fielded at least two teams every year, and according to the yearbook, battled for the Cup for the school championship. On average, 25 to 30 women tried out each year and 15 to 17 were chosen. Women considered for the team had to maintain a C average in their studies. The teams consisted of two classes and could be any combination of seniors, juniors, sophomores and freshmen. 1922 produced a mild winter and no teams were chosen, but the women did practice. There was enough interest in 1923 to field three teams, but by 1927 women were interested in other winter sports — basketball and swimming — and there were only enough players for two teams. These players practiced stick-handling, checking, passing and shooting in the gymnasium until after the Christmas break, when they laced up their skates and practiced on the skating rink at Northrop Field. Emil Iverson, coach of the men's hockey team, advised the women on how to improve their game. According to the 1929 yearbook, for the first time in the history of ice hockey at Minnesota, the women had a skating rink of their own constructed on the hockey field behind the old library. This allowed more regular practices. The growth of the women's program was short-lived, however, as the team played only until the early 1930s.

COURTESY LYNN OLSON

Members of one of three women's hockey teams at the University of Minnesota in 1925.

Other women's hockey teams formed during the 1920s as well. In January 1995, the *Duluth News-Tribune* published a photo taken in the mid-1920s of women playing hockey on the Iron Range in Northern Minnesota. In 1928, a team formed at Carleton College in Northfield, Minnesota, and enjoyed early success. The women played against town teams and other nearby college teams, including women's teams, co-ed teams and men's teams. By 1932, Carleton had two women's teams — and no men's team.

The Depression of the 1930s crippled the nation, and its aftermath affected women and sports for years to come. Once the Depression began to subside, there seemed to be little time, money or energy for women to make a serious commitment to sports.

World War II also led to many changes for women. With so much of the male working population fighting the war in Europe, women entered the workforce to keep America running and support their families. Many women enjoyed an independence they had not had before. Women's team sports were the only game in town in most areas. The trend of industry-backed teams continued, as Allen Guttmann reported in his book, *Women's Sports: A History*: 38.3 percent of 639 firms surveyed in 1940 sponsored sports for employees. Women's softball, basketball and bowling in particular were popular, and very well attended, with leagues and teams all over the country. But as soon as the men returned from the war, the women were expected to assume their roles as spectators instead of athletes. After the war, however, there was a decline in heavy industry and an increase in service industries. This allowed many middle-class women to continue on in the paid workforce after marriage. As employment rose and people had more money to spend on recreational sports, spectator sports of all kinds began to appear on television, inspiring men and women to become interested and active. By the 1950s, athletes, musicians and movie stars had replaced political leaders, authors and educators as role models for teenagers. While American colleges were still hesitant to field women's teams, they had to concede that exercise was not detrimental to young women's health and some colleges even endorsed moderate physical activity.

The 1960s brought about the second women's movement in the century. Women demanded equality in all areas of their lives, including sports. This called for equal opportunities in contact sports such as soccer, football and ice hockey. Women were granted equality of opportunity through Title IX legislation in 1972, but an important clause still legally prohibited them from playing contact sports. Soon after Title IX was established, the US Court of Appeals for the 6th District of Michigan ruled in *Morris v. Michigan Board of Ed.* (1973) that girls had the right to try out for boys' teams even if a girls' team in the same sport already existed.

By the 1970s, government programs and big business began to focus their attention on fitness for everyone, and towards the end of the decade, schools and communities had developed fitness programs for women and girls of all backgrounds. Businesses began to focus on the middle class, specifically women with purchasing power. Women continued to exercise through dance and aerobics in the 1980s, but all too often the emphasis was placed on developing a thin, "attractive" body rather than increasing a woman's athleticism.

Towards the end of the 1960s and into the 1970s, partly because of efforts to entrench Title IX legislation, American colleges finally began to accept women as athletes and sponsor women's teams. In 1971, representatives from 278 colleges and universities formed the Association for Intercollegiate Athletics for Women (AIAW), an organization dedicated to making sure that women's sports received an equal amount of publicity and game scheduling as men's sports. The AIAW gained so much support that in 1980 the National Collegiate Athletic Association (NCAA), which formulates rules and directs national championships for men's and women's collegiate sports nationwide, voted to hold national championships for women's sports at Division II and Division III schools. In 1981, national championships were created for Division I schools for women's basketball, cross-country, field hockey, gymnastics, swimming, track and field, tennis and volleyball. The next year AIAW folded, but the rewards for its support and promotion of women's athletics were already being reaped. During the 1971-1972 school year, 31,000 women were enrolled in varsity sports at the collegiate level. By 1981-1982, that number had swelled to 70,000. Women's athletic scholarship funding had also increased from one percent of the total amount of money awarded in 1974, to 22 percent in 1984, and the number of colleges and universities that offered athletic scholarships had risen from 60 to 500. During the 1970s, community-based (grassroots) hockey also emerged, mostly in the Northeast and Minnesota, with peewee (age 15 and under) and midget (age 19 and under) teams.

While Title IX legislation was a major influence on sport in the US, another factor in favour of women athletes was that some sports were becoming moneymakers. Throughout the 1980s, collegiate sports evolved from primarily extracurricular activity to big business that could earn money to be used to fund other athletic or educational programs. By the 1990s, some schools were able to finance their entire athletic budget from proceeds earned from the men's football program. In the 1990s, medical studies were also beginning to reveal the benefits of exercise and sports to women's health. Some studies indicated a decreased risk of breast cancer among women who were more physically active. Other studies found that women who participated in sports usually had more self-esteem and confidence, and that girls who played sports in high school were less likely to become pregnant or drop out of school. Today, in 1997, girls account for more than one-third of high school athletes.

One of the biggest contributions to women's sport came from Billie Jean King. In the 1970s, she was the top women's professional tennis player in the US, and she came to represent the feats female athletes were capable of achieving. King defeated professional male tennis champion Bobbie Riggs in a tennis match broadcast around the country. King not only revolutionized her sport of tennis, but changed the public's perception of all women athletes. King also fought for equality in prize money and created a magazine, *Women Sports*, devoted specifically to women athletes.

USA HOCKEY

USA Hockey was first formed in 1936 as the governing association of amateur ice hockey in the United States. In 1980, USA Hockey organized the first national championship for girls in the peewee and midget divisions. That year, Taylor, Michigan won the Peewee Championship and Wayzata, Minnesota took home the Midget Championship. Women's senior A and B divisions were added to the championship the following year, with Assabet Valley winning the first Senior A Championship and Cape Cod receiving the Senior B title.

The girls' and women's section of USA Hockey was established in 1989. The purpose of the new division was to determine the rules and regulations that would govern the girls' part of the program, to assist with running national tournaments and development camps for girls 15 to 18 years old, and to oversee the development of the girls' program throughout the country. Lynn Olson, a longtime advocate of, and volunteer in, women's hockey in Minnesota, was named director and held the position for six years. The first problem Olson faced was recognition: "When I first started, the girls' program was not really recognized," she said. "That's the way I felt and so did a lot of the rest of the country and we were very happy to see that USA Hockey was appointing a director to help establish a better program. We grew from 150 teams to over 700 teams; just the visibility that was created and the credibility of being a part of USA Hockey helped establish that." Olson believes that even today there are still some people who are not comfortable with the idea of girls playing hockey: "I believe USA Hockey is firmly behind the program but not everybody at the amateur level is necessarily interested in promoting it because it takes time away from their sons. It has been a problem over the years, but it's getting better."

MINNESOTA MAKES WOMEN'S HOCKEY HISTORY

Since 1994, participation in girls' ice hockey in Minnesota has been about three times larger than in any other state. It's all because of a survey and the hard work of volunteers such as Mitzi Witchger, who founded Girls Really Expect A Team! (GREAT!) in 1993. When the Minnesota State High School League conducted a survey in 1993 to gain an accurate assessment of the sports high school girls were most interested in playing, it found that more than eight thousand girls were interested in playing ice hockey. After girls and parents signed petitions to add ice hockey to the athletic schedule, their requests were approved by school committees across the state. On March 21, 1994, the Minnesota State High School League sanctioned girls' ice hockey as a varsity sport; it was the first state in the US to do so. Twenty-four teams fielded girls' varsity ice hockey teams that first year and just a little over a year later, Apple Valley was named state high school champion when it defeated South St. Paul 2-0. The league nearly doubled in 1995-1996, with 47 teams, and grew to 63 teams for the 1996-1997 season.

Hockey, including women's hockey, has a long heritage in Minnesota. In 1925, a women's team played at the University of Minnesota, and presumably played against mostly Canadian teams, since there was little competition in the US. Women continued to play over the years but there weren't any women-only programs until a few teams formed in the late 1960s. In the 1970s, girls' ice hockey programs were included in the athletic programs of some school districts. Most teams folded within a few years, but some stayed together and continued to play into the late 1970s. Many of these girls now play as senior women, which accounts for Minnesota having such a large senior women's program long before its youth programs were fully developed. About a dozen of these girls' teams lasted into the 1980s, but it wasn't until 1993 — when girls' ice hockey became a high school sport — that the girls' program in Minnesota really took off.

In addition to her work for the USA Hockey girls' and women's section, Lynn Olson is the director of girls' and women's hockey in Minnesota, a position she has held off and on since 1989. She was the first woman on the board of directors of the Minnesota Amateur Hockey Association and helped start the women's league, becoming its first president. Olson expects the explosion of girls' ice hockey at the high school level to continue. In 1996, 24 midget girls' high school teams were organizing, hoping to spend a year or two improving and then gradually enter into the state high school league. Eventually, Olson would like the

DENNY DeGRISSELES

Apple Valley High captured the first Minnesota girls' ice hockey state championship in 1995.

number of girls' high school teams to equal the number of boys' teams, which in 1996 totalled 140.

High school hockey in Minnesota is a tremendously popular spectator event, and the girls' games are no exception. According to Olson, "The 1996 high school hockey championship for girls was the best attended high school event and it just blew the socks off the state high school league. As a matter of fact, the first year they put it in a place that held about 2,000 people and they had the fire marshall upset because the place was overpacked. They had 7,000 fans for four games. It was unbelievable how many people attended."

Olson thinks a lot of the interest can be traced back to the people of Minnesota. "They are just much more forward about allowing girls to participate," she said, "And our legislature has had a lot to do with it. We have a lot of women legislators who skate. They have a team that plays at the state capital. They come out and play every Sunday night. A lot of these legislator women are not all that good but they're out there every Sunday and they love every minute of it. I think they just feel that 'If I can do this, every kid should be able to do this, every boy or girl.'"

Legislators have done much more than just encourage girls to play. They have taken action. In 1996, the Minnesota legislature passed a bill requiring that 15 percent of all ice time in 1994 and 1995, in both public and private rinks, be reserved for girls, increasing to 30 percent in 1995-96 and 50 percent in 1997. Rink owners could no longer give the girls undesirable hours, like 6:00 a.m. or 11:00 p.m. and report that they had filled their quota. In addition, the Minnesota Amateur Sports Commission, which runs all amateur sports in the state, received funds through the legislature to build new ice facilities or improve existing facilities. The grants ranged from $50,000 to $250,000 and nearly $19 million was awarded over two years.

USA Hockey community volunteers have been helpful too. In 1994, each of the USA Hockey directors in Minnesota selected a girls' coordinator to work with them to help get the girls' programs rolling, since many of the directors couldn't devote enough time to both the boys' and the girls' programs. The 12 hockey districts in Minnesota meet five times a year and Olson continues to be a proponent of girls' hockey. She urges directors to start initiation programs at the earliest level. If girls won't participate because they have to play with boys, Olson asks the directors to find enough girls to play on an all-girls team, even if the directors have to go to the next town to find players.

Some northern areas of the state still don't have girls teams, but Olson thinks that within 10 years the fathers and mothers who played themselves will start girls' programs: "So many of the fathers have much more to do with their daughters' lives than the fathers who are now over 50 did. As soon as that over-50 generation gets out of the picture and the new fathers come in, I don't think we'll have any problems getting programs started anyplace in the United States. It seems to be in males over 50 or 55 that we have the worst attitude — those who think that girls shouldn't play hockey."

Clearly, Minnesota is an example of what girls' and women's hockey can become. Table 3-1 illustrates the huge growth of women's hockey in Minnesota from 1986 to 1997. Other states do have girls' high school teams, but these aren't recognized by the high school leagues and there are no state championships. Some teams have formed their own leagues — for example, in 1996, the Eastern Massachusetts Girls' Public High School Ice Hockey League was formed, consisting of 14 teams from public high schools in eastern Massachusetts. Outside of that league, only a handful of public high schools in New England offer women's ice hockey as a varsity sport.

Table 3-1

Growth of Women's Hockey in Minnesota, 1986-1997

Year	Number of Female Teams	
1997	332*	(235 youth + 68 high school +17 JV + 12 college)
1996	236	(187 youth + 49 high school)
1995	143	(119 youth + 24 high school)
1994	86	(78 youth + 8 high school)
1993	41	
1992	33	
1991	27	
1990	29	
1988	40	
1986	35	

Breakdown of ages of teams:

	Ages 10-12	Ages 13-15	Ages 16-19	Senior 20+
1995	36	39	13	31
1996	72	57	25	35
1997*	100	75	25	35

*projected

PREPARATORY (PREP) SCHOOLS

Unlike state-run schools, prep schools — which are private schools in the US — began offering ice hockey to girls around 1971. Almost all Eastern schools offered the sport, but most were not very competitive, with only a few good players spread throughout the league. As girls' ice hockey became more popular in the late 1980s, the number of prep schools offering ice hockey increased, and the quality of the teams and players rose as well. During that time, many of the better players were also members of the best club, or community, teams in the area — the Connecticut Polar Bears and the Assabet Valley team in Concord, Massachusetts. With more teams, a tournament was in order, so female hockey advocate Tony Dennis, along with Chuck Bruno Vernon, initiated the New England Prep School Girls Tournament, which began in March 1987. Four teams competed the first year.

In 1996, approximately 100 prep schools in New England had varsity girls' teams. What makes prep schools such an attractive option for many girls is the fact that they are among the few places that offer programs where girls' ice hockey is on a par with boys'. Nearly everything is provided by the school, from coaches, referees and score keepers to on-site trainers and buses. The teams play an average of 15 to 20 games per year from the end of November to the end of February. Although they do not have an intensive game schedule, prep schools produce many topnotch players. In 1996, almost half of the players on women's college varsity ice hockey teams in the eastern US came out of prep school programs.

COLLEGES AND UNIVERSITIES

American colleges and universities have always been the feeder system for women's elite hockey. As early as 1910, some American colleges and universities iced women's hockey teams. The Depression and World War II. forced the teams to disband and many lay dormant for nearly 50 years. In 1964, Brown University in Providence, Rhode Island became the first college to ice a women's ice hockey team in post-war America when student Nancy Schieffelin, class of 1967, got the program started with the help of athletic director Arlene Gorton. Three years later, under the leadership of Brown hockey player Linda Fox Phillips (class of 1968), the program produced the first intercollegiate women's team in the US, playing against Canadian universities. In 1975 the team gained varsity status, the first collegiate women's ice hockey team to do so. Aside from Brown's success, growth of women's ice hockey at colleges in the 1970s was slow. By 1972, only one other school iced a team — Cornell University in Ithaca, New York. Since there were so few female teams, American college teams often played against Canadian colleges.

These early American teams shared many of the struggles of their Canadian counterparts in organizing and maintaining themselves. For example, many of the women at Cornell University, who began their program in 1972, had never skated in an organized hockey program and were recruited for the team by radio advertisements. Ice time was a problem — it was scheduled in the school's lone rink after practices by men's teams from Cornell and two other nearby colleges, and after public skating. The Cornell team also had trouble getting the school to pay for road trips in its first year — all four of them.

Many athletic departments felt that money would be better spent on men's programs. One team to fall victim to this attitude was at Clarkson University in New York. A varsity team was formed in 1974, but folded after 10 years. Over 20 years later, in January 1996, the women were back on the ice, thanks to Clarkson student and hockey player Abby Clabough, who put together a club team. The team was given free ice four times a week and has gained some support from school officials, largely because of Clabough and the team's efforts. The Clarkson team played only a couple of games in 1996, but the women were enthusiastic and have persevered.

Another college which formed a team in 1974 was Hamilton College in Clinton, New York. In the first years, competition was hard to find. The team played as few as three games a year. After 21 years of struggling to find opportunities to play, as well as to improve the calibre of play, Hamilton College competed as a varsity team in 1996-1997 in the Eastern College Athletic Conference (ECAC) Women's Hockey Alliance.

While the overall quality of college teams was poor, some individual players were very skilled. Kathy Lawler skated for State University College at Potsdam in New York State in the mid-1970s. Lawler got her start when she was 10 and soon was the top scorer for an all-boys local youth hockey team in an all-boys league. She went on to play on her high school boys' varsity team. In just 87 games during her senior year at Potsdam, she scored 279 goals.

In 1981, Providence College, the University of New Hampshire and Northeastern University began offering athletic scholarships to women hockey players. Meanwhile, Ivy League schools, which included eight colleges and universities in the East with similar high academic standards, were prohibited from offering athletic scholarships. They could, however, extend scholastic scholarships based on need. With over one thousand girls' hockey teams in Canada in 1985, compared to 114 in the US, many American coaches looked north to strengthen their teams. There were problems, however, in scouting all the teams in Canada. Most college coaches doubled as scouts and simply didn't have the time to scour Canada in search of players. Their solution was to attend major tournaments to find the best players, a practice which still occurs today.

ANNE DIFFILY/BROWN UNIVERSITY

Brown University's Martha Schmidtt attempts to score on Connecticut in the first round of the Brown Invitational Tournament in February 1976.

In the mid-1980s, the Northeastern University women's hockey program was almost cut because of budget constraints. The team managed to stay afloat, but the scholarship program was axed. Providence College and the University of New Hampshire (UNH) followed suit and dropped their scholarships. A few years later, scholarships were reinstated at Providence and the other schools began offering scholarships again too. In 1996 the University of Minnesota became the first school in the country to offer scholarships to 18 players — the most allowed under NCAA rules. The number of scholarships will continue to rise since the NCAA has designated women's hockey an "emerging sport." There is no NCAA national championship yet, but women's hockey is recognized by the NCAA, which means Division I varsity women's teams follow the same rules as men's teams, including the right to recruit players and offer scholarships.

In 1984, the NCAA approved the formation of the Eastern College Athletic Conference, which determines a champion for varsity clubs in the eastern US and abides by Division I hockey rules. Providence College and UNH have dominated the league, claiming 12 out of 14 championship titles (through 1997) between them. Traditionally, colleges and universities are categorized as Division I, Division II or Division III according to population, with Division I schools having the largest student enrollment. Division I schools usually have larger athletic budgets than the other divisions and are able to recruit the best athletes by offering athletic scholarships and fully funded athletic programs. To create fair competition, teams compete against other teams within their division. Through the 1980s, the number of schools producing women's ice hockey teams was so small that all the teams played in the same division, regardless of the size of the school or ability of the team. In 1989, the teams were separated into two divisions — I and III — according to skill level, and champions were crowned in both divisions.

CORNELL UNIVERSITY

Cornell University women's ice hockey, one of the first women's college hockey programs since the 1920s, was established in 1972. By 1979, they had skated to their third consecutive Ivy League championship.

In 1992, ECAC was restructured to eliminate the division label. Teams were not organized according to the school's size but according to ability. In 1995, an ECAC League was formed to include former Division I varsity teams, and an ECAC Alliance was established which consisted of both varsity and club teams formerly labeled Division III. The teams involved in the ECAC League and Alliance in 1996-1997 are shown in Table 3-2. At the end of the regular season, the top eight of the 12 teams that make up the ECAC advance to the playoffs. The 1996 ECAC Women's Championship proved to be historic, as UNH edged Providence 3-2 after an amazing five overtime periods. In the eighth period, more than 145 minutes into the game, New Hampshire left wing Brandy Fisher scored off the post, putting an end to the longest collegiate hockey game in history. Table 3-3 summarizes the ECAC Conference champions from 1989 to 1997.

Within the ECAC is the Ivy League. Six of the eight Ivy League schools ice women's varsity hockey teams — Brown University, Cornell University, Dartmouth College, Harvard University, Princeton University and Yale University.

The team highest in the ECAC standings at the end of the season is crowned the Ivy League champion. Table 3-4 summarizes the Ivy League champions from 1977 to 1997.

Former national team member Ellen Weinberg finds that East Coast colleges have an advantage over other women's leagues in the US or Canada. "You're not paying for travel and are given a per diem when you're on the road," she said. "It's almost the only way of being a professional athlete. Even the girls that go to Switzerland [on professional teams] are not making money. These women have an opportunity to get an education while playing hockey for their schools."

Even without the advantages of the East Coast leagues, more women's hockey conferences were formed in 1996 — the Midwestern Collegiate Women's Hockey Alliance (MCWHA) and the

JOHN FORASTE/BROWN UNIVERSITY

Players battle in the corner during the "Mayor's Cup", the annual tilt between Providence College and Brown University, in Providence, Rhode Island. (c. 1975)

Central Collegiate Women's Ice Hockey Association (CCWHA). Tables 3-5 and 3-6 show the colleges and universities involved in these new leagues. While there is only one varsity team that plays in each league, the formation of the leagues is an important step in establishing an NCAA national championship. The MCWHA, made up of teams from Minnesota and Wisconsin, joins the ECAC League and ECAC Alliance as the three college leagues available to women.

Andy Twombly is founder of the CCWHA — which consists solely of club teams from Michigan, Ohio, Illinois and Wisconsin — and coach of the Lake Forest team. In an interview with Rosann Mando in *Women's Hockey* magazine in 1997, Twombly said one of the goals of the league is to help the teams and schools draw the attention of potential women student hockey players from the Midwest and New England high schools and prep schools. Many of the teams in the league have applied for varsity status but have not yet been accepted. In an interview with

THOMAS MAGUIRE JR./PROVIDENCE COLLEGE

Cammi Granato, fourth from left in the front row, captained the 1992-93 Providence College team to an ECAC championship.

Joshua Weisbrod in the *Brown Daily Herald* in 1994, Joan Taylor, Associate Director of Athletics at Brown University, said that a minimum of 40 schools must sponsor a Division I varsity women's ice hockey program in order to gain NCAA recognition and establish a national championship. The NCAA, however, has tagged women's ice hockey as an emerging sport and is willing to decrease that minimum number to make the championship possible. Since the American colleges are divided into conferences according to their geographic location, however, there is a need for more conferences to be established in women's hockey to determine champions from different parts of the country.

Some states are taking the necessary steps towards establishing a national championship. Minnesota leads women's hockey in the Midwest. Augsburg College in Minneapolis fully funded its women's varsity program in 1995, the first in the state and in the country to do so, and the University of Minnesota team followed suit by turning varsity in 1996-1997. The University of Minnesota established a varsity team in part because of the demand for women's hockey in the state, but also in response to the gender equity issues that continually surface in college athletics. Both the Big 10 Athletic Conference (covering the Great Lakes region and Midwest), to which Minnesota belongs, and the NCAA have strict rules about equity and providing an equal number of sports for both male and female

Table 3-2	
Eastern Collegiate Athletic Conference, 1996-1997 season	
Women's League (Division I-style)	Women's Alliance (Division III-style)
Boston College	*East*
Brown University	Amherst College
Colby College	Bowdoin College
Cornell University	Connecticut College
Dartmouth College	University of Maine*
Harvard University	Wesleyan University
Northeastern Universtiy	Williams College
Princeton University	
Providence College	*West*
St. Lawrence University	Colgate College*
University of New Hampshire	Hamilton College
Yale University	Middlebury College
Rochester Institute of Technology	
Rensselaer Polytechnic Institute	
Vermont College*	
	Teams to be added for 1998-1999 season: Bates College* Sacred Heart University*
	*club team

Table 3-3

Eastern College Athletic Conference Champions, 1984-1997

Division I

1984	Providence College
1985	Providence College
1986	University of New Hampshire
1987	University of New Hampshire
1988	Northeastern University
1989	Northeastern University
1990	University of New Hampshire
1991	University of New Hampshire
1992	Providence College
1993	Providence College
1994	Providence College
1995	Providence College
1996	University of New Hampshire
1997	Northeastern University

Division III

1989	Rochester Institute of Technology
1990	St Lawrence University
1991	St Lawrence University
1992	St Lawrence University

Alliance

1996	Middlebury College
1997	Middlebury College

Table 3-4	
Ivy League Champions, 1977-1997	
1977	Cornell University
1978	Cornell University
1979	Cornell University
1980	Cornell University
1981	Cornell University;
	Brown University
1982	Princeton University
1983	Princeton University
1984	Princeton University
1985	Brown University
1986	Brown University
1987	Harvard University
1988	Harvard University
1989	Harvard University
1990	Cornell University
1991	Dartmouth College
1992	Princeton University
1993	Dartmouth College
1994	Brown University
1995	Dartmouth College;
	Princeton University
1996	Cornell University
1997	Brown University

Table 3-5

Midwestern Collegiate Women's Hockey Alliance, 1996-1997

Augsburg College

Carleton College

Gustavus Adolphus

University of Minnesota

University of Minnesota-Duluth

St. Catherine/St. Thomas

St. Cloud State University

St. Mary's

St. Olaf

University of Wisconsin (at Madison)

University of Wisconsin (at Eau Claire)

University of Wisconsin (at River Falls)

Table 3-6

Central Collegiate Women's Ice Hockey Association, 1996-1997

Bowling Green State University

University of Illinois (at Champaign)

Lake Forest College

University of Michigan

Michigan State University

Ohio State University

Western Michigan University

University of Wisconsin

Table 3-7

US Colleges and Universities offering Women's Ice Hockey, 1996-1997

Club

Amherst College, MA
Bates College, ME
Boston University, MA
Bowling Green State University, OH
Carleton College, MN
Chatham College, PA
Clarkson University, NY
Colgate University, NY
College of the Holy Cross, MA
Colorado College
Connecticut College
Gustavus Adolphus, MN
Iowa State University
Lake Forest College, IL
Mankota State, MN
Massachusetts Institute of Technology
Michigan State University
Michigan Tech University
Mount Holyoke College, MA
Niagara University, NY
North County Community College, NY
Ohio State University
Pennsylvania State University
Sacred Heart University, CT
Skidmore College, NY
Smith College, MA
Southern Maine University
St. Catherine & St. Thomas, MN
St. Cloud State University, MN
St. Mary's College, MN
St. Michael's College, VT
St. Olaf's College, MN
Union College, NY
University of Colorado (at Boulder)
University of Connecticut
University of Illinois (at Champaign)
University of Maine (at Orono)
University of Massachusetts (at Amherst)

University of Michigan
University of Minnesota (at Duluth)
University of Pennsylvania
University of Vermont
University of Wisconsin (at Eau Claire)
University of Wisconsin (at Madison)
University of Wisconsin (at River Falls)
Western Michigan University
Wheaton College, MA
William Smith College, NY

Varsity

Augsburg College, MN
Boston College, MA
Bowdoin College, ME
Brown University, RI
Colby College, ME
Cornell University, NY
Dartmouth College, NH
Hamilton College, NY
Harvard University, MA
Middlebury College, VT
Northeastern University, MA
Princeton University, NJ
Providence College, RI
Rensselaer Polytechnic Institute, NY
Rochester Institute of Technology, NY
St. Lawrence University, NY
University of Minnesota
University of New Hampshire
Wesleyan University, CT
Williams College, MA
Yale University, CT

MONTY RAND/UNIVERSITY OF NEW HAMPSHIRE

The University of New Hampshire Wildcats celebrate their 1995-96 ECAC championship win.

athletes. This was one way to satisfy them. One problem that the varsity status created was competition. During the first year, only Augsburg College offered competition on the same level of play as Minnesota. Laura Halldorson, head coach of the Minnesota team and former Colby College coach, scheduled as many games against eastern opponents as possible and budgeted three trips east. The University of Minnesota is very active in marketing and promoting all of its sports, and as a result, Halldorson expects her team to have more fan support than any other women's hockey team in the country. She has done promotion herself in the past, usually on a shoestring budget. "At Colby, we made the flyers, and put them around town and called the papers. We definitely gained an audience at Colby, but a lot of that was because we had a couple of really good players who got national media attention," Halldorson said. "So the key for me is to put a good product together, to make it successful right away and keep the people coming back. Minnesota fans are used to good hockey, so they want to bring in the best." The team will remain independent and will not join a women's league until more varsity teams are formed in the Midwest.

Colleges and universities across the USA continue to add or upgrade women's ice hockey programs. In 1996-1997, 903 colleges were part of the NCAA. Of these, 131 offered men's varsity hockey and more offered club hockey. Fifty of the 131 schools were Division I, 13 were Division II and 68 were Division III. Only 21 colleges offered varsity ice hockey to women and 48 more had women's club teams. As usual, colleges in New England led the pack with the most varsity programs — 13. As Table 3-7 shows, there are many colleges and universities in the US offering women's ice hockey, although the number is not large compared to other sports or to men's hockey programs. Notably absent, however, are varsity or club

University of New Hampshire coach Karen Kay rallies the troops before a 1997 matchup against rival Providence College.

teams from the West and the South. Ice hockey has been slow to catch on in these regions, in part because of the warm climate and lack of ice rinks.

IF YOU ASK, THEY WILL COME

The rise in the number of colleges offering women's hockey can be attributed to two factors: Title IX legislation, and the sudden growth of girls' community hockey clubs in the eastern US in the early 1970s. States across the nation offered girls' hockey in the 1960s, including New York, Delaware, West Virginia, Michigan and Ohio. In 1967, Michigan girls' hockey started up with four teams. By 1976 there were nearly 50. Unlike in most programs, the girls were not lacking for competition, as they were part of the Michigan/Ontario Ladies Hockey League, and could compete in both Canada and the US. But none of these states foresaw the explosion of interest and participation that occurred in Massachusetts in the 1970s. One of the people responsible for this explosion was Tony Marmo.

"Wanted: Girls interested in becoming nice hockey players." In 1970, when Tony Marmo put this ad in the local paper to recruit girls for an ice hockey team, he never expected the kind of response he received. Over 100 girls showed up for the first practice. In that group were some girls who could skate and knew the basics of the game, but most had never even played hockey before and were just curious about Marmo's intentions to form a girls' hockey team. After a few weeks of practice, the best skaters and the most deeply interested and dedicated players, about 40 in all, formed two travel teams, A and B. In November 1970, the Massport Jets were born.

Marmo was born into a family of four sisters and three brothers. He played youth hockey as a boy in East Boston but noticed that his sisters did not get the same opportunity. "Schools and recreation departments offered baseball, football, basketball, hockey, tennis, boxing, swimming — everything a kid could want. There was nothing for girls," Marmo said. "My sisters inspired me. They were denied while the boys were spoiled. If my sister ever asked to play hockey, she would get a slap in the face. And I always said if I got the chance someday, I'd do something about it." Marmo got his chance in 1970, when he was commissioner of youth hockey at the Porrazzo Municipal rink in East Boston. He was also a certified American Hockey Association referee, and a former semi-professional player in the New England League, where he had played for the Windsor, Connecticut hockey club and the East Boston Pros. Bobby Orr and the Boston Bruins had just won the Stanley Cup and hockey fever had gripped the state. Ice arenas were built, particularly in metropolitan Boston. Girls and boys also took to frozen ponds and streams in the winter and the asphalt in the summer, all of them emulating the Big Bad Bruins.

The name "Massport Jets" was derived from the Massachusetts Port Authority, or Massport, operators of Logan International Airport. Massport was located in East Boston, the home of Marmo and the team. Massport assisted in the initial organization of the Jets, providing jerseys and socks for the girls, and in some instances, bus transportation to tournaments and games. The Boston Police Association provided the goalie equipment. It also helped that Marmo was a boyhood friend and former youth hockey team-mate of former Massachusetts Governor Ed King, the executive director of Massport.

For the first few weeks, the girls showed up to practice in second-hand equipment and figure skates. By the second season, the girls looked like any boys' team, with hockey skates, new equipment and jerseys. But Marmo knew the equipment was designed for boys and would not properly protect girls. He developed a chest protector which incorporated additional plastic that attached to the shoulder pads and covered the breasts. He designed a cup for girls and women, and insisted that his players wear it to guard against injury to their genitals.

During the first year of the Jets, the girls, most of whom were high school age,

DONALD YOUNG/COURTESY TONY MARMO

Many members of the Massport Jets of East Boston, Massachusetts started off wearing figure skates and very little padding when the team was formed in 1971.

were taught the basics of ice hockey and the rules of the game. Several press releases and newspaper articles were printed featuring Marmo and his Jets, and these generated even more interest in girls' ice hockey. Girls from the North Shore of Massachusetts to Cape Cod wanted to be a part of the Massport Jets. Within a year, the Jets had grown to include a house league of four teams of younger, less-experienced girls who could work their way up to the travelling team. Marmo also received inquiries from towns and communities interested in forming their own girls' teams and wanting to find out how to get started. By the end of 1972, Marmo and other Massport Jets staff, who were all volunteers, had assisted many towns in the Boston area in developing girls' hockey, including Billerica, Canton, East Cambridge, Framingham, Holliston, Marblehead, Needham, Norwood and Warwick, Rhode Island. This nucleus of teams formed the American Girls Hockey Association (AGHA). The objective of the AGHA was to promote girls' hockey in as many communities as possible and the staff was readily available to help any community with an interest in girls' hockey.

While many girls participated, there were many others who wanted to play but weren't allowed to do so. Marmo acknowledges that parents were sometimes the biggest obstacle. "Most of the fathers went along with it when I brought it up. They said they thought it was a great idea," he said. "But then they'd go home and tell their wives if I asked them [to allow their daughters to play] to say no." The mothers, however, were generally supportive. Marmo believes that many mothers saw it as an opportunity for their daughters that they hadn't had, and did not want to deny their daughters that opportunity. Another concern of parents was that their daughters could get injured and that they would not appear "lady-like." In fact, Marmo recalls, the worst injuries over the years were a broken thumb and a facial fracture. Most boys' teams were against the girls, too. Some parents of players on opposing boys' teams were not supportive of girls who could beat their sons, with the result that many boys' teams fought against letting girls play competitive hockey.

Marmo not only battled parents; he battled youth hockey organizations as well, especially coaches and male players were not keen on sharing ice time. But behind Marmo were dedicated and persistent community activists such as Bobby Travaglini, Chick Geraci, Al Morelli, Billy Penicelli and Harold Jones. With their support, girls' hockey skated on, even though it was two years before Title IX would legally force equality.

The Jets remained in East Boston and became the best girls' hockey team in the state. They established an unbroken record of wins and found it necessary to travel beyond Massachusetts to find teams with more experience. In February 1972, the Jets were invited to Montreal, Quebec to play McGill University, Loyola College and MacDonald College. They returned from Canada undefeated.

The Jets received quite a bit of publicity in local newspapers about being the first girls' hockey team in the area. In March 1972, after their return from Canada, the Jets put on the first-ever exhibition of girls' hockey at the Boston Garden with a 10-minute exhibition game between the first and second period of a Boston Braves–Providence Reds game of the American Hockey League. The girls were warmly received by over 14,000 hockey fans. In January 1973, the Jets were the subject of a half-hour documentary on a local television magazine show, *Bostonia*. In March 1975, Jets player Patty Jones was interviewed by colour commentator Johnny Pearson in between periods of a Boston Bruins game. Throughout the 1970s, the girls also appeared in national magazines such as

COURTESY TONY MARMO

By 1973, the Massport Jets had hockey skates, full gear and matching uniforms.

Women Sports, *Popular Sports Face-Off*, and *The Sportswoman*.

In March 1973, the Massport Jets were invited to participate in the First Invitational Women's Hockey Tournament at Cornell University in Ithaca, New York. Other participants included Loyola University and McGill University from Montreal, both considered among the top teams in Canada. The format of the tournament was a one-game elimination. Round one pitted the Jets against Loyola. The Jets rolled over the competition 7-0. In the championship game, the Jets faced off against McGill and shut them out 8-0 to be crowned Northeast American Champions. After 95 games, the Jets remained undefeated.

In addition to tournaments and games against other girls' teams, the Jets played exhibition games against boys' teams to promote girls' hockey and assist other communities in forming teams. The Jets won about half of the games they played against boys, but were always competitive and donated much of the proceeds in the exhibition games to further promote girls' hockey in the community. Two sets of tickets were sold for each girls-versus-boys exhibition game. Whatever amount the boys made they kept for their organization and whatever the girls sold went to equipment and uniforms in that community. The girls also sponsored raffles, sticker drives and other fundraising activities to pay for transportation to tournaments (when it wasn't provided by Massport), ice time and other costs. Marmo instituted a unique policy among the Jets whereby each member of the team had a bank account. As the player sold tickets or stickers, the money would go into her account. Because any additional cost for transportation and registration had to be paid by the player's family, this gave the players incentive to promote the sport and help out their families.

The AGHA continued to grow. By April 1973, teams from Wakefield, Arlington, Burlington, Concord, Rockport, Gloucester, Lexington, Medford, Peabody, Saugus and Nashua, New Hampshire were added. By the end of the year, the AGHA encompassed 2,000 girls on 28 teams. Marmo estimated that there were at least 25 more teams in Massachusetts that were not part of the AGHA.

Even as participation in girls' hockey in Massachusetts skyrocketed, groups tried to halt it. In December 1974, it had come to the attention of the Massachusetts Secondary Schools Principal's Association that several of the girls on the Jets might be in violation of Headmaster's Rule 19. Rule 19 stated that no athlete may play varsity sports in school and take part on an organized team outside the school during the same season. The rule was supposed to prevent high school varsity athletes, both boys and girls, from overexerting themselves by playing on and/or practicing with more than one team. A team was defined as an organization with a coach, a schedule and a consistent roster for each game. The headmasters hoped that Rule 19 would allow many athletes in the community to play on teams instead of the outstanding athletes who excelled at many sports dominating all the sports in town. (For example, Jets star Lee Johnson played basketball in Swampscott at the same time as she suited up for the Jets.) The headmasters were not successful in limiting the activities of athletes and Rule 19 was fought by high school athletic directors, who naturally wanted the star athletes to play in school teams, and was soon banished.

The Jets team was more than just a form of recreation for its players. Marmo ran a strict practice and tried to develop healthy minds and bodies. There was a strict no-smoking rule and the girls carried and put on their own equipment. They were suspended if their grades became unsatisfactory. He approached school guidance counsellors to ensure that his players would have opportunities beyond high school. Parents who didn't approve of Marmo's methods were asked to remove their daughters from the program. Marmo also sponsored clinics in coaching and refereeing so that his players could eventually take over the coaching duties of the Jets. By 1975, the B squad was coached by standout A team players Patty Jones and Lee Johnson.

The Jets continued to play against Canadian powerhouses and continued to win. By February 1975, the Jets had played in 10 women's tournaments in Canada. The Toronto Agincourts, with much more experienced and slightly older (19- and 20-year-old) players, and winners of 117 straight games, split a two-game series with the Jets. The East Boston team won the first game 6-3, but dropped the second 5-2. It was the first time either team had ever lost to another girls' team. Both games featured bodychecking, a style the Jets did not usually play. A Toronto television station aired the game and newspaper reporters from Toronto and Boston covered the event.

The Jets faced off against some of the best women hockey teams in Canada, including the Montreal Cougars (the North American Champions), the Kingston Red Barons, Toronto Ladies and Peterborough Fontaine Cycles. All of their losses were at the hands of Canadian teams, but usually the Jets prevailed, despite the greater experience of their opponents and the age difference between the teams. The average age of the Jets players was 16, while it was not uncommon for the Canadian players to be cheered on by their own children in the stands. By April 1975, the Massport Jets had amassed an incredible 128-6 record.

Other successful girls' teams also emerged from the AGHA. In 1972, Janet Ryan, a sophomore member of the Jets, no longer wanted to travel 20 miles to Boston from her home to play hockey. She put up posters in her high school girls' locker room and the local sporting goods store, inquiring if there were any girls were interested in forming a hockey team. Twenty girls responded. The resulting Suburban Eagles iced a team with girls from Framingham, Natick, Sherborn, Sudbury, Wayland and Cochituate. Within a couple of years, the Eagles boasted girls aged eight to 18 and had formed three teams — A, B and C — and played 25 to 30 games a season. They quickly emerged as one of the top teams in the state, winning 10 straight games and a tournament in Saugus their first year. Some of the girls took their hockey very seriously. Marsha Hunter was a puckstopper for the Eagles when the team was formed. At 16, as a junior at Natick High School, Hunter aspired to play professional ice hockey. She kept a diary with statistics and critiques of her own and teammates' performances for the entire season. She had a 1.10 goals against average the team's first year but was unable to play beyond college.

The Massport Jets dissolved in the early 1980s, ironically because of all the teams they had helped to create. The original group of girls who had answered

Tony Marmo's ad for a "nice hockey team" had moved on to college or careers. Other players who might have been replacements opted to play in their own hometowns. While there is no longer a team in East Boston sporting the Jets uniform, there are now thousands of girls playing youth hockey in over a hundred communities in Massachusetts, and the opportunities that Marmo and his Jets helped create will last into the next century.

4 / WE JUST WANT TO PLAY HOCKEY
Putting Girls in the Game

TITLE IX LEGISLATION IN THE US

The ice crunches beneath the short choppy strides of Meghan Roy's skates. She races down the left wing back to her position on defence in a game against the Dover (New Hampshire) Dino-mites. Her eight-year-old legs wobble as she reaches for the puck and swipes it away from a Dino-mite player before he can gain control, then she falls to the ice. Meghan picks herself back up and moves back to her position on defence. The whistle blows and Meghan skates over to the bench, receiving praise from her coach and team-mates. Meghan is one of four girls playing for the Rochester (New Hampshire) Blackhawks, an initiation team comprised of six- to eight-year-olds who until this year have never played hockey. The other players see Meghan as a team-mate, an integral part of what helps them win, lose and, more importantly, have fun.

After the game, Meghan changes out of her uniform and equipment, soaked with a combination of sweat and melted ice, and tosses sticks, skates and pads into a long duffel bag. Like every other member of the Blackhawks, she tugs at the bag as best she can until her mother carries it the rest of the way to the sea of minivans and cars in the parking lot.

Meghan is excited about playing every game and thousands of girls share in her enthusiasm. That's why it's hard to believe that just over two and a half decades ago in the US, and a little more than 10 years ago in Canada, many girls were denied the chance to play the game, develop their skills and have fun because they were just that — girls.

Had Meghan been a young girl in the 1960s, the sports opportunities available to her would have been significantly fewer. Although the women's movement surfaced at that time, equality in athletics was still unknown. Even in the early 1970s, most high schools and colleges across the US had minimal or no athletic programs for women. The United States Congress attempted to correct the imbalance in school athletics in 1972 with Title IX of the Education Amendments. It states, in part, that no person in the United States shall, on the basis of sex, be excluded from participation in, denied the benefits of, or be subject to discrimination under any education program or activity receiving federal financial assistance.

An immediate problem arose regarding exactly which programs were covered under Title IX. The Department of Health, Education and Welfare (HEW) was assigned to make that decision. It interpreted the Act to apply to every program within a school that received any federal financial assistance, as opposed to only those programs that received direct government financial aid. In 1975, HEW issued its first set of proposed regulations regarding Title IX and cited interscholastic and intercollegiate athletics as specific departments covered under the law.

Athletic directors were then faced with determining what they were required to provide female athletes such as Meghan. To clear up the misconceptions, the Department of Education issued a Title IX Policy Interpretation in December 1979. The Policy provided for equal treatment for all athletes in the areas of financial assistance, scholarships, practice and competitive facilities, coaching, recruitment and other program benefits.

The Policy Interpretation also called for equal opportunity in the selection of sports and levels of competition. This did not mean that schools were required to integrate sports or offer the same sports to male and female athletes. It did mean that all women and girls would be allowed to try out for any non-contact sport. If the demand for a specific sport was high enough, the school would be asked to sponsor a women's team. For Meghan, the Policy's claim of equality was deceptive. Women were still prohibited from trying out for contact sports, such as football or ice hockey. Concern for the health and safety of women and girls was used as justification.

Despite HEW's recommendations, it remained unclear whether, by law, Title IX applied only to those departments within an institution receiving federal funds or to all departments of an institution receiving federal funds. The decision was vital in determining whether athletics would be covered, since few athletic departments received direct government funding. The issue was decided by the Supreme Court in *Grove City College v. Bell* in 1984. The Court ruled that Title IX would pertain to only those departments and programs that received direct federal aid.

Gender equity proponents fought to have the Supreme Court's decision overturned and in March 1988, Congress enacted the Civil Rights Restoration Act of

Table 4-1	
Increase in women's participation in high school and college sports	
Percentage of total athletes	
1972	15%
1989	33.7%
1995	36.9%
sources: The Civil Rights Restoration Act of 1987 by M. Villalobos and the 1994-95 NCAA participation study.	

1987. The future for female athletes like Meghan brightened. For them the new Act meant that if the school received federal aid for any program, all programs were included under Title IX and other federal anti-discrimination laws. Around the same time, many states found the contact sport exception to be unconstitutional and the girls were soon executing skating and passing drills in tryouts alongside the boys.

As a result of the legislation, many female athletes like Meghan seized the opportunity to participate in sports. Prior to Title IX, women accounted for 15 percent of the total number of athletes in high school and college sports. By 1989, women comprised just over one-third of all athletes and this number was still rising in 1995. Table 4-1 illustrates this increase in women's participation in athletics.

While more women and girls were participating in athletics, they were still not receiving their fair share of funding. Women's programs received less than 18 percent of the available athletic budget in 1989. In 1992, the National Collegiate Athletic Association (NCAA) commissioned a Gender Equity Task Force to review the issue. While the percentage of male and female students was equal, the percentage of varsity athletic participants, scholarship money received, athletic budget received and recruiting budget received was grossly skewed in favour of male athletes. Five years later, in 1997, the twenty-fifth anniversary of Title IX, the NCAA released results of a second gender equity study which began in June 1996. While the percentage of money for women's programs increased slightly in most areas, it was still far from equal. Table 4-2 shows the results of the 1992 and 1996 surveys.

Table 4-2

NCAA Gender-Equity Study

| | March 1992 | | April 1997 | |
	Male	Female	Male	Female
Student Body	50%	50%	47%	53%
Varsity Athletic Participation	69%	31%	63%	37%
Scholarship Money Received	69.6%	30.4%	62%	38%
Athletic Department Budget Received	77.4%	22.6%	77%	23%
Recruiting Budget Received	82.8%	17.2%	73%	27%

Table 4-3

NCAA Gender-Equity Study — Division I Ice hockey

April 1997

	Male	Female
Scholarship Money Received	79%	21%
Ice Hockey Dept. Budget Received	74.5%	25.5%
Recruiting Budget Received	83.2%	16.8%
source: NCAA Gender-Equity Study, April 1997		

How did women's hockey compare with men's hockey in the 1996 NCAA study? Women fared slightly better in hockey than in other women's sports in terms of their percentage of the operating budget, but were below average in recruiting and scholarship monies. Overall, the women's ice hockey teams received only a quarter of what the men's teams received. Table 4-3 summarizes the findings of the study for Division I ice hockey.

In 1992, it appeared there was a breakthrough in persuading athletic departments to comply with Title IX when the Supreme Court handed down its decision in *Franklin v. Gwinnett County Public Schools*. The case involved a female high school student who brought a Title IX sexual harassment suit against a Georgia school district, alleging that school officials had failed to stop the unwanted sexual advances of a teacher for more than a year. The Supreme Court ruled unanimously that not only was the school in violation of Title IX, but the student deserved compensation, as would all victims of deliberate Title IX discrimination. What did this decision mean to girls like Meghan? Previously, the danger of failure to comply with Title IX was merely the potential loss of federal funding. After *Franklin v. Gwinnett County Public Schools*, the cost of gender discrimination, including court costs and possible compensation, could exceed the cost of adding entire sports programs for women.

Equity in ice hockey was the issue in the 1990 case of *Cook et al. v. Colgate University*. Five members of the Colgate women's hockey club team contended that Colgate had violated Title IX by repeatedly denying varsity status to members. A varsity designation would promote the team to official representatives of the school with full-time coaches and specific competitive playing schedules. Varsity teams were also provided with equipment, practice facilities and travel accommodations. Club teams were more recreational in nature, with informal practices and competitions and a distinctly smaller budget. The men's varsity hockey team had a budget of over $238,000 per year, while the women were allotted $4,600 for their team — which was equivalent to the amount the men's team paid for sticks in one season. The court ruled that the university had violated Title IX by not providing the women's ice hockey team with athletic opportunities comparable to the men's team. The women's program was inferior to the men's in the areas of financial support, equipment, locker room facilities, travel expenses, practice time and coaching. The women were granted varsity status for the 1993-1994 season. The case marked the first time in which Title IX was used for a sport-specific comparison of women's and men's teams, as opposed to program-wide equality. Colgate appealed, and in 1993 the 2nd District Court of New York ruled the matter moot, as the plaintiffs had graduated from school before the team was granted varsity status. The Colgate women's ice hockey team gained varsity level status for 1997-1998 season.

Although the Colgate women ultimately lost the case, other women's teams began to examine their own programs. In 1992, members of the Bowdoin College women's ice hockey team in Maine filed a sexual discrimination complaint with the US Department of Education, alleging the school favoured men's team sports. Five graduates filed suit on behalf of the team, citing the school was in violation of Title IX in the scheduling of events, treatment of the coaching staff and awarding scholarships. As of 1997, the status of the case was unknown.

In 1995, integrated youth hockey was examined legally. Amy Poole, a 15-year-old member of the Waunakee Youth Hockey Association, filed a complaint against the Association, claiming she was treated unfairly because of gender. Poole, the only girl her age on a hockey team in Waunakee, Wisconsin, said she quit the team after six months of discrimination. In the complaint, Poole accused the head coach of the Association of discouraging her from joining the boys' team before seeing her play. Instead, he gave her the names of two girls' teams in Madison, 10 miles south. But Poole preferred to play with a team where she lived. The complaint also alleged that team-mates called her names and the coach did not play her while team-mates sat in the penalty box. The team also voted to ban her from the locker room, forcing Poole to change in the hallway, missing out on pre-game bonding and instructions from the coach. Six other girls in the district were competing on boys' teams in the 12-15 age group. As of 1997, the case was still pending in the Wisconsin court system.

Other high school teams and hockey associations integrated girls into boys' teams without objection or fanfare. Four girls participated in the 50-team Suffolk County High School Hockey League, a club league in New York. The girls changed alongside their team-mates in the men's dressing room. While the girls were not permitted to strip beyond their underwear, and in some cases were not allowed to wear less than a T-shirt and shorts, all the girls felt that changing in the dressing room was an important part of the game. Kimberly Fezza played for the junior varsity club team of Longwood in Hauppauge, New York, and was named assistant captain her junior year of high school. She participated in pre-game and post-game meetings and was a vocal leader on her team. In an interview with Rocky Bonanno of *Newsday* in 1994, she said that her presence in the locker room was an integral part of her acceptance and success on the team. Marisa Steckis, a junior left wing in the Police Athletic League in New York, also changed beside her team-mates. Her comments, also made in an interview with Bonanno in 1994, echoed Fezza's: "It made me feel more like a part of the team. The locker room was where the whole team got psyched and that helped me play better."

Title IX compliance is determined by comparing the overall percentage of athletes in men's and women's sports programs to the male-female student body ratio. Compliance problems immediately arise for schools offering football, as women do not have a corresponding sport requiring such a large number of

Table 4-4	
Intercollegiate sports offered to women: Division I Schools	
	Number of sports
1972	2.5
1977	5.6
1984	6.9
1988	7.3
source: Women & Athletics: A Twenty Year Retrospective on Title IX by D. Heckman (1992)	

athletes. Thus, the participation ratio is drastically skewed in favour of men. College football, however, is vitally important to many schools' athletic departments. It is the largest revenue-producing sport in many institutions and is a factor in funding other sports at the college or university. While many colleges and universities realize the importance of gender equity, budget cuts and lack of funds make the task even more difficult. With no money to fund more women's programs, the course many schools take to improve their female sports participation ratios is to cut men's programs. As a result, a law intended to provide equal opportunities for men and women, and thereby to increase opportunities for women in sport, has become what some call a quota-filling system.

While cutting men's programs is not what Title IX was meant to accomplish, the implementation of gender equity legislation has at least increased awareness of the imbalance in athletics. Some progress has been made. As Table 4-4 shows, many schools have added girls' and women's sports programs, creating opportunities for young women to learn or compete in a new sport, such as ice hockey.

CANADIAN GIRLS PLAYING BOYS' HOCKEY

If Meghan had lived in Canada, the battle for athletic equality would have been fought without the benefit of legislation like Title IX. Except for national teams, sports in Canada are organized and administered on a provincial and community level, with equity varying from province to province. Significant progress towards women's rights in sports, specifically hockey, began with the controversy Abigail Hoffman created in 1955, when she cut her hair and suited up to play for a boys' hockey team. It was an event that signalled a change in attitude and a new era in women's hockey.

Eight-year-old Abigail Hoffman had grown up playing hockey with her brothers and registered in the Toronto Hockey League, an all-boys league. Undaunted by the unwritten rule of "no girls allowed," Abigail called herself "Ab" and handed officials her birth certificate. No one checked the gender on the certificate and Ab was assigned to a team. She became a star at defence, matching her teammates and opponents stride for stride, and was named to the all-star team during the season.

When it was rumoured that a girl was playing on the team, the officials rechecked birth certificates and discovered "Ab" was a girl. Her celebrity skyrocketed, as newspapers, magazines and television stations jumped on the story. Hoffman was allowed to continue to play with her team, but was given her own dressing room. The following season she succumbed to pressure from players and coaches to quit the boys' team, although she was not forbidden to try out. She joined a girls' league, but they had difficulty scheduling games and eventually Hoffman decided to quit hockey to pursue other sports. Hoffman never intended to challenge the system — she just wanted to play hockey — but, in the process, she proved she was capable of playing hockey as well as any boy her age.

The question of whether girls should be allowed to play on boys' hockey teams was reintroduced on a much larger scale in 1977. Eleven-year-old Gail Cummings of Huntsville, Ontario joined a boys' team as a goalie in October 1976 because no girls' team existed in the area with a higher level of competition than house league. Cummings won four games and posted a shutout for the Atoms All-Stars before the Ontario Minor Hockey Association (OMHA) refused to acknowledge her as a member because she was a girl. The OMHA also refused to allow her to participate in any more games. They claimed her participation was against their rules, and they had no intentions of changing the rules or making an exception. Cummings' mother, Dorothy, asked the Ontario Human Rights Commission to investigate whether there was a case for a charge of gender discrimination. The investigation was based on the grounds that Cummings was denied access to public services and facilities because of her gender, which constituted a breach of the 1962 Ontario Human Rights Code. The OMHA contended it was a private organization and not subject to public rules. It was the first case under the Human Rights Code to question girls' rights to play sports on teams with boys.

The case sparked a major debate between those who felt the girls should be given a chance to play, even if it meant playing on a boys' team, and those who still felt that girls shouldn't play hockey at all. In an interview with the *Toronto Star*, Al Moore, president of the OMHA, explained his decision to ban Cummings from the league: "There are problems when you start mixing sexes. Dressing rooms might have to be changed to accommodate girls and many of the facilities that we play in just don't have the space. We make the regulations for all members, not for isolated individuals. I'm not so sure hockey is such a great thing for girls to be playing anyway."

Moore and the OMHA were not alone in their concern that girls should not play boys' hockey. Some boys' hockey executives felt that boys might lose respect for girls who played hockey against them and that girls were just not physically strong enough to compete. Many officials in minor hockey were so steadfast in their opinion they threatened to resign if girls were allowed to play.

But not everyone was convinced that girls on boys' teams was such a bad idea. Some believed that boys and girls should be able to play sports together without any problems until age 13 or 14, when puberty begins to alter their bodies. Many felt that as long as the girls were qualified to play and had proven their skill level was at least equal to the boys', the girls should be given the opportunity to learn, compete and grow as players on a boys' team. Barry Webb, who coached Cummings, testified before the commission that there was no difference between her and the boy players on the team. "I thought she played well. I was disappointed when I found out she wouldn't be allowed to play," Webb said.

Abby Hoffman also testified at the inquiry and, because of her own experience, was in a good position to discuss the merits and handicaps of girls playing on boys' teams. Hoffman said there is "no inherent reason in girls prior to puberty to make them less suitable for competitive sports. In fact, in flexibility and skills girls are often better than boys at that age." According to Brian McFarlane's book, *Proud Past, Bright Future*, Hoffman said in an interview with Anita Latner of the *Toronto Star* that "there is a lack of opportunity and little encouragement for girls to enter sports. If a girl is exceptional, she's accepted as an athlete. But if she's just average, she's questioned as to why she's trying to be like a man."

The board of inquiry gave its ruling on November 2, 1977. The OMHA was in violation of the Human Rights Code in banning Gail Cummings from competition on the basis of gender alone. A 20-page report by University of Toronto law professor Mary Eberts, who headed the board, declared that the OMHA was not sufficiently private to escape the reach of Section 2 of the Code, which dealt with "services or facilities available in any place to which the public is customarily admitted." Eberts maintained that the OMHA would be in compliance with the Code only if it were to "accept for registration any female player within its geographical and age jurisdiction who had been judged by the appropriate coach as skilled enough to play on a competitive team." Eberts went on to say that the decision reached beyond the age group for which Cummings was disputing to include all ranks and levels of the OMHA.

The OMHA appealed the ruling and refused to play against any team that dressed a female player. At a tournament in Chicago, a Kitchener, Ontario team refused to line up against a team from Waukegan, Illinois when their goaltender, nine-year-old Kelly Emerson, skated out to the net. Kitchener was forced to forfeit the game, but the OMHA's tenacity paid off when the Divisional Court of the Supreme Court of Ontario overturned the board of inquiry's ruling in August 1978. By mid-1979 the Divisional Court's ruling was appealed to the Ontario Court of Appeals. The judges decided the Canadian Amateur Hockey Association, who held jurisdiction over the OMHA, did not follow the proper steps to be recognized under Canadian law, and the case was dismissed. Cummings was ultimately not allowed to play on the boys' team, but this one little girl's desire to play hockey had turned into a case of national proportion that would open the doors for other girls across Canada.

Cummings' case prompted young girls and their parents to question the hockey programs in their own area. Seven-year-old Samantha Sniderman of Montreal faced the same situation as Cummings. When Sniderman's parents threatened to bring suit against the City of Montreal and the League, organizers permitted Sniderman to play. In 1978 in Yarmouth, Nova Scotia, an 11-year-old girl became the first female member of the Yarmouth Minor Hockey Association after a judge ruled the association was in violation of the Nova Scotia Human Rights Commission by not allowing her to play. In western Canada, the situation was much the same, as four girls were barred from competitive play during the 1980-1981 season. One coach, however, stood by his player and her right to play. Jerry Hartwell, coach of the Pirate Community Club's Tier Four minor peewee hockey team in Winnipeg, Manitoba, allowed assistant captain Heather Kramble to compete in the team's opening playoff game against the East End Wings. Hartwell was told by the Winnipeg Minor Hockey Association, which subscribed to the implied male-only policy of the Canadian Amateur Hockey Association (CAHA), that he could lose his position as coach and be barred indefinitely if Kramble played. Kramble was on the ice during the Pirates 2-1 loss to East End. The players and parents fully supported Hartwell's position. Bryan Kramble, Heather's father, commented in an interview with the *Globe & Mail* in 1981 that "if one or two girls can poison minor hockey in Winnipeg, then it's in rough shape." Hartwell was suspended after the game. City councillors immediately adopted a resolution to allow girls to play, prompting the Winnipeg Minor Hockey Association to lift the suspension. They refused, however, to reverse the decision on girls. It was becoming clear that the old "club-house" thinking of the male-run hockey associations was outdated and many youth hockey associations had to reassess their rules if they did not want to go to court.

The girls-in-boys'-hockey controversy remained focused in Ontario and the Ontario government eventually organized a task force to study the matter of females being allowed to participate on all-male teams. As a result, in 1982, Section 19 (2) was adopted into the Human Rights Code, which prohibited women from filing discrimination charges when all-male amateur athletic clubs refused them a tryout. Ontario became the only province with specific legislation designed to segregate sports on the basis of gender.

In 1982 the Canadian Association for the Advancement of Women and Sport (CAAWS) was established to promote the interests of women in sport. The group included sports administrators, educators and former athletes who wished to change attitudes and laws that discouraged women from playing sports that involved direct physical contact. While CAAWS has not had any direct impact on women's hockey, it has shown continued support for the development of the sport, including publishing favourable articles in its newsletter, *Action Bulletin*. Other agencies have also shown progress on equality issues. Fitness Canada established a women's program in 1988, the same year a national task force stated that all publicly funded agencies must promote gender equality in programs and services.

Just to confuse things, as Ontario was cracking down on integration, the CAHA passed a policy in May 1984 that allowed girls 12 and under to play on boys' teams, but only in areas where girls' teams did not exist. As a result of the new CAHA rule, the Don Valley Village Hockey association was suspended from the

Metropolitan Toronto Hockey League (MTHL) in 1984 when it allowed six girls to play on house league teams. The MTHL claimed Don Valley was in violation of the CAHA — while Don Valley did not have a girls' team in their league, girls' leagues were available in North York and Scarborough, just a few miles away. Keith Burrow, vice-president of the Don Valley group, said in a 1984 interview with Lois Kalchman of the *Toronto Star* that it was not attacking the MTHL but felt the rules were outdated. Many provincial and local hockey officials supported the CAHA rule, claiming it was designed to give all girls a chance to play hockey and not to promote integration. Even the Ontario Women's Hockey Association (OWHA), longtime proponents of women's hockey, was in favour of the CAHA rule, claiming it was an issue about opportunity, not integration.

Other hockey groups thought that by refusing to allow girls to play on boys' teams, even if comparable girls' teams existed, the CAHA and its supporters were refusing girls a chance to play up to their skill level and denying them the opportunity to become better players. Other MTHL teams followed the lead of Don Valley and allowed girls to play. The Queensway Canadian House league in Etobicoke risked suspension by permitting five girls to suit up and play on boys' teams. In an interview with Lois Kalchman of the *Toronto Star* in 1984, Queensway director Karl Heck said he could not understand why girls were not allowed to play on boys' teams, particularly at young ages, and refused to back down even when threatened with suspension for him and the team.

North York controller Barbara Greene was not as resistant to integration as the OWHA and set out to do something about organized hockey's discrimination against female players in the Toronto area. Greene felt the CAHA rule was discriminatory, and to allow such actions to take place in facilities or sponsored programs was a violation of Canada's 1982 Charter of Rights and Freedoms, a code similar to the US Bill of Rights. "The object is to compete on ability and not by sex," Greene said in a 1984 interview with Lois Kalchman. In 1984, Greene drafted a motion to block the CAHA from further discriminatory practice, but it was voted down by the North York council, which felt it had no jurisdiction over the CAHA. Ellen Mills, senior policy advisor for social issues for the Ontario Women's Directorate, supported Greene's motion. Mills further proposed to put an end to the issue once and for all when she suggested a legislative amendment to the Ontario Human Rights code to forbid sex discrimination in sports.

While the MTHL was refusing to adhere to female players' demands, the

Quebec Ice Hockey Federation (QIHF) had been accepting and welcoming female players since 1978, when a Quebec court ruling forced them to stop banning players on the basis of gender. QIHF executive director Gil Cardinal said in an interview with Lois Kalchman that of the 91,000 players registered on 6,000 men's teams in Quebec in 1985, approximately 200 were female, less than one quarter of 1 percent. These numbers quell the theory that allowing girls and women to play on boys' and men's teams would create a mass exodus from existing women's teams. Cardinal also said that young women usually realized when they had outgrown the league, or rather the league had outgrown them, at around age 13 or 14 when the boys began to bulk up and the girls did not. With the checking allowed in competitive boy's hockey in that age group and above, girls realized they would have problems playing against 6-foot, 200-pound opponents. Girls who did stay with the boys' teams were usually goaltenders. As Cardinal noted, a 14-year-old girl playing bantam AA was the best goalie in her division.

The MTHL remained adamant about its position, refusing to consider female players as members. Their determination was matched, however, by that of 12-year-old Justine Blainey of the Toronto Olympics, a minor peewee A team. In 1985, Blainey lobbied the Ontario Human Rights Commission for the right to play on the boys' team, even though comparable girls' teams existed in her age and skill level. Opponents, including the Ontario Hockey Association (OHA), which had jurisdiction over the MTHL, and the OWHA, contended that allowing Blainey to play on the boys' team would undermine the development of women's hockey in Canada, and that numerous opportunities currently existed within the women's program.

It was clear to Blainey and other young women that they did not have equal opportunities on women's teams, as the OWHA contended. Why did the girls want to play on boys' teams? Skating with the boys gave the girls an opportunity for more competition, more practices, more games and generally a higher standard of play. Many of the girls were more challenged by playing with the boys and had access to more experienced and skilled coaches, not to mention the opportunity to play in a rink closer to home. For Blainey, the issue was bodychecking and slapshots, both prohibited in the women's game. Even though a girls' team could accommodate Blainey, she felt her hockey skills might not have the chance to develop in the same manner as they would on a boys' team.

It appeared Blainey would be able to declare victory when Ontario Attorney-General Ian Scott announced a repeal of Section 19 (2) of the Code in July of 1985, a month before the scheduled court date. The case continued and the Ontario Court of Appeal ruled in 1986 that Section 19 (2) of the Ontario Human Rights Code was unconstitutional on the basis that it allowed sex discrimination in sport. Although the section was repealed, Blainey was still not permitted to suit up. An OHA regulation stated that only boys could be OHA members and play on its teams. Even though she was chosen to play for the Etobicoke Canucks during their tryouts in 1986, Blainey was still not allowed to play.

An appeal by the OHA in the Divisional Court of Ontario ruled against Blainey, but the case eventually went to the Supreme Court of Canada. In May 1987, Blainey won the right for qualified girls to play on the most skilled boys' teams through their teen years and beyond, seemingly putting an end to gender discrimination in organized hockey in Canada. In January 1988, Blainey played her first game in a minor bantam league. She skated with the boys for three years and then attended the University of Toronto, where she joined the varsity women's team. Her case created debate over the rights of a girl to play hockey versus the overall need to develop girls' hockey.

Hockey associations across Canada continued to ease their antiquated rules of boys-only hockey. In 1993 the Greater Montreal Athletic Association, the ruling sports body for 56 Montreal-area schools, voted to let girls try out for ice hockey and tackle football. The decision came on the heels of a request by 14-year-old Michelle Fauteux, who wanted to join the boys' hockey team at John Rennie High School. Fauteux had been trying to join the team since the start of the school year. She had played for a boys' bantam A team the season before.

More and more girls across the United States and Canada are discovering hockey for the first time and benefiting from the teamwork and friendships that develop. The prehistoric mentality that only boys can play hockey is slowly crumbling and someday, perhaps when Rochester's Meghan Roy has a daughter of her own, girls playing on the rink will be as much a part of the game as off-sides and icing.

5 / GRASSROOTS HOCKEY
Building Strong Networks

DIFFERENCES BETWEEN CANADA AND THE UNITED STATES

Grassroots hockey includes all the girls (and boys) who play on their community and school teams. It is the 5-year-old girl who is just learning to skate; it is the 10-year-old girl who is a figure-skater-turned-hockey-player; it is the 13-year-old who has been playing organized hockey in her community for eight years; and it is the 16-year-old who is playing on her high school's first-ever girls' ice hockey team. Grassroots hockey helps develop competitive national, state and provincial championships, and feeds the elite levels of the Canadian and US national teams. Without this broad base of players in grassroots hockey, competitions such as national tournaments, world championships and Olympic events would not be possible.

Both the Canadian Hockey Association (CHA) and USA Hockey have specific minor hockey programs which target players under the age of 18 (in Canada) and 19 (in the United States). Table 5-1 outlines the age classifications in youth hockey for the United States and Canada. The category names differ slightly between the two countries but the age divisions are generally the same. USA Hockey has developed an initiation program for boys and girls aged eight and under. In Canada, the initiation program targets beginner players, typically girls and boys aged nine and under. Most areas of the US don't have enough girls at the youngest age levels, especially squirts (12 and under), to create teams or leagues. As a result, many young girls play on boys' teams until the boys start bodychecking at 11 or 12 years old. At that point many girls either quit because of the aggressiveness of the boys, or, if they are serious about the game, travel beyond their region to find a girls' team.

There has been a huge acceleration in female hockey registration in North America since 1990. In Canada between 1987 and 1996, male hockey registration increased 13 percent, whereas female hockey registration grew 250 percent. In the United States, female registration increased 260 percent between 1991 and 1996, while male registration increased by 80 percent.

Table 5-1

Youth Hockey Age Classifications, 1997

United States		Canada
Boys	Girls	Boys and Girls
Midget (17 and under)	Midget (19 and under)	Midget (17 and under)
Bantam (14 and under)	Peewee (15 and under)	Bantam (15 and under)
Peewee (12 and under)	Squirt (12 and under)	PeeWee (13 and under)
Squirt (10 and under)		Atom (11 and under)
Mite (8 and under)		Novice (9 and under)
Mini-Mite (6 and under)		

For girls' hockey in the United States, forming girls' hockey teams has always been the focus of attention — the grassroots has always been quite strong. In Canada, on the other hand, female hockey has historically been top-heavy — that is, most of the participants were on women's teams and there were comparatively few youth teams involved. This became a problem for growth since there were very few young players to move up onto women's teams when the older players decided to hang up their skates. This was particularly obvious in the mid-1980s, when female hockey in Canada showed minimal growth, and even declined, in its numbers because the women's teams were folding.

In the province of Ontario, balancing registration between the women's categories and the minor hockey divisions has always been a challenge. In 1981, there were 197 women's teams registered in the province and 103 of these — over half — were at the senior level. Eight years later the total number of teams had increased to 285, but senior teams only comprised 31 percent of the total. By the 1995-1996 season, the total registration for the Ontario Women's Hockey Association (OWHA) was 12,296 playes, of whom only 3,709, about one-third, played in women's divisions — a slight increase over six years.

Since the 1970s, many states in the US have seen a steady increase in their girls' hockey registrations. As Table 5-2 illustrates, by 1990-1991, total female registration in the United States was 5,573 — only about 2,500 shy of Canada — and by 1996, this difference remained about the same as both countries experienced a boom in the female game. Registration numbers for young American

Table 5-2

Female hockey registration in Canada since 1990-1991

Year	Canada	United States
1990-91	8,146	5,573
1991-92	11,341	6,805
1992-93	12,418	8,991
1993-94	15,467	12,577
1994-95	19,050	17,573
1995-96	23,922	20,319
1996-97	27,305	not available at press time

players are quite accurate because the totals include girls who play on boys' teams: The total is of all girls playing hockey, not just girls who play hockey on girls' teams. USA Hockey estimates that approximately half of all females registered with USA Hockey in 1996 play on boys' or men's teams. Getting accurate registration numbers is a problem for female hockey in Canada. As of May 1997, some provinces reported that the registration numbers for female hockey in their area failed to capture players on boys' teams. For example, in Quebec the registration numbers only included girls' teams and didn't count about one thousand girls playing with boys. Numbers are just as inaccurate in other provinces, where many girls who play on boys' teams are simply counted among the boys' youth hockey totals.

The growth in female hockey can also be compared among different regions. As Table 5-3 shows, USA Hockey is divided into 11 different districts, whereas Canada has 11 different branches. (In May 1997, the Northwest Territories became the newest — and eleventh — branch of the CHA.) In 1995-1996, the US Minnkota District, the region including Minnesota, North Dakota and South Dakota, had the most female registrants with 4,455, nearly one-fifth of the total. In Canada, Ontario's OWHA ranked highest in 1996-1997 with 15,116 registrants, over half of the total for all of Canada. British Columbia, with the second-highest total, had only 2,872 registrants.

Even though women's hockey has increased in popularity, it is important for its future health that growth happen amongst younger players to avoid forming

Table 5-3

Female Hockey Registration in North America by District and Branch

United States, 1995-1996*		Canada, 1996-1997	
Minnkota	4,455	Ontario	15,116
Massachusetts	3,006	British Columbia	2,872
New England	2,224	Quebec	2,205
New York	2,124	Alberta	1,960
Michigan	1,923	Manitoba	1,667
Central	1,896	Nova Scotia	969
Pacific	1,693	Saskatchewan	878
Mid-American	945	New Brunswick	558
Rocky Mountain	809	Newfoundland	516
Atlantic	687	Prince Edward Island	404
Southeast	557	Other	160

* 1996-1997 female hockey registration for the US not available at press time

an upside-down pyramid, with an abundance of women's teams and very few girls' teams. In 1996 in Massachusetts, for example, the squirt and peewee divisions, the two youngest ages, had the highest numbers, illustrating how strong the grassroots base is in the state. By contrast, in 1996 in Ontario, senior women's hockey was still the category with the highest number of players. Peewee had the second highest number. Fortunately for the OWHA, the atom division, 11 and under, was third largest and showed signs of continuing to grow. Even though women still make up the hub of the OWHA membership, the grassroots growth will certainly help make a stronger, younger base for the association.

In both the US and Canada, some areas have very active female hockey participation and others don't. Why? In many cases, it depends on the opportunities girls have to play hockey — how minor hockey is organized. Another factor is the history and popularity of the sport. The Northeast and upper Midwest of the US have always been hockey hotbeds, but the sport was only introduced to Florida and Arizona in the last five years. In Massachusetts, there are many teams and leagues; in Texas, girls' hockey is just starting. The same comparison can be made for Ontario and Newfoundland in Canada. In other regions, such as Rhode Island in the United

States, and Alberta, British Columbia, Saskatchewan and Manitoba in western Canada, girls' hockey is still developing.

HOW DOES IT ALL START?

If someone were to ask how girls' hockey is organized in Canada and the United States, there wouldn't be a clear answer. For boys, the system is the same in every province and every state. But for girls, the opportunity to play hockey depends on where you live and what is available. Generally, a girl who wants to play hockey has two main options — play with the boys or play with the girls. Sometimes an all-girls team will play in a league against boys' teams. There is tremendous debate among players, parents and administrators over the best development strategy for girls' hockey.

In many cases, the first step towards getting girls involved in hockey is to have them play minor hockey on a boys' team. When more girls become involved, all-girls teams can begin to form. This is usually the second step in the growth cycle. Sometimes there is only one girls' team in an age category, such as novice or peewee. In these situations the all-girls team will play in a house league against boys' teams. Sometimes when the girls are new to the game they have a hard time fitting into a category that matches their calibre. In these cases, the girls' team will just arrange exhibition games rather than play in a formal league for the season. Once the girls gain experience, they join the boys' house league in their area. The third growth stage is reached when there are enough girls to form numerous girls' teams that can play against each other in their own league.

In Canada and in the United States, the setup varies even from town to town because communities do whatever it takes just to get the girls playing. The same plan cannot be used everywhere. If ice time is difficult to obtain, girls and boys may have to play together. If it is a rural area, far away from other towns and other teams, the girls' team may have to play in a boys' house league and travel every now and then to play in girls' hockey tournaments. If it is a large city with many female hockey volunteers, there may be a very large girls' hockey association and a league that includes different ages. Here, the girls play with and against other girls. Girls on boys' teams may also play on a girls' team in tournaments. For example, in Saskatchewan, the provincial hockey association requires girls on boys' teams to register on a girls' team in order to continue to develop female hockey in the province.

The top players in women's hockey today are examples of the variety of ways in which girls can become involved in hockey. Shirley Cameron, who played on Team Canada at the 1990 Women's World Hockey Championship, never played organized hockey when she was growing up. Cameron was born in 1952 and grew up on a farm just outside of Bonnyville, Alberta. Before the age of 20, she played hockey with her brothers on the frozen sloughs, similar to small marshes, in the fields around the farm. When asked why she got into the game so late, Cameron replied, "There were no other options. Where I came from, rural Alberta, the girls did not play with the boys. So there wasn't that option for me." She elaborated: "I don't know if there was an attitude difference or if it was just that nobody did it. I was on a farm and wasn't really encouraged by my parents. None of us were — my brothers didn't even really play organized hockey. What we played was in this small area [where] there were three Cameron families and so we would gather all the time at the slough that was kind of in between the three farms and we would play hockey every single night in the winter and on Saturday and Sunday. We were farm kids so I never even thought there would be such a thing as playing on an organized team."

Cameron's first experience in organized hockey came in the early 1970s after she moved to Edmonton, Alberta. She heard a radio ad asking women to come out and play pick-up hockey. The first year she played, it was like a women's night at the hockey rink: "The first year we came out there were enough girls to put two teams together and you were either the Sunday night girls' team or the Tuesday night girls' team. You had one ice session and all we did was kind of practiced. We had everything, from people who couldn't even stand on skates, to people who could kind of skate. Some were in figure skates, and some were in equipment." This was the first year. Little did Cameron know that the Tuesday and Sunday night gang would later form the team known as the Edmonton Chimos. The Chimos have dominated women's hockey in Alberta since the late 1970s and have won all but one provincial championship since 1982. In 1997, the Chimos won the Esso Women's Canadian Hockey Championship.

Judy Diduck, a four-time gold medallist with Team Canada, also was late to play organized hockey — in fact, although she played ringette, she did not play hockey at all until she was 19 years old. She didn't even realize she could play hockey until a high school acquaintance, who lived across the street and was playing hockey, said, "Why don't you come out?" Diduck commented, "I always

COURTESY MICHAEL DESJARDINS

Judy Diduck, four-time gold medallist with Team Canada, covers defence with her club team the Edmonton Chimos at the 1997 Esso Women's National Hockey Championship.

loved hockey. Hockey is a great sport! I just never realized it was there for me to play — that it was available to females. There was no turning back once I started." The conversion of ringette players into hockey players has become a common occurrence. What is so exceptional about Diduck is that even though she only started to play in her late teens, by the age of 24, she was a world champion with Team Canada. Diduck had strong skating skills from playing ringette but she still had to develop her puck control and shooting skills. She

COURTESY MICHAEL DESJARDINS

Dawn McGuire, captain of Alberta provincial champions the Edmonton Chimos, follows the play during the 1997 Esso Women's National Hockey Championship.

plays defence, so the tactical and technical aspects are an important part of her game — she quarterbacks the play.

Dawn McGuire, one of Shirley Cameron's team-mates on the Chimos, is an example of someone who started to play with the boys and joined girls' hockey later on. (McGuire played withthe Chimos until 1997; Cameron was her coach during the last few seasons she played.) Although these two women followed similar paths to national and international success, McGuire started to play organized hockey at a much younger age than Cameron. McGuire was born in 1960 in Stonewall, Manitoba and spent a lot of time in Stoney Mountain near Winnipeg when she was growing up. She first joined minor hockey when she was seven years old. "For the first four years of hockey I played with the boys — one year in Balmoral, and then we moved and I played with the Stonewall and Stoney Mountain boys," reflected McGuire. Why did she join boys' minor hockey? "I went to watch two cousins play, and Balmoral had only 500 people at the time, so they were short. I asked Dad if I could play and I actually started playing with them. I started to play in net. I played goal the first couple of years and just went from there." Once McGuire was 12 years old, she started playing on an all-girls team in Winnipeg, which meant a 25-mile drive into the city from where she lived.

Another top player who grew up in the boys' hockey system is American Maria Dennis. In 1962, when she was six, Maria's dad signed up her and an older brother for youth hockey in South Windsor, Connecticut. Dennis was one of only two girls in the program of 200 boys. She immediately fell in love with the game. She started out in the beginner's program with all the other six-year-olds, learning how to skate properly and use a hockey stick. Dennis graduated to a travel team, playing centre, and stayed with them until trying out for peewees at age 11. The coach then told her that he wasn't going to choose her because she was a girl and he was worried she might get hurt. Since there were no girls' teams at that time in Connecticut, Dennis found a boys' program in Enfield, and played for them through bantam. In her second year of high school she went to private school. Dennis first attended Taft School in Watertown, Connecticut, then decided to try out for the junior varsity boys' team, which was closer to the level at which she played. The junior varsity coach was willing to take Dennis on the team, but needed to ask permission from the athletic director. Dennis was shocked at the director's vehement refusal. The headmaster was also not willing to give her a chance. "Maria, you're never going to get any better, so why try?" he said. So Dennis left Taft and finished her senior year at Loomis Chaffee, playing for the girls' team. Dennis commented on her next decision — to play for Yale University in 1984: "The best women's hockey in the world is in the Northeast United States and that's where I was and that's who I was playing against. It was really great and I had a successful career even though my team didn't. I got a lot of scoring awards."

Dennis developed into an elite player because she wanted to play hockey as much as she could: "I loved it and I'm the type of person that if I love something, I want to be the best at it, so I really push myself and try to be the best I can be. So I was always trying out for travel teams and trying to go to national tournaments and just really striving, whether scoring the most goals or getting the most assists or just having the best record as a team. I was always trying to do that, and in college, I had the highest scoring average over my four years at Yale, the highest scoring average of women and men in the history of Yale. I think I had 160 points, which is goals and assists, over four years. The guy who had 158 points actually made it to the NHL."

Jane Robinson, another Team Canada player who won a gold medal at the 1994 Women's World Championship, followed a path similar to McGuire's — she started with boys' hockey then moved into girls'. For Robinson, however, moving into girls' hockey meant playing on a senior women's team at the age of 12. Robinson started to play when she was nine years old. She is one of eight children and grew up in a large hockey family. Her first team was in Wainwright, Alberta, in their minor hockey association. "It was great," Robinson said. "Another girl and I played and were probably the top two players, so there was never an issue about me or her being female and playing on a guys' team. It was never a problem. We played for two years and then we joined the ladies' team in Wainwright, though we were both very young."

Once Robinson overcame the challenge of being a young teenager on a women's team, the second hurdle was finding teams to play. Robinson remembered travelling every weekend just so they could participate in the Edmonton league: "The last year, when I was in Grade 12, our team was allowed to join the Edmonton league under the condition that we would go to Edmonton for all our league games. We loved to get together for road trips, so we agreed to travel. We drove to Edmonton basically every other weekend. We ended up placing first in the league that year. Because we were so young and loved the game immensely, the travelling did not seem to affect our play."

A few top female players never did play on girls' teams. Ellen Weinberg is the success story of a girl who graduated from an American grassroots system in Texas and excelled. Ice hockey is relatively new to Texans, for boys and girls alike. The first pro team, the Dallas Stars, just moved to Texas from Minnesota in 1993. But if Weinberg had not moved to Texas, she might never have become a hockey player. She was born in St. Louis, Missouri in 1968, and when she was six her older brother started playing hockey. She wanted to try it too. In the state of Missouri, however, boys' teams did not have to let girls play.

A year later, the Weinberg family moved to Dallas, Texas, and Ellen began playing on a boys' hockey team right away. She was the only girl on the team. Since there was little competition in Dallas, or anywhere in Texas, the team travelled as far as St. Louis, Kansas City and Colorado to play games, usually more than 40 a year. Weinberg never experienced any discrimination on her own team, but when they played teams in St. Louis, Chicago or any other hockey hotbed, she was usually greeted

CSI/F. SCOTT GRANT

Team Canada forward Jane Robinson sprints into action at the 1994 World Championship.

with "Girls can't play hockey." She tried to use that mentality to her advantage. "I think it makes you that much better and you are that much more competitive," she said. "And one of my assets to this day is my speed and my quickness. I'm small compared to a lot of women, and I think that the reason I have been able to play at such a high level is because of my speed, which I think I learned with quickness of playing boys. And when I say quickness, I mean quick decision-making and that type of thing, because you are playing with guys at an early level. Also, if you are not a big kid and you are playing in a checking league, it teaches you at an early age how to be strong on your skates."

Weinberg continued playing hockey through her sophomore year of high school, then switched to soccer. When she became a senior, she was recruited by schools all over the country to play soccer, but she wanted to play hockey as well. The University of New Hampshire (UNH) recruited her for soccer and offered a full scholarship. A few weeks into her freshman year, she contacted the women's hockey coach, Russ McCurdy, and asked about the hockey team. He was not encouraging about her chances. It was already a month into the hockey season by the time Weinberg's soccer season was over, and he also figured a girl from Dallas wouldn't know much about hockey. Bob Johnson, who had coached Weinberg at summer camps in Wisconsin for years, called McCurdy and urged him to take a careful look at Weinberg. McCurdy agreed to give her a week-long tryout, since the girls on the team were already in shape. After the first practice McCurdy invited Weinberg to join the team and later she went on to become captain and win three Eastern College Athletic Conference (ECAC) championships at UNH. She missed the 1990 World Championship during her junior year because of an injury, but she stayed on at UNH as McCurdy's assistant coach for two years while she obtained her master's degree.

Girls' and women's hockey teams have emerged in Texas since Weinberg played, but most of the competition still comes from boys' teams. In Dallas, peewee and midget girls both have teams. Women's leagues are still in the development stages, as most of the women who are interested in playing are part of the senior recreational men's league.

Canadian gold medallist Danielle Dubé is also an exception to the typical path of hockey development for women. Like Weinberg, she played with the boys and never switched to a girls' minor hockey team. Unlike Weinberg, Dubé continued to play competitive boys' hockey even into her late teens and early twenties. In fact, she never played on a girls' or women's team until her late teens when she played net for Team British Columbia in the 1991 Canada Games. Her team won the silver medal, losing to Team Alberta.

Starting at the age of four, Dubé played minor boys' hockey for Grandview Minor Hockey in Vancouver, British Columbia. After 13 years, Danielle was skilled enough to try out for junior men's hockey. At age 16 she tried out for the Penticton Panthers, and at age 17 played for the Grandview Steelers, a junior B men's hockey team. For the 1995-1996 season, she played with the Bakersfield Fog in the semi-pro West Coast Hockey League. In the fall of 1996, she played for the Central Texas Stampede of the Western Professional Hockey League until late November, when she broke her collar bone.

After playing for Team BC in the Canada Games, Dubé was invited to compete with Team Canada for the 1993 USA Olympic Festival in San Antonio, Texas. It was a great learning experience for her and since that time she has climbed the ranks to become one of Canada's strongest netminders. She was selected to the 1995 and 1996 Pacific Rim teams and to the 1996 Three Nations Cup team. She also won a gold medal with Team Canada at the 1997 World Championship. Except for these stints with Team Canada and Team BC, however, Dubé has always played boys' and men's hockey.

THE PACIFIC DISTRICT OF THE USA AND WESTERN CANADA

Growth in female hockey in the Pacific District of the US isn't at the same level as in the East, but girls' teams are popping up even in the non-traditional states and regions.

One new team in the US, the Northwest Admirals, is the first girls' travel team in Washington state, playing in the midget division. The girls play in the female Canadian league, travel across the country to tournaments and vie for regional and national championships. The program began a few years ago and quickly expanded to include a squirt "house" team, which plays against boys' house teams, and a midget house team which plays in a female Canadian league. The girls start in a beginner program (ages 5-8) for both boys and girls.

Growth in California is only just underway. In January 1997, only five all-girls teams were registered in the state. An elite midget team, Team California, including girls from both northern and southern California, has been playing since 1993. An elite peewee team, consisting of mostly 15-and-under Southern California girls, was formed in 1994, and they also go by the name Team California. In 1996, two squirt teams for girls 12 and under were created — Team California South and the Nor Cal Rep Blue Diamonds. When Team California South met the Nor Cal Rep Blue Diamonds in December 1996, it was the first time in California that an all-girls team played another all-girls team of the same level. In January 1997, the Nor Cal Rep Blue Diamonds also played a newly formed girls' 19-and-under team from Phoenix, Arizona, in Los Angeles. Most often, the teams rack up their playing time in tournaments and in encounters with boys' teams.

In California, the state youth hockey program currently concentrates more on the youth all-star team to vie for regionals and nationals. While girls may play on the all-star team, it does not promote the growth and development of girls' programs. State teams like Team California and Team Alaska recruit players from across the US. This presents difficulties for the hometown players who are shut out when more talented out-of-state players make the all-star team. It also robs players from other states trying to develop a girls' program. Two teams have folded in eastern Washington state because so many players left to play for state

COURTESY PEGGY CUNHA

In the past few years, girls' hockey has taken off in California. Girls who once had to join boys' teams to be challenged are now finding girls' teams like the So Cal Rays II provide comparable competition.

all-star teams. Many youth organizations are looking to USA Hockey for a ruling on whether all-star teams can be comprised of out-of-state players.

Many see the California system as neglecting the grassroots system and prohibiting the development of girls' hockey. There are only a few USA Hockey initiation programs for girls in the state. Most of the girls who play hockey are talented enough and aggressive enough to make the boys' house or travel teams. This practice ignores the hundreds of girls who might be interested in hockey but do not have the proper channels available to them to learn the game.

In western Canada, there are some all-girls teams. Depending on the province and the area, these teams play other boys' and/or girls' teams. One way to compare the development of female hockey in western Canada is to contrast two associations: the Edmonton Girls' Hockey Association and Calgary Girls' Hockey.

Tom Devaney has been an enthusiast of female hockey in Edmonton. In April 1992, Devaney, along with some other hockey volunteers, held "Hockey Fun Days" for girls. The event encouraged girls, many of whom had never played hockey, to come out and try the game. The event was such a success that a second fun day was held a couple of months later. That September, the Edmonton Girls' Hockey Association (EGHA) was formed. Its current goal is to expand the number of girls' teams at all levels, from novice to midget.

The boys versus the girls...

The following is a brief look at the experience of Anais Cunha, a young woman playing hockey in California, as told to Joanna Avery, via the Internet, by Anais' mother:

Anais Cunha is 18 and lives in California. When she was 12, she preferred to play with the boys' teams because the level of play was much higher than with the all-girls teams. Girls' hockey and all-girls teams in California were in the early stages of development at the time, and were not as competitive as boys' teams. Cunha played co-ed midget in-house hockey from ages 12 to 16, meaning that there might be one or two other girls on the team. After two years of trying out for various leagues, she found a boys' midget C team that would take her. After all the effort trying to get onto a boys' team, it was not as gratifying as she thought it would be. Having to sit out the play because her team was on the penalty kill due to a team-mate losing his temper angered her. For the past two years, Anais has also played for the So Cal Rays, a women's tournament team. The team has improved so much since she joined, she now finds the challenge and competition she wants without going to a boys' team and now prefers playing with women. After playing on the boys' team, Cunha finds that she stands out on the girls' team in her willingness to take the body of either a male or female player. In the girls' game, this translates to a player that is not afraid to move someone off the puck and fight for it aggressively.

The EGHA had eight teams during the 1996-1997 season, and works closely with the Edmonton Minor Hockey Association to develop the girls' teams, which play in the city house leagues against boys' teams. The leagues include different tiers, or levels, and the girls' teams are ranked and placed in a tier equal to their calibre. Many girls play on boys' teams in the city and are therefore not part of the EGHA. These girls join a team in their part of the city, whereas the EGHA draws players city-wide in order to have enough girls to form teams. In 1996-1997, the EGHA made a conscious effort to improve the youngest division, the novice, by subsidizing novice players so that registration wasn't so costly. The EGHA hopes that making the game affordable will continue to attract new players.

Calgary Girls' Hockey is the girls' hockey branch within the Calgary Minor Hockey Association. In 1989, when girls' hockey began in Calgary, the focus was on the peewee age category. Gradually, the number of girls involved in the program grew and different age categories developed. Like the EGHA, the Calgary association focuses on developing girls' hockey teams, but has also extended that goal to include the formation of all-girls leagues; that is, they have made a conscious decision to encourage girls to move from boys' teams and play on all-girls teams. Initially, girls' teams are formed within a category. Once the number of teams reaches four, a girls' league is created. Calgary has found that all-girls leagues attract more players. Calgary Girls' Hockey had 15 teams for the 1996-1997 season and project they will have over 50 girls' teams by the year 2000.

FIRST FEMALE PROGRAM IN THE NEW ENGLAND DISTRICT

The Rhode Island Panthers were the first female program established in the New England district of USA Hockey. Bob and Jackie Bagosian were part of the original co-founders of the program, at first called the Cranston Amateur Women's League, and then the Cranston Panthers. At that time, the late 1960s, no girls were allowed to play in the youth groups — they had all the boys they needed and did not let the girls in — so organizers started a girls' team. The first team, an all-star team, consisted of girls 13 through 18 years old. By the second year, there were enough girls to skate twice a week — an above-average amount of time for a girls' team in the early 1970s — and scrimmage against themselves. Eventually they travelled to Massachusetts to play against the girls' and women's teams that had been established there. As with most of the girls' teams that had emerged, the first years were a struggle, and the Panthers were not exempt from the familiar fight for ice time and respect. Ice time remains a problem, as many of the rinks are privately owned and there are only so many teams that can be accommodated. As for respect, as the team improved, respect for them did as well.

The Panthers remained as one team until 1980, when Fred Miller took over the program. As more and more players became interested in the program, peewee and senior women's teams were added. Players were placed on teams according to their age instead of all ages playing on one team. The organization's name was changed to the Rhode Island Panthers as girls and women from all over Rhode Island became involved in the program. Now, the peewee girls play in a community league against boys' teams and other girls' teams in their own area, usually within a 25-mile radius. That provides them with a lot of competition with boys' teams, usually exhibition games, and provides the girls with more chances to improve their skills. The peewee girls' classification is 15 years and under, which means the players are two to three years older than their male counterparts. "Right now we are running a 27-1 winning streak against the boys' peewee league," Fred Miller said in December 1996. He finds the girls every bit as competitive as boys at that age, and much better students: "I find with the girls you tend to teach hockey more than with boys. You let the boys check a lot more. With girls, it's teaching true hockey. Hockey skill means skating, and not hitting people."

To provide themselves with more competition against girls' teams, since 1988 the Panthers have hosted the Rhode Island Panthers Thanksgiving Tournament, the second largest tournament of its kind in New England. In 1996, 50 teams participated, including representatives from California and Alaska.

There were seven female hockey teams in Rhode Island in 1996 — two squirt teams, two peewee teams, one midget, and two senior women's teams. Girls under nine play on the boys' instructional teams and then move up to the Panthers. Panthers players have moved on to play in competitive ice hockey programs such as those at Brown University and the University of New Hampshire.

DOMINANT REGIONS IN THE US: MASSACHUSETTS AND CONNECTICUT

In 1972, Carl Gray began what has become one of the most powerful female hockey programs in Massachusetts. Although it wasn't the first girls' hockey program in Massachusetts, Assabet Valley quickly became one of the best. In the beginning, Assabet iced two teams and played against six other female teams. By 1975 they were the Boston Arena Tournament Champions, beating teams with players twice their age and experience. The next year they were US National Champions in the teen division. By 1996, Assabet had won 111 titles, including 16 US national championships, 16 US national runner-ups, 26 state-regional championships, 17 league championships, and 36 tournament championships.

Gray's involvement with women's hockey was actually a result of his participating in Little League baseball. He had never played contact sports as a boy — a car accident when he was nine left one leg shorter than the other. But he wanted to get involved with sports for his children. In 1971 he was coaching Little League baseball for 11- and 12-year-olds. "There was a girl who had come down to the field. Her name was Kelly Fitzgerald from Concord," Gray said. "She had four older brothers and she came out and played with us and I let her get involved in practices with us, but the local baseball league refused to allow her to participate because she was female. She was a better athlete than any of the boys I had on the field." Gray petitioned the Little League organization, but they still refused to allow a girl to play. Gray got angry, thinking of his own children, a boy and two girls at that time, and the opportunities they might miss just because of their gender. As a professional engineer, Gray had seen first-hand what women could do: "I felt from my interaction with female astronauts that girls could contribute to society as well, and I wanted my two daughters to have that level of confidence." It's confidence that has made the difference for his hockey players, according to Gray. Eight of the 20 players in the 1990, 1992 and 1994 national teams, and nine players on the 1995 team, came out of the Assabet program. And 10 of the 26 candidates for the 1996 US national women's team were present or former Assabet Valley players.

Back in 1971, Gray was looking for a sport where he could get girls involved. He turned to ice hockey. He knew of girls' teams in the area, and was involved in the formation of the Concord Youth Hockey program for boys, but he would only participate in the program if girls were allowed to play. Gray became president of Concord Youth Hockey and was involved in setting the tone, pace and the direction of the organization. After the first year, the head of the girls' team said the girls should only practice and play amongst themselves. Gray disagreed, saying they should play competitively. That's when he decided to form his own girls' program, Assabet Valley. All the girls, almost 40, moved over to Gray's program and were registered with USA Hockey. Two teams were formed and began playing against other girls' teams in the area, including Woburn, Burlington, Waltham and Natick, about 15 games a year. Gray, who coached some of the teams, didn't have the problem with ice time that most teams experienced. With seven other people, he had recently purchased the Valley Sports ice arena in Concord, Massachusetts. Within three years, Assabet Valley was travelling to Minnesota to compete with teams there and had won the 1995 Boston Arena Tournament over the powerful Massport Jets.

Gray develops both players and coaches. "Over 60 percent of our coaching staff is female," he said. His program has produced two US National Women's Ice Hockey Team coaches — 1994 and 1995 head coach Karen Kay, and 1996 assistant coach Julie Andeberhan. "I try to involve mothers who are skaters, too,"

Gray added. Gray has always emphasized quality hockey over quantity, and as a result his teams have excelled. It also helps to have the right people in the program, the most skilled coaches and the most organized administrators. He has always tried to instil a level of intensity in his players and coaches. "It's like a pyramid," he said. "The closer you get to that net the more you want to beat it. I would say that I've been fortunate — I've had some good athletes and success breeds success."

And the athletes get better. Gray said that players among the 11- and 12-year-olds he had playing for him in 1996 had more potential to become national elite players than any other group in his 25 years with the program: "They're six years away from getting close to demonstrating their peak level performance, which will be between ages 18 to 24, but I've been there before and I can see it in their eyes and I can see it in the way they handle themselves." Gray also emphasizes academics. Over the past four years every player has gone on to college, many to Ivy League colleges, and over the years, his players have received over $2 million in scholarship money.

Each year Gray spends between $5,000 and $10,000 of his own money to sponsor his teams, paying for registration fees, transportation and hotel accommodations. "That's what it takes," Gray said. "You've got to be able to stand behind it and make it happen." Gray has been making it happen for more than two decades. In September 1996, the Assabet program entered its twenty-fourth season with 16 teams, including squirt, peewee, midget and senior levels. The program also offered a beginner program for girls at least six years old. The teams play at least one regularly scheduled league game a week, attend one practice per week, one skill session per month and participate in invitational games, international competition and post-season tournament play for qualifying teams.

In Connecticut, Tony Dennis has also been organizing female hockey. Dennis became interested in girls' hockey the way many men and women do — he had a daughter, Maria, who played. Maria eventually played on the US women's national team in 1990, but she started off playing on a boys' team in South Windsor, Connecticut.

While Maria Dennis was playing on a boys' team, Tony Dennis was the USA Hockey registrar for the state of Connecticut and president of the state association. But it wasn't until Maria went off to college that Tony Dennis began to organize a women's program for Connecticut. "When Maria got into Yale, I had a little time on my hands and more freedom in my job. As registrar, I had the rosters from around the state," Dennis said. "There was a bunch of female players and I decided to try to put a team together. We started out with about eight players, had a practice and played a couple of games against boys' teams, and then [co-founder of the program] Mark Fitz and I decided to form a team and go to the Nationals." Dennis and Fitz gathered about 16 peewee-aged girls together in the fall of 1985, called themselves the Connecticut Polar Bears and began playing boys' teams in the area. "Some teams were willing to play against the girls' team, and if they lost — and most of the time those games were relatively good games, and we won some and lost some — the boys and the parents were secure and open-minded enough that they didn't mind," Dennis said. The Polar Bears also encountered other girls' teams from Connecticut and Rhode Island, but were not able to beat them that season. The Polar Bears did, however, represent the New England District, which includes Maine, New Hampshire, Vermont, Connecticut and Rhode Island, in the peewee division at the national championship in Detroit.

In the first game of their first-ever national championship competition, the Polar Bears faced an experienced team from Michigan and beat them 7-3. The next morning the Polar Bears managed a tie against Stoneham, Massachusetts, and earned a trip to the semi-finals. Michigan was the opponent in the semis, which Connecticut won 3-0. In the finals it was Assabet Valley and the Polar Bears. Connecticut grabbed an early two-goal lead and went on to win by a score of 7-0.

In 1993, Dennis wanted to expand the Polar Bears and put together a squirts team of 20 girls aged eight to 11. The girls were all playing on boys' teams at the time, but Dennis wanted to give them the opportunity to play on a girls' team against other girls as well. "We had four practices and 10 games, and we played a couple of boys' teams," Dennis said. "We won one very big, we did not win another game, another game we lost big. We also played a couple of high school girls JV [junior varsity]." The squirts clobbered the high school team and, as a result, were able to schedule more games against girls' teams. The squirts, called the Connecticut Cubs, were merged with the Polar Bears the following year because Dennis could no longer commit to the team.

Dennis also was behind the creation of the Connecticut Polar Bears Christmas Tournament. In 1986, it consisted of four teams — three boys' teams and

Connecticut has been well-represented at US national championships with a combined seven titles in the peewee and midget divisions since 1980. The 1986 Polar Bears peewee team was the first to claim a title for Connecticut.

the Polar Bears, all from Connecticut. Ten years later, it was the largest women's youth hockey tournament in the United States and included 63 women's youth hockey teams from across Canada and the US playing in seven levels of competition.

Dennis was active with women's hockey at a higher level as well. In the 1980s, at the same time as the Polar Bears were starting out, Dennis was also active at the national level and was on the first Women's National Committee that met in Hartford. A committee of four developed a five-year plan for national camps and national teams. Within a couple of years, national camps were held at Lake Placid in New York and St. Cloud in Minnesota. Dennis served as camp director and chief counsellor for one of the camps in St. Cloud. "There were over 100 females, including a senior group of 40 players, and we tried to pick a national team. We also had 66 midget and under-18 players, and college coaches and whatnot for the whole week up in St. Cloud. And that's been an ongoing thing," Dennis said.

Ten years after it started, there were over 90 players in the Connecticut Polar Bears system. A few other girls' teams have emerged throughout the state, but the Polar Bears still play against boys' teams and also against colleges to find more competition.

The Connecticut Polar Bears captured their third straight US National Championship in the peewee division in 1997.

DOMINANT REGIONS IN CANADA: ONTARIO AND MANITOBA

In 1964, Roy Morris formed the Brampton Canadettes, a girls' hockey association, and organized the first youth house league for girls in Ontario. There was such a mixture of ages and abilities that helmets were colour coded to make sure girls played against others of similar calibre. In 1967, the Canadettes, under Morris, held the first Dominion Ladies Hockey Tournament, with 22 teams entered in three divisions. The tournament is still held today, every Easter, and for many girls' and women's teams it is a much anticipated way to close off the season. The 1997 Brampton Canadettes Dominion Tournament had 344 teams — 232 from Canada, 110 from the US and one each from Russia, Japan and Kazakhstan. The Dominion Tournament is the largest female hockey tournament in the world.

The Canadettes organization became the model for other communities trying to start girls' hockey. Because of the Dominion Tournament, volunteers from across Ontario were able to meet and chat. These conversations ultimately led, in 1975, to the formation of a new, provincial girls' hockey body — the Ontario Women's Hockey Association (OWHA), which is the only hockey association in Canada, and even the world, devoted solely to the development of female hockey. Like state associations in the US, the OWHA manages all the girls' and women's hockey activity in Ontario and has one purpose — to develop all-girls teams and all-girls leagues. This has been the main focus of every girls' hockey association that has formed in the province ever since.

Other regions of Canada did not set this goal outright, but have evolved towards it as more girls begin to play hockey. Initially, these associations simply wanted to get girls playing. If that meant playing with boys, so be it. It soon became clear from the players themselves, however, that it was important for girls to play with other girls. They wanted to play with their friends and against girls' teams, just as in school sports. Many associations started to develop all-girls teams which then grew into all-girls leagues. One such association is the Winnipeg Girls' Hockey League.

Playing girls' hockey in Winnipeg, Manitoba in the early 1990s typically meant you were a girl playing hockey with boys in the Winnipeg Minor Hockey Association. A vice-president for female hockey within the association, and representatives from around the city, would get together each month to discuss the issues and concerns of the female program. The sole purpose of this committee was to establish a female league. Because of the committee's efforts, the first female midget league was launched in Winnipeg in 1991. Four city teams and two rural teams were organized for the league. The city teams included all girls aged 11 to 17 who were part of the Winnipeg Minor Hockey Association. Rural teams expanded the age range to include nine- to 17-year-olds who were playing on boys' teams but wanted to play on girls' teams. Altogether, about 105 girls played in the league that first season. Directors of female hockey from 11 area associations worked with the vice-president of female hockey in the Winnipeg association in order to manage the league.

In one year, the girls' minor hockey league had grown to include about 250 girls aged nine to 17, forming 12 midget teams and four peewee teams. As a result of the increase in players, the league formed two divisions — one midget and one peewee. As the calibre of play improved, the midget division began to show signs of becoming competitive. There were some very strong, dominant teams, and some less skilled teams. Tiering was done for the 1993-1994 season to keep the program fair. Tiering is done to place teams at a level of play that is appropriate to their calibre. Many house leagues have multiple tiers to ensure teams are competing against teams of a similar calibre. At the same time, numbers continued to increase in the pewee league. Concerns grew over 13-year-olds playing against nine-year-olds, so a new atom division was added to the league. By September 1994, the girls' division included 450 players and 28 teams — all this in only three years.

"OLD SCHOOL" THINKING

There are many differences in how girls' minor, or youth, hockey can be organized, and each top Canadian or American player tells a different story. For Shirley Cameron there was no minor hockey for girls — not even playing with the boys. She started to play when she was older and joined a women's club. On the other hand, Dawn McGuire started to play organized hockey at the age of seven and her early years in youth hockey were with boys. She didn't play on a girls' teams until her teen years. Maria Dennis played on a boys' team through her second year of high school and then switched over to girls' private school hockey. Jane Robinson played with the boys until peewee level, and then, at 12, joined a women's team that travelled on weekends to play other teams. She never played girls' bantam or midget hockey. Ellen Weinberg played boys' hockey until she was in her second year of high school, then switched sports. Fortunately, she was able to return to hockey later. Danielle Dubé started out playing with boys and continues to play on male teams to this day. Judy Diduck didn't even play hockey until she was 18 years old.

The stories about how these players became involved in hockey do little to reveal the reality of their struggle once they were at the rink. When asked if she faced any challenges as a girl playing with and against boys, McGuire said that it was difficult to understand those issues as a kid: "Actually, when I think back … I guess I did face some problems. I suppose even on my team there were always some parents who didn't care for the fact that I was on their team — possibly because I was taking their son's ice time away. They didn't look at me as just another hockey player. Maybe I even had a little bit more skill, but they wouldn't look at it that way. It was a different issue because I was female and they thought I shouldn't be playing in the boys' system." The attitudes of parents are a major factor when it comes to girls playing hockey. In most cases, the biggest hurdle is to get parents to sign their daughters up for hockey. The true challenge, however, is in trying to overcome the negative attitudes of other parents, whose sons are playing with and against the girls. This issue can be as much a problem in the 1990s as it was for Dawn McGuire in the 1960s.

In the US, girls playing on boys' teams often encountered negative attitudes from opposing teams. Boys on opposing teams would often take a run at the girl players. It was not uncommon for coaches or parents to encourage this behaviour. Conversely, the girls seldom experienced any discrimination on their own teams. The boys they played with usually realized how talented the girls were and found it in their best interest to protect rather than taunt the girls.

A few players experienced little difficulty in playing in boys' leagues. Although Jane Robinson started out playing with boys, she doesn't remember any problems: "I never experienced the attitude that a female shouldn't be playing hockey. Even in the school yard, nothing was said about joining in the boys' activities. I don't remember anybody saying anything." Danielle Dubé did experience negative attitudes in the older levels, but saw it as nothing special: "For me it was normal because I started with the boys and I was just part of the team. I grew up with those boys all the way through minor hockey, right up to bantam. It was normal for me. There was more reaction, I think, from the opposing teams." Playing in the all-boys system wasn't always smooth skating for Dubé. When she entered the junior hockey ranks, she moved into new areas or played on new teams. Here, the male players didn't know her as well and handled the situation a little differently than her home-town friends had. She commented, "The players can have one of two reactions to me. They will be so determined to score on me that they mess up all the time, or they try to do really well. They will either be thinking, 'I can't shoot at her because she's a girl,' or they'll be firing at me to try and get me out of there. But, like I said, you get out there and you start playing. They don't forget you're a girl but they do remember you're a team-mate." It took a while for Dubé to fit in, especially with the players who didn't know her from minor hockey days. She said, "I grew up with the same group. Once I got into the junior levels, when I was 15, I started trying out for junior. When I was that young, the guys were good to me. They were looking out for me because I was a young girl. As you get older it becomes tougher. It's a difficult age for guys, I think, between 15 and 20. It takes them a while to accept you. Once they see me play, though, they see I'm just another player."

In Canada, 12 or 13 years of age is the generally accepted cut-off point when girls no longer play on boys' teams. After this age, girls either drop out of the game or are lucky enough to find a girls' or women's team on which to play. For a girl to switch over to all-girls hockey may require a commitment on the part of her family, however. In some cases, a lot of driving is required if the girls' team is in the next town or county. In other cases, she may need to make a huge jump up to senior hockey because there is more likely to be a women's team in the area than a team for 14- to 17-year-olds. As a result of Justine Blainey's victory in the Supreme Court in 1987, the Canadian Hockey Association has an integration policy for girls, but it only applies up to the peewee level. After peewee, the physical differences between boys and girls become an issue. Both girls and boys enter puberty around that age and physical size differences become obvious. In bantam, the category for 14- and 15-year-old players, bodychecking is allowed in male hockey, but it is never allowed at any level of female hockey. In some cases the physical differences between females and males makes it dangerous for girls to bodycheck with the boys. The second change brought about by puberty is in emotional and sexual maturity. Simply put, at this age it becomes awkward for boys and girls to share dressing rooms. These are the two main reasons why most girls don't play integrated hockey after the age of 13.

There are some exceptions, especially for very talented girls who can play competitive bantam and midget (16 and 17 years of age) boys' hockey. Generally, these girls use their own change rooms and join the team only for the pre-game talk. As a result, the female player may be involved in very competitive hockey, but she probably won't feel like a part of the team. Then again, there's Danielle Dubé, who thoroughly enjoyed playing boys' hockey and continues to enjoy playing men's hockey. It seems that goaltenders like Dubé can stay on male teams because they don't need to play the physical, bodychecking game. "It's less of an issue. Usually, when young girls say they want to play hockey, I recommend they go with the guys until the age where the change rooms have to split and the hitting comes in," commented Dubé. "It's helped my life skills to be able to hang out with guys and girls. It's opened my eyes to a whole bunch of experiences."

In the United States there are other avenues open to girls once they reach puberty. If there isn't a girls' peewee team in the area, one option is to play for a girls' varsity prep-school team. This is a costly alternative and often requires moving away from home, but it can be a sound investment in a girls' hockey career if she has no other choice. The prep schools, mostly in the East, offer a very competitive brand of hockey. And since they are privately run, there are no problems with finding enough ice time or proper equipment and training for girls. It is all provided by the school.

Table 5-4

Canadian Hockey Association

Winners of Women's and Girls' National Championships, 1982 to 1997

	Women's Senior		Midget and Under 18
1982	Agincourt Canadians (Ontario)		
1983	Burlington Ladies (Ontario)		
1984	Edmonton Chimos (Alberta)		
1985	Edmonton Chimos (Alberta)		
1986	Hamilton Hawks (Ontario)		
1987	Hamilton Hawks (Ontario)		
1988	Sherbrooke (Quebec)		
1989	Sherbrooke (Quebec)		
1990	Sherbrooke (Quebec)		
1991	Toronto Aeros (Ontario)		
1992	Edmonton Chimos (Alberta)		
1993	Toronto Aeros (Ontario)	1993	Team Ontario (Red)*
1994	Team Quebec (provincial select team)		
1995	Team Quebec (provincial select team)		
1996	Team Quebec (provincial select team)		
1997	Edmonton Chimos (Alberta)	1997	Team Quebec**

*Under-18 Pilot Event

**National Midget Championship

Table 5-5.1

USA Hockey

Winners of Girls' National Championships, 1980 to 1997

	Girls's Peewee		Girls's Midget
1980	Taylor, MI	1980	Wayzata, MI
1981	Clarence, NY	1981	Minneapolis, MI
1982	Clarence, NY	1982	Massena, NY
1983	Livonia, MI	1983	Stoneham, MA
1984	Livonia, MI	1984	Buffalo, NY
1985	Stoneham, MA	1985	Assabet Valley, MA
1986	Hartford, CT	1986	Assabet Valley, MA
1987	Assabet Valley, MA	1987	Stoneham, MA
1988	Assabet Valley, MA	1988	Stoneham, MA
1989	Assabet Valley, MA	1989	Assabet Valley, MA
1990	Chelmsford, MA	1990	Team Connecticut
1991	Assabet Valley, MA	1991	Team Connecticut
1992	New Hampshire Selects	1992	Assabet Valley, MA
1993	Chelmsford, MA	1993	Michigan
1994	Chelmsford, MA	1994	Assabet Valley, MA
1995	Connecticut Polar Bears	1995	Wisconsin Challengers
1996	Connecticut Polar Bears	1996	Alaska Firebirds
1997	Connecticut Polar Bears	1997	Connecticut Polar Bears

Table 5-5.2

USA Hockey

Winners of Women's National Championship, 1981 to 1997

Women's Senior A		Women's Senior B	
1981	Assabet Valley, MA	1981	Cape Cod, MA
1982	Minneapolis, MN	1982	Cape Cod, MA
1983	Stoneham, MA	1983	Chelmsford, MA
1984	no competition	1984	Cape Cod, MA
1985	no competition	1985	Waltham, MA
1986	Assabet Valley, MA	1986	Cape Cod, MA
1987	Stoneham, MA	1987	Wayne, MI
1988	Stoneham, MA	1988	Wayne, MI
1989	Stoneham, MA	1989	Wayne, MI
1990	Stoneham, MA	1990	Cheektowaga, NY
1991	Assabet Valley, MA	1991	Needham, MA
1992	Assabet Valley, MA	1992	Hobomock, MA
1993	Assabet Valley, MA	1993	Needham, MA
1994	Hudson, MA	1994	Lincoln Park Chiefs, MI
1995	Needham, MA	1995	Minnesota Northern Lights
1996	Minnesota Northern Lights	1996	Michigan O'Leary Hawks
1997	Team Southeast	1997	Springfield She Devils, MA

CURRENT CHALLENGES

What are some of the current challenges facing grassroots hockey? For girls, there is an increased number of competitive opportunities and this will be a big part of their future success. There is no doubt that, with the addition of national and international events, high performance play is the fastest growing segment of female hockey. Striving to become an excellent hockey player may be a challenge for certain athletes. As Jane Robinson commented, "There are going to be more challenges, as far as the competition, than there ever were before, and more commitment to the sport. Not that some athletes aren't putting in a lot of time now, but we are going to have to look at new ideas in training to meet these challenges, and with that comes an increase in pressure to be on top of your game all the time. It may be tougher now for girls to make provincial and national teams than it was in 1990, but at least these programs are in place."

In 1989 there were no world championships for female hockey players, no Canada Games and no minor or youth hockey categories in the Regional Shields. There are now two regional hockey competitions for women in Canada. British Columbia, Alberta, Saskatchewan and Manitoba compete in the Western Shield Championship, which includes two senior women's divisions and one midget division. Prince Edward Island, New Brunswick, Nova Scotia and Newfoundland participate in the Atlantic Challenge Cup development event, which includes a women's under-18 division. This is definitely progress. Shirley Cameron believes female hockey is completely different now than when she was a girl — different in many positive ways. It's also more acceptable for girls to play hockey. She said, "I would say there are probably fewer challenges today. When I was younger, it was not acceptable for females to be playing and it was not as encouraged as it is today. There were more struggles and you weren't given a whole lot of encouragement. Young girls are encouraged to play now and I doubt they are going to have anywhere near the struggles we had back then when we tried to play, tried to get funding, tried to get ice time and sponsorships."

Cameron is one hockey enthusiast who responded very strongly to the question, Is female hockey growing too fast? "Not for me!" she said. "For me it feels like it has grown slowly because I have seen when female hockey was nothing compared to what it is now. It seems like the growth wasn't fast enough. When I went to the 1996 Pacific Rim Tournament, I found the play hard to watch because I thought, 'this is what I missed out on.' I got a little taste of how much women's hockey has grown in 1990, when I went to the World Championship. I didn't really know what to expect because it was the first World Championship. When we got there and we were given the Team Canada sweater, I thought, 'Wow, this is big!' Then all of a sudden we had practices and there was media attention. We were pulled into signing autographs and all that. So we just got a little taste of what it was like. When I went to the 1996 Pacific Rim, there was a line-up around the arena to get in and a line-up to get autographs. I thought, 'Oh man. It didn't go fast enough for me!'"

But are all the changes at the competitive levels, even within minor hockey, actually helping the grassroots? Jane Robinson would say that the answer probably depends on who you ask: "There is an incredible focus on the [women's] national team. The bulk of us at the top level of hockey have always wanted to see how far we can go. Being caught up in this, our energy is directed towards personal goals. The CHA may be focussing on the National Team because it is still new. But as years go by and the pioneers of the sport retire from playing and turn to coaching and/or administration, we will see individuals turning to help the newcomers in the sport. But because the sport is new and it is growing and it is in the Olympics, it only makes sense the focus is going to be on the top players right now. The spinoff that occurs as a result of the elite teams is going to be very positive for our younger players. Maybe there will be a lag effect when it comes to grassroots development. Maybe there will be a period of time before the impact of the Olympics, or even the World Championships, will be felt in girls' hockey."

In the meantime, does the focus on elite athletes hinder the grassroots? In Canada, the CHA runs all national events, including championships. Provincial branches send teams to these events and sometimes these teams are funded to go. For many years, female hockey had only one national championship, the Women's Senior National, which was first held in 1982. In February 1997, a second event, the National Midget Championship, was held and involved nine provinces. Table 5-4 summarizes the winners of these championships. As Tables 5-5.1 and 5-5.2 show, this represents considerably less opportunity than is available in the United States at the grassroots level. USA Hockey stages four national events for women and girls — peewee and midget championships since 1980, senior A and senior B since 1981. At the 1997 nationals, squirts teams from around the US played in an exhibition tournament, with the Wisconsin

The squirt division was introduced in the 1997 US National Championship as an exhibition match. Finalist Assabet Valley await their runner-up medals...

Challengers winning the competition.

Canadian resources continue to be torn between elite and grassroots hockey. In Canada, midget is considered part of grassroots hockey. When the branches send a team to a midget championship, they select the best players from the province to be on the team. The athletes and coaches come together for that event, in a fashion similar to what happens when the national team

...as the Wisconsin Challengers celebrate their victory.

plays. Branch money is given to cover the cost of the team, including selections and training camps. This means that branches are putting money into grassroots hockey, but that money is for elite competitions, not for programs for the everyday player. In the US, the midget and peewee teams attending the national championships are club teams that have played together all season and won the right to represent their district at the nationals. They are independent teams and cover their own costs of going to the championship. In Canada, the question is whether funding should still be focused on getting girls into the game, or on those who are already playing.

Shirley Cameron notes the need to find a balance between the two levels —
elite and grassroots. She sees support for grassroots hockey continuing only if
people remember it is an important part of female hockey development. She remarked, "I think it'll be okay so long as each province doesn't get too hung up
on the elite athletes and as long as the money within each province isn't poured
only into the elite players. Then I think we will be okay. Some provinces select
all-star teams to compete as the provincial team at the senior Canadian national
championships. These programs cost thousands of dollars over a period of a few
years yet they only serve around 25 players and two or three coaches. Just think
what that money could accomplish if it was channelled toward learn-to-play-
hockey programs for young girls. Provinces could still send club teams, or even
an all-star team, to the championship — but must all the money go to them?"

When talking about the growth of girls' hockey, Jane Robinson felt more grassroots programs were being developed. She remarked, "Players today will have a
lot more opportunity than we ever had. The doors are now open for today's players to participate in events that the older players had always wished for. But
somebody has to break the ground and open those doors." Danielle Dubé perhaps said it best: "That's the whole idea — to get as many girls as possible interested in hockey and go out and play."

Why is grassroots hockey so important to the female game? Because it is the
future of the game. Without the involvement of youth, female hockey will not
survive. Unfortunately, the reality of the sports world is that a sport isn't
considred "real" until there is a national championship, a world championship
and even an Olympic competition. In its struggle to gain a profile and legitimacy,
female hockey has focused on these high performance goals. For years, many
women and girls in both the United States and Canada simply played the game.
There is no denying that being in the Olympics is very exciting for female hockey,
and that participating in the Olympics is a wonderful opportunity for players.
But how many women will actually go to the Olympics? The official roster has
space for 20 women. How many women and girls play hockey overall? Right now,
there are over 20,000 players in each of the two countries.

Female hockey volunteers have to maintain a delicate balance between the
grassroots and the elite high performance game. It is a hard job. Maybe, when
the CHA and USA Hockey are deciding what to do with programs and money,
they should remember what Shirley Cameron said: "NHL players will tell you

they always had these dreams of playing in the Stanley Cup finals. But when I was growing up, I always dreamed of playing on a girls' team — an all-girls team where you had uniforms and there were referees and it was an actual game. When I was growing up, I dreamt of the possibility that I could actually play a game other than the stuff on the slough."

6 / THE US NATIONAL TEAM

THE EARLY YEARS

Team USA, the women's hockey team representing the United States, was initially assembled in 1987 to play in the first Women's Invitational Tournament, which was held in Ontario. The Amateur Hockey Association of the United States (AHAUS) had sanctioned a select team to participate in the tournament. The players from Team USA were selected from mini-camps held in Massachusetts, New York, Michigan and Minnesota. The selection process was quick, lasting less than two months from start to finish, but team administrators were confident they had assembled the best talent in the US. Team USA was coached by Chris Hartung, coach of the Stoneham (Massachusetts) Unicorns in the Senior A Division, who had won the AHAUS 1987 Senior A Championship. Assisting Hartung was Assabet Valley founder Carl Gray and his son, Eric. Some members of the original Team USA — like Cindy Curley — went on to participate in later national teams that were a part of the Women's World Championships.

By the time the 1990 World Championship rolled around, it was an International Ice Hockey Federation (IIHF)-sanctioned event and included participants from European countries. Nobody knew what to expect from the event and USA Hockey did little to promote it to coaches and players. The training camps and tryouts were disorganized and not as frequent as they could have been. Maria Dennis was a member of the 1990 national team. She was a standout on the women's varsity ice hockey team at Yale University and was in her second year at law school at Georgetown University when she heard about the national tryouts. She was playing on the men's club team and was an active member of USA Hockey, serving on committees. Dennis continued with law school while trying out for the national team. The tryout camps were spread so far apart, she was able to finish her second year of law school and play on the national team at the same time. "USA Hockey didn't know how to schedule [camps]; they didn't throw the money in right away," she said. "It was the first team, the first tournament, so we were basically doing things off the cuff on a first-hand basis. We really got together five days before the tournament and practiced as a team and then we were shipped up to Ottawa."

Since USA Hockey had not stressed the importance of the World Championship to players or coaches, players who did find out about the team were not urged to try out. Karyn Bye grew up in River Falls, Wisconsin. At age seven, she began playing hockey for the local boys' youth hockey team. She played centre in the organization through ninth grade, when she also made the junior varsity high school hockey team. In her sophomore year, she made the varsity team. She graduated in 1989 and went to the University of New Hampshire (UNH) on a hockey scholarship. During her freshman year, Bye heard about tryouts for the national team that would go to the World Championship. Like most players, she didn't really know what the national team was or the ramifications it would have for women's hockey. So Bye didn't even bother to try out. "I didn't really know the extent of the team, and I just heard there was some tryout for some team," she said. "I talked to my coach about it and he didn't make it sound like it was a big deal. I was playing tennis at the time. He just told me to focus on my tennis, and to not worry about it." After the selection of the 1990 team, Team USA scrimmaged against UNH and the coach of Team USA asked Bye why she hadn't tried out for the team. She has been on the Team USA ever since.

Despite the disorganization before the event, the 1990 World Championship holds a special place in the hearts of the players who attended. As Maria Dennis commented, "I don't think you could ever replace the first World Championship. There was something very special about being a part of that. The female hockey players were experiencing the type of recognition and appreciation that other elite players had always experienced. There was coverage on the news every night and in the newspapers the next morning, and there were athletic trainers and massage therapists at the players' disposal."

Julie Andeberhan was another member of Team USA in 1990 and, like Dennis, she was thrilled to be part of the event. Andeberhan had graduated from Harvard in 1988 and stayed on as an assistant coach in soccer, hockey and softball. She was still active in hockey, playing in the women's division at Assabet Valley, when she heard about the national team selection for the first Women's World Championship. She went to the tryouts at Northeastern University and was selected by the panel, which included some Division I women's hockey coaches. "I remember it just being a great thrill because we didn't really take things for granted then," she reminisced. "You know, we were so appreciative of having the opportunity to play and I just loved it. All you really focus on is playing well, and although our opportunities, now that I look at it, were limited compared to what's available now, we were happy. We were intoxicated with the sport and weren't fully aware that our ice times were not quite as good as the men's ice times, and that our equipment budget was not as big and so on. At that time we were really thrilled with the sport. I think women still play the sport for really pure reasons. There's no NHL to look forward to and so the women in the sport love the game."

The 1990 Championship was the first time Andeberhan and many other American players had ever played against a Canadian team. Canadian university teams would occasionally face off against American college teams, but Team USA was an all-star team gleaned from women's hockey all over the United States. It was also the first time Andeberhan wasn't the star of her team: "It was such a different experience. It was such an eye opener. I think it really helped me a lot with my coaching to recognize the different roles that players have and recognize that as you go to higher and higher levels, people play different roles and you can't have your 12 forwards all be centres. That happens when you get these teams together. People are used to playing certain positions."

Team USA's reception in Canada was probably the biggest surprise for the players. "It was just fantastic," Andeberhan said. "We played in several different venues around Ottawa and the organizers there had done a great job marketing the tournament. We were all surprised and amused that Canada chose to wear those loud, bright pink uniforms. Everyone has their own opinion about it, but whether it's pro or con, their marketing strategy really worked. Every single venue was packed, whether it held 600 or 10,000 spectators. I'll never forget where our dressing room was ... I can picture where I sat and I'll never forget walking out ... it was where the Zamboni entrance was. The two doors opened and they put the plank down for us. I remember just running out to that final game to this sea of pink pompoms, pink everywhere, and a deafening crowd too. We had no expectations going into it. Just playing against the foreign teams, Sweden and Canada and Finland, was a new and different experience. It was so exciting."

Clearly, the 1990 US national team was not ready for gold. "I remember just being so thrilled to be part of it, just being so happy to be there," Andeberhan said. Team USA wasn't beaten by a lack of competitiveness, but instead by a lack of experience. "Until you're in that international arena, it's really difficult to know what to expect and to know how different the game is," Andeberhan explained. "It's mostly just the pace at which it's played, the skill level and the physical dimension, and the speed of play — the speed at which players make decisions."

Cammi Granato, another Team USA player in 1990, is considered by many to be the best female player in the US today. Granato started playing at age five, following in the footsteps of her older brothers. She played with the boys from the start, since there were no girls' teams in or around her home of Downers Grove, Illinois. She played forward, usually centre, for the Downers Grove Huskies, a travelling team, through her second year in high school. Granato was forced to stop playing when the boys got too big, and she focused her talents on other sports until she went to college. When the time came to choose a college, hockey was very much on her mind. Granato heard about Providence College through a friend of her brother. She got in touch with a girls' hockey team in the eastern US when she was 16 and went out to play a game with them. The next year she was offered a scholarship by Providence College, although the coach hadn't even seen her play. His offer was based on her family reputation and the playing analysis of a friend who had seen her play. Since no other teams knew about Granato — no one scouted for players in the Midwest at that time — she was scooped up by Providence College and proceeded to bring their program to new heights. As a freshman in 1989, Granato earned Eastern College Athletic Conference (ECAC) Division I rookie of the year honours, notching 24 goals and 22 assists in 24 games. The next year she knocked in 26 goals and added 20 assists in 22 games, good for ECAC co-player of the year. Granato earned the distinction of ECAC player of the year three times in her four years at Providence and was named the 1996 USA Hockey Women's player of the year. Granato was in her freshman year when she heard about tryouts for the national team. She was still in transition from playing with boys, but the Women's World Championship quickly showed her what women's hockey was all about. "It was the most fun I ever had," she said.

In 1992 the World Championship shifted to Tampere, Finland, and the atmosphere of the event changed. There was a language barrier, and the European culture was not as accepting of women in traditionally male sports. Many of the players from the 1990 national team were on the 1992 team, as USA Hockey had still not made a big commitment to the women's team in terms of recruiting, financing and training. In 1994 the Championship moved to Lake Placid, New York, but USA Hockey had done little to promote the event. The US squad was more talented and experienced than the previous teams and was

COURTESY MARIA DENNIS

The 1990 US National Team at the Women's World Ice Hockey Championship in Ottawa. *Front (from left)*: Kelly Dyer, Maria Dennis, Heidi Chalupnik, Lisa Brown, Tina Cardinale (Captain), Kim Eisenreid, Mary Jones. *Middle (from left)*: Kulraj Sidhu (Equipment Manager), Karen Kay (Assistant Coach), Don MacLeod (Head Coach), Jeanine Sobek, Sue Merz, Julie Sasner, Cindy Curley, Beth Beagan, Sharon Stidsen, Kelly O'Leary, Lynn Olsen (Assistant General Manager), Debbie White Lyons (Trainer), Dr. V. George Nagobads (Physician). *Top (from left)*: Bob Allen (General Manager), Judy Parish, Kelly Owen, Lauren Apollo, Yvonne Percy, Shawna Davidson, Cammi Granato. *Missing*: Julie Andeberhan

hoping to repeat the 1980 Olympic gold-medal-winning performance by the men's US national team, this time for the women. But the "Miracle On Ice" didn't happen. "Actually we played really well," Kelly Dyer, netminder for the 1994 team, remarked. "The shots were pretty even that year — they were 23-22. But still we came up on the short side of the stick on that one." The Canadians collected another gold medal while the US took home silver.

PLAYER POOL

The first Team USA of 1987 consisted of only USA Hockey players, in part because the college programs were at a less advanced level than they are today. Many of the players on that team were the elite peewees of the 1970s and had already graduated from college or were playing on community teams as well as varsity teams. American colleges and universities, particularly those in the East, have been the feeder system for the national team. Cammi Granato, for example,

PHILLIP MacCALLUM/FREESTYLE PHOTOGRAPHY

Cammi Granato was named ECAC Player of the Year for three out of her four years at Providence College, and was 1996 USA Hockey Women's player of the year. Here she collides with Canadian forward Hayley Wickenheiser at the Three Nations Cup.

probably would never had heard about tryouts for the national team had she gone to college in the Midwest or stayed in Downers Grove.

The amount of female hockey talent in the US has grown over the past few years and will undoubtedly continue to do so with the increased participation of girls and women in the grassroots system. Obviously the Olympics is the goal of every player trying out for the national team. But, with the new crop of talent coming from colleges and the youth hockey systems, the players realize that no one has an automatic berth on the team. Karyn Bye appreciates the competition:

"I think just making the team that is going to the Olympics is going to be quite an accomplishment for anybody."

Despite all the new talent, four of the players who skated on the 1990 US women's national team still have a shot at making the Olympic team: Lisa Brown, Cammi Granato, Sue Merz and Jeanine Sobek. For them, US college hockey is no longer an option and the women's community programs are just not as developed or competitive as they are in Canada. To continue playing at a competitive level after they graduate from college, some US players head north. For instance, Cammi Granato attended Concordia University in Montreal, Quebec, to extend her playing career. She had intended to stay for only a year, but three years later was still there. "I've learned more than I learned in college," she said. "I've got a whole new coaching angle, and I've learned another style of hockey." Granato calls the Canadian style more physical, with more clutch and grab than the American style. The season is longer in Canada as well. Granato typically plays an average of 45 games a season and is on the ice from September to April. On the other hand, the US college season lasts from November to March, and players will participate in only about 25 games. The extended season was the biggest attraction for Granato: "I don't think I would ever have found that anywhere if I played in a club team after college. So that's where I think I've really been fortunate."

Karyn Bye chose the same route as Granato for the same reasons. After playing for UNH, Bye left to play for Concordia University in 1993, the same year as Granato. As a graduate student, Bye played on Concordia's undergraduate team for two years.

USA Hockey has also taken steps to ensure that talent is being developed at the lower levels, not just with the elite national players. Select teams are often put together for girls of various age groups, such as 15 to 18, or 18 to 21. Select teams are recognized by USA Hockey, but are not sanctioned, meaning that USA Hockey will not pay any of their expenses for trips to foreign countries or special tournaments. Out of these select teams, the women's national junior team was established in 1990. It started out with development camps where the young women would try out. A core of about 80 players continued to train with the national junior team and the first team of 21 players played against the Canadian women's developmental team a few years later.

In 1995, for the first time ever, the US junior team went to Ottawa and competed in a four-game series against Team Canada juniors. The competitions were used for training purposes and to give the coaches a chance to see how the players are developing, how they react in various situations and who might be ready for the national team in a couple of years. National team players are generally more experienced and mature, usually college-aged players or older, although there is no age minimum.

Julie Andeberhan became involved with coaching the junior team in 1996. "According to USA Hockey administrators who have sort of seen the thing through the whole cycle, these are the first couple of years when we've had real tough competition for spots," she said. "1995 was the first year that the US selected a team out of the development camp. So those players just weren't used to it. They were used to more of a supportive development camp environment, and apparently some of the coaches who worked with the players this year in the class said the cuts, selections, and everything, went so much smoother and the kids are so much more in tune with what was happening, and what the focus was, and had a much more competitive spirit about the whole situation. But it takes time. It takes a couple years."

There are more signs of growth in the player pool and the level of talent it is producing. USA Hockey will continue to focus on junior activities, developing more select teams and looking at teams with different calibres of play, such as 12-year-olds who are nearly ready to break into the senior national team, but are not quite seasoned enough. Also, 1995 marked the first time USA Hockey hosted a junior elite camp with both female and male goalies. The boys have had an elite goalie camp for years, but it was the first year girls also participated.

COMPETITION

Although Team USA has improved since the 1990 World Championship, so has their competition. To sharpen their skills for international events, US teams are picked from the various training camps to play tournaments against specific European and Asian women's national teams. In 1995, Team USA travelled to Finland and played Team Finland in Sampari, Verimaki and Helsinki. The games were round-robin format. Kelly Dyer believes such tournaments are a great way to gain international experience without feeling the anxiety of a world championship. "We play a lot of countries, but don't have the pressure of the world championships," she said. "We may want to try a new power play and it might be kind of radical or whatever. Last time, we just went crazy and tried all sorts of things, and people played real loose, and we outscored the other country in our four-game series, something like 18-2 overall. So it was a lot of fun, it was a really good tour. We had played outside the country before, but only for world championships, for sanctioned events. It's the first time we had a training activity with another country."

With women's hockey now an Olympic sport, new international competition has emerged, including teams from Russia and Italy. USA Hockey tried to organize a tournament of the best Russian players and a US select team of women 21 and under. The Russians decided not to compete, waiting to unveil their players in the Olympics. In January 1997, however, Team USA trekked to China to meet Team China in a tournament similar to the 1995 one in Finland.

There are ways to learn about other women's programs without directly playing with the team. In 1993, Ellen Weinberg, a member of the 1992 national team, travelled to Norway to work with the Norwegian Ice Hockey Federation, establishing and then training with their women's national team for five months. The women's team played in a league with junior men to try to increase the women's ability and intensity and bring their play to a higher level. Weinberg also flew to different clubs that played women's hockey throughout the countryside, and conducted clinics there. While the calibre of women's hockey is lower than it is in Canada and the USA, and there are only 17 rinks in Norway, Weinberg found that there were television cameras and newspaper reporters wherever she went. She found that for women athletes in Norway, equality with male athletes was much more important, and real, than it was in the United States.

CONSISTENCY AND COMMITMENT

One complaint that players had about Team USA was its lack of consistency. New coaches were introduced every year (except when Karen Kay coached in 1992 and 1994), bringing a different style of hockey and expectations with them. Training camps and events were sporadic, making it difficult to create a "team" feeling. The camps were tournament-based, with the players coming together a few weeks before an event to train and then returning to college or their community teams until the next event. Camp was usually held from Christmas to New Year's and also during the summer, with a few weeks scattered in between — every two or three months. Among the World Championship, the Pacific Rim Tournament, and the Three Nations Cup Tournament, which was introduced in October 1996, there was at least one major tournament every year. Getting together a few times a year for development and a couple of weeks before an event for training was all the coaches had to work with back in 1990.

In order to make a serious bid for a medal in the Olympics, USA Hockey decided to make a much stronger commitment to its women's team. This included hiring a full-time coach. When, on June 3, 1996, Ben Smith was named head coach of the US women's national and Olympic teams as well as director of the women's development program for three years, many players felt their chances of winning a gold medal had improved. Smith had served as head coach for the Northeastern University men's team from 1991 to 1996. While he had no experience coaching women, he did have experience with national and Olympic teams. Smith was the assistant coach for three US men's national junior teams (1985, 1986 and 1987), and was on the coaching staff for the US men's national team that went to the World Championships in 1987 and 1990. Smith was also an assistant coach for the 1988 US Olympic Ice Hockey Team.

Kelly Dyer saw Smith's hiring as an important commitment by USA Hockey: "Coach Smith will be in charge of all the other coaches, so there will be more consistency in the structure and hopefully a consistency in the philosophy. Maybe it won't be as specific as your forecheck and back check, but the problem we had before this was that every year we've had a new coach, except for Coach Kay who we've had for back-to-back assignments. The consistency problem exists more for the forwards than for the goalies. These poor girls are already coming from really diverse situations ... like Cammi Granato, who was playing for Concordia University in Montreal, versus Chris Bailey who's coaching at Providence College in the States. Everybody has such diverse backgrounds already, and now you have a different coach and a different philosophy every six months. It's pretty hard on the players, especially the defence. One coach would say, 'Stand up on the blue line, pitch in hard,' and the next would say 'No, don't stand up on the blue line, come back, protect your zone.' The defences have the hardest time of all. As a goalie, you just don't care — you just stop the puck."

Team USA now had a commitment from USA Hockey for consistent coaching — at least for three years. With that kind of dedication to the women's program from USA Hockey, many players reciprocated with their own type of dedication. They left jobs, families and colleges to train full-time for the national team and the Olympics. Some began training with strength and conditioning coaches. And Smith was serious about the responsibility he had just undertaken. Within months, he had implemented a program of holding camp at the Iorio Rink in Walpole, Massachusetts every month for one to two weeks, with scrimmages scheduled against local teams. Many of the scrimmages were against men's teams of varying levels, from boys' junior varsity to former NHL players.

The monthly camps released a lot of pressure from the players, who felt they constantly needed to impress several different coaches, and sometimes adapt their playing style accordingly, to make the team. Now they were able to concentrate on improving their skills. It also gave Smith a chance to get to know his players and look at more players, since there were more opportunities for the women to try out. The players think it's a fair system and it allows the national team truly to be comprised of the best players in the nation.

Smith has not refused any player a tryout and gives the players the most opportunities he can to make the team. Ellen Weinberg was a member of the national team that played at the 1992 Women's World Championship, but retired afterwards, since she was out of college and couldn't afford to train for the next World Championship. In 1992, there was no money in USA Hockey's budget for women to train for the World Hockey Championship. Weinberg tried to stay in shape, hoping for a chance to someday skate in the Olympics. When she heard women's hockey would be an Olympic event in 1998, she began training in the summer of 1996 and tried out for the training pool in September. While she was training for the Three Nations Cup, she blew out her knee. After surgery she began to rehabilitate and hoped to recover in time to go to Nagano. Coach Smith was encouraging. "He could have easily said, 'It's going to be tough, you know, you are a little bit older,'" Weinberg said. "But he was really positive and it makes your training that much better."

THE PLAN

With a new head coach firmly in place, it was time to make some other changes. Smith was preparing aggressively for the upcoming tournaments. Karyn Bye saw a distinct difference in the schedule. "This year [1996] I've actually spent more time training than any other year," she said. "We got together in August for two weeks. We were together for a week in September, three weeks in October, two weeks in November, and two more weeks in December. I think starting in August

[1997] the team will get together, and live together, and be together until the Olympics. Until then it's like a stepping stone. They don't want us to get sick of each other, and get burned out." In 1997, the team went to China from January 1 to 14 and played Team China and Team Finland. After they returned, they had a week and a half off and were back on the ice the last week in January. They got together again for two weeks in February, and then trained together for a month starting on March 8, which took

Team USA head coach Ben Smith behind the bench at the 1997 Women's World Championship.

them to the World Championship the first week in April. "At least two weeks out of each month we've been getting together, which is a lot different from any other year," Bye continued. "In the past we've just been getting together for a couple weeks in August, a couple weeks in December, and a couple weeks in March, so it's a lot different."

The team can have a different makeup at any given competition. Depending on the event, it can be the top 20 players, or a couple of prospects on the fringe of making the team, or some of the younger elite players. The makeup of the team also depends on some of the players' college schedules.

While the new members of the team are stronger and very skilled, one aspect that concerns Bye is their lack of experience. She feels, though, that acquiring experience is one of the purposes of having these select teams. "Some of [the college] players tried out for the national team, and some of them have made it," she said. "The only thing they're lacking is experience. And we're giving the opportunity to gain experience to a lot of these younger kids. You know, we've had some 16- and 17-year-olds on our team going to these last few tournaments. Therefore they're getting some of that experience." As an example, in August 1996, Team USA swept Team Sweden in a three-game exhibition series with scores of 7-1, 4-1 and 2-1. The purpose of the series was not only to get some competition from another national team, but also for coach Ben Smith to look at the younger players on his squad and consider who among them might have the potential to be Olympians.

PHILLIP MacCALLUM/FREESTYLE PHOTOGRAPHY

Team USA huddles up at the bench to listen to head coach Ben Smith during the 1996 Three Nations Cup tournament.

Smith wanted to make sure he had the best team possible for the World Championship and subsequently the Olympics. The team that competed in the World Championship in Kitchener, Ontario was not selected until two weeks before the tournament and the Olympic team was not picked until early fall 1997. The players took it one camp at a time. "All you can do is keep yourself the best prepared you can at all times," was the advice of Kelly Dyer. "That's what I do. It sort of helps to just keep a nice even keel. You can't get over-focused about what's coming next and what's two or three years down the line. Just stay prepared, always challenge yourself by playing at a higher level of hockey and work to find some consistency in your game."

One criticism of the US National Team has been their inability to express themselves on the ice and to be creative with the play. Those criticisms have dissolved under Smith, who many players say encourages exactly that sort of behaviour. Under his guidance, the team is focusing on becoming stronger and faster and is making itself the best team it can be for the 1998 Olympics and beyond.

ANDRÉ RINGUETTE/FREESTYLE PHOTOGRAPHY

Team USA forward Karyn Bye at the 1996 Three Nations Cup.

BEATING THE CANADIANS

Canada has always been the team for the US to beat. Team USA has never won a tournament over Canada, and it was not until April 1995 that Team USA won its first game over Team Canada in international tournament play at the Pacific Rim Tournament. Many Canadians dismissed the loss by saying that the tournament was not representative of the best Canadian women. But Canada did send their best to the Three Nations Cup in October 1996 and were defeated by Team USA in round-robin play 2-1 in overtime. It appears that the gap between the teams is closing. Julie Andeberhan doesn't see much difference in talent between the two countries. She believes the biggest edge Canada has over the United States is in how the sport is perceived by its citizens. "At the junior national team competition [in 1995], I noticed the coach

ANDRÉ RINGUETTE/FREESTYLE PHOTOGRAPHY

An American trio set for the faceoff: Shelley Looney (no. 15), Colleen Coyne (no. 5) and Jeanine Sobek (no. 17) at the Three Nations Cup.

and the players had T-shirts that said on the front, 'Hockey is Canada,' and on the back, 'Canada is Hockey' — and I think they really feel that," Andeberhan said. "They really feel that, and as a result, I think there's less distraction. I think they probably get more of the best athletes playing hockey. The athletes don't get distracted into playing other sports, and maybe there aren't as many other sport options available as in the United States."

Why has Team USA had so much difficulty beating the Canadians? Former national team member Kelly Dyer believes that in tournament play before 1997, the Canadians had more depth, greater consistency of style, and a greater depth chart and player pool. "They've got the dominance which has given them more confidence," she said. "We go into games with a 'we can't beat them' or 'we *have* to beat them' mentality. I always thought it would be more interesting if we had a series playoff instead of just one game. I think we would probably do better because once we got our jitters out we'd have better control. We have a lot of talented players. I also think that once we have more consistency in the philosophy of our coaches it'll help our girls play one pattern. You never see Canada really get flustered. Even when we came out to a two-goal lead, and they kept with their game, they didn't change anything. So I think that's going to be a key for us. And we have that mental hurdle. We know we can win. We do have the skills, we do have the talent. I kept saying, 'Now, our motto is we don't want to waste it on the little one, we're just saving it for the big one [the Olympics].' So that's what everyone started saying [in 1996]."

SUPPORT FROM USA HOCKEY

USA Hockey received much flak from women's hockey supporters for the poor attendance at the 1994 Women's World Championship held in Lake Placid, New York. The event was not well publicized and many feel that this was a result of USA Hockey's attitude towards women's hockey at the time. USA Hockey still wasn't taking the women's program seriously and thought that it might be a passing phase. This was evident on the cover of the tournament's program, which was a photograph of two male hockey players in action. Less than a thousand people showed up for the US game against Finland in which Team USA won the B pool. USA Hockey officials admitted that their decision to hold the games in Lake Placid, the site of the men's US National Team "Miracle on Ice" gold medal performance, was not the right choice. Lake Placid was not the best location to attract new fans, nor was there a strong base of women players or fans who might attend the games.

Lynn Olson, director of the girls' and women's section of USA Hockey at the time, affirms that the debacle at Lake Placid was a result of USA Hockey not taking the program seriously enough. USA Hockey does the promotion for the World Championships. "Everything comes out of their public relations office," she said. "I'm a volunteer. All the positions as directors are volunteer. I always had lots of suggestions and oftentimes they fell on deaf ears." USA Hockey blamed the poor promotion on the tight budget, but Olson thought otherwise. "I don't know if they thought it would be a passing fancy or what but I think at some point they realized, 'Gee, if this goes Olympic, then the Olympic Committee will give funds for [the players] to train and money will come into USA Hockey for that,' and then the IIHF started giving some funds for some of the international competitions like the Pacific Rim which was held in California. So at some point they finally realized that the girls weren't going to go away and they might as well all get on the bandwagon and start trying to promote ... and since then it's been pretty

Team Canada forward France St. Louis battles Team USA defender Kelly O'Leary in front of netminder Erin Whitten at the 1996 Three Nations Cup.

good," Olson said. For the Olympics, she is hoping for a world tour similar to the men's programs in the past, where Team USA would play exhibition games against other women's national teams. She has suggested the US Olympic team meet the Canadian national team in Minneapolis, because of the fan support already established there for women's hockey: "We probably have 350 teams and if we can't fill a stadium with fans to come and watch the national Olympic program, it would be bizarre."

For some time, many girls' hockey enthusiasts have been critical of USA Hockey. Tony Dennis, former USA Hockey registrar for Connecticut, has always been a proponent of women's hockey and is not afraid to let people know when he thinks the system isn't supporting women: "I was interviewed by the *Hartford Courant*, because I was coaching [girls'] teams that were doing very well and [the interviewer] said, 'How's the national organization doing?' And I said, 'Well, they are not doing much at all for women's hockey.' I said, 'It's an old boys' network, and I don't think they are doing a damn thing for women's hockey.'" Dennis got a call from Bob Johnson, who was the executive director of USA Hockey at the time, but Dennis didn't back down. He does admit that since he made that statement (around 1990), USA Hockey has improved its program for women and has provided players with a lot of opportunities. But there are still improvements to be made. Dennis believes that USA Hockey still retains the attitude that the female athlete and the male athlete should be treated differently.

According to Karen Kay, head coach of the 1994 national team, USA Hockey's commitment to women's hockey has changed dramatically since 1990. "When we went to the first world tournament we had one weekend tryout in Boston and then we skated together for three days and then played in the world tournament, which is amazing," she said. "Then, in 1992, they did a little bit more. They had maybe a two-week training camp and played maybe one or two exhibition games and then played [in the World Championship]. In 1994, when I had the team, we had open tryouts around the country. We had four open tryouts to rate the players. We brought the players to camps throughout the year, and then we picked the team. It's the same thing [in 1996]. Now we have finally made the commitment and now they've done what I feel is necessary — they've hired a full-time coach. We're at the point where we need to do that. It had to be done. I'm really happy for the program that they decided to do that. Obviously, now, making that kind of commitment and giving the coach a three-year contract and providing full-time training for the players — they're working out all the time — and having them in camps, it's just a huge difference. Before they would just pick a team and go play a tournament and that was about it. And it's all happened in a really short amount of time. When you think of the change that has occured in that amount of time, it's unbelievable. I don't think there are too many other sports where things progress that fast."

Cammi Granato has seen improvement in the national team over the years as well: "I think everything has improved — every aspect that you look at. Even the physical shape that we're in, I think maybe that's the biggest difference. Especially now, we have time to prepare, we know how serious the [World] Championship is, and we understand how important it is to train."

USA Hockey made further commitment to women's hockey in 1996 at the Pacific Rim Tournament. Karen Kay, Ben Smith and Bill Beaney, the men's coach at Middlebury College, each scouted one of the other countries. They watched the other teams practice and play and wrote a report on each team for USA Hockey. It was the first time USA Hockey had ever given that type of assignment to coaches.

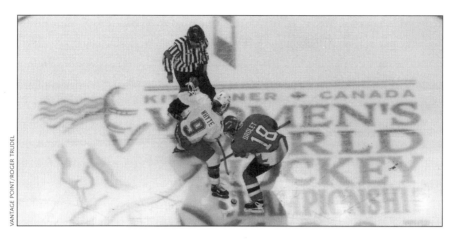

Facing off for gold: USA versus Canada at the gold-medal game of the 1997 World Women's Championships in Kitchener, Ontario.

Financially, support of the women's program has improved since 1990, when players had to pay their own expenses. Now that women's hockey is a recognized sport with world tournaments and Olympic status, players can receive grants from the US Olympic Committee. Any players who have used up their college eligibility can take advantage of the grant money, but it usually goes to the top players in the pool. It was this type of financial support that allowed Karyn Bye to begin training immediately for the national team and the Olympics after receiving her graduate degree in 1995. Players can also become involved in the Olympic job opportunities program. The program is set up by the Olympic Committee for all athletes and pairs them with various companies that allow the athletes to work part of the day and still have time for training. USA Hockey implemented a residency program to include housing, ice time and equipment (through sponsorship) once the whole team began training full-time for the Olympics in the fall of 1997. USA Hockey funds all of its programs with money received from registration of all players and teams throughout the country.

At the administrative level, women are given a voice, although small, through the player representatives on the Board of Directors, the policy-making body of USA Hockey. Maria Dennis, former Team USA player and an attorney specializing in business and sports law since 1991, currently serves on the USA Hockey Board of Directors as a player representative. Dennis, a member of the 1990 national

179

team, didn't participate in the 1992 World Championship because she didn't want to delay her career. Although she works for a law firm in Los Angeles, she is still active in hockey, playing in a Division I men's league. Dennis took her commitment to player's rights a step further when she was named the USA Hockey player representative to the US Olympic Committee.

Player representatives were created as a result of the Amateur Sports Act of 1978, which reviewed the United States Olympic Committee (USOC) and the manner in which national amateur sports organizations were governed in the US. The Act determined that the governing bodies of all amateur sports, and the USOC, must have 20 percent player representation at all board and committee meetings and on any level at which decisions and policy regarding the sport are made.

As of 1996, all player representatives of USA Hockey are voted in by their peers. Candidates eligible to become or vote on a representative must have played on an elite level, such as the Olympics, world championships or junior world championships, within the past 10 years. Each athlete representative has a tenure of 10 years. There are currently 13 player representatives, four women and nine men, who have a chance to voice their concerns and opinions on behalf of all the players registered with USA Hockey. Besides sitting on the Board of Directors, all representatives are assigned to a committee which explores and discusses a specific issue or problem facing hockey players today. These committees include: the International Council, which focuses on the elite athletes competing internationally; the Youth Council, which ensures that USA Hockey is serving the youth competing on an amateur level; and the Safety and Protective committee, headed by a doctor who makes sure that players are wearing the safest equipment.

The commitment of the players and of USA Hockey has certainly strengthened the women's national team program. As Karen Kay commented, "Our players at that level are sacrificing a lot in their lives to make that commitment and they're not going to get a big financial reward afterwards. They're not going to get a pro contract. They're not going to get any of those things. But that's the beauty of it. That's what's so special about working with those athletes — they have a passion for the sport."

7 / PROFILE
Kelly Dyer — Team USA

FROM FIGURE SKATER TO PRO HOCKEY PLAYER

Although she started playing hockey at a time when opportunities for girls were severely limited, Kelly Dyer has been in the right place at the right time for a large part of her hockey career. She has played goal for one of the strongest women's programs in the country — Assabet Valley in Concord, Massachusetts — guided Northeastern University to two Eastern College Athletic Conference (ECAC) championships, played men's professional hockey in two minor leagues and played in goal for three USA women's national teams.

Dyer was born in 1966 in Princeton, New Jersey, but her family moved to Acton, Massachusetts when she was six months old. Like many female hockey hopefuls in the 1970s, she began her career as a figure skater. For four years she skated at the Colonial Figure-Skating Club in Acton-Boxboro, but in 1977, at age 11, she made the switch to ice hockey. Growing up in a neighbourhood of boys and having a hockey-playing older brother made the transition a natural one. "I always used to go and watch my brother play," Dyer said. "I'd finish my figure lessons and go over to the other side and watch him. And I said, 'Jeez, that looks like a lot more fun.'" That was the era when Bobby Orr had established himself as the best defenceman ever to play the game with the Boston Bruins. As a result, the Boston area boomed with new ice rinks, and boys and girls from hundreds of miles around picked up sticks and gloves trying to emulate the flashy moves and scoring finesse of Number 4. "I grew up in a neighbourhood that was pretty much all boys, and they always played," Dyer continued. "We'd come home from whatever organized activity we had and we just played street hockey until dark, or until we broke all the windows in the garage and had to come in. And because I was the youngest in the neighbourhood, they used to just throw me in the net." And a goalie was born.

Dyer was a natural athlete. She played soccer and basketball and made the swim team. Not only was she comfortable on skates, she was also fond of the pigskin. Her dad, however, didn't want her putting a lot of time and energy into sports that had no future for girls, and Dyer was forced to choose between hockey and football. Once it was determined what Dyer wanted to do, it was time to determine where she could do it. At the time, the Dyers didn't know there was organized girls' hockey. But some investigation uncovered an organization called Assabet Valley, located in Concord, Massachusetts and headed by Carl Gray.

The Assabet team was not a second-rate team of girls fooling around in ill-fitting equipment. They were serious about their hockey and expected newcomers to be as well. "I remember my first time out there," Dyer recalled. "I had my brother's equipment on and my figure skates. And I was a laughing stock. Everybody made fun of me." But she was not deterred. She played a wing position for the first two years, as Assabet already had a strong goalie when Dyer entered the program. Finally, Dyer got her chance when the starting goalie didn't show up and she was asked to take the position between the pipes. Dyer was impressive, even wearing just her regular hockey equipment, and earned herself the starting position.

Within a year at Assabet, Dyer was on the A team. It was still the late 1970s, but several girls' and women's teams had emerged throughout the area to provide some female competition. Boys' teams provided additional practice and scrimmage time, but Dyer played against Massachusetts girls' teams from Stoneham, Chelmsford and Hudson, and also the Assabet midget team, made up of 17- and 18-year-olds.

While at Assabet, Dyer was in the net for 12 out of a possible 14 national championships. She continued her career there through high school. At the same time she played with the boys' varsity hockey team at Acton-Boxboro High School, the same school that produced NHL goaltender Tom Barrasso. Dyer was the first girl to play Division I boys' hockey. Today, due to USA Hockey rules, Dyer would not be able to play for both her high school team and a USA Hockey-sanctioned youth hockey team, but in the early 1980s, Dyer was allowed to suit up for both.

Playing on boys' teams, Dyer received some harrassment from players and other coaches, but she feels it was minimal and it never intimidated her into pursuing another sport. Dyer insists that, despite some initial trepidation, the last person to give her a hard time because she was female was Ned Bunyan. He was at the New England Hockey School in Contoocook, New Hampshire, which she attended when she was 15 years old. "I was there right in between junior age and the senior age of the campers and it was an all-boys hockey school and a girls' figure skating school," Dyer explained. "So I lived with the figure skaters and went to the hockey school. They couldn't decide whether to put me in the junior or the senior [division], so the first day they said, 'All right, go with the junior and go with the seniors and we'll see which [to keep you in],' so I just played both the whole time. Bunyan came up to me and said, 'Don't you know that women should be in the kitchen baking brownies?' I didn't take it too personally. And it turned out he was one of the head referees for the men in the ECAC Division I, which was the division I played in. That is a pretty big spot for a ref and he'd come to our female games and he'd just look at me and shake his head. I'd say, 'Want a brownie, there, ref Bunyan?'"

There was also tension surrounding Dyer at Acton-Boxboro because of Tom Barrasso, who was a hot prospect for the NHL. Dyer said some people in the community were under the impression that the presence of a girl in the league would make NHL scouts think it was a lesser league and would therefore make Barrasso less of a prospect. Their concerns were unwarranted. Barrasso played with the Buffalo Sabres right out of high school at age 18 and went on to win the Veniza Trophy for Outstanding Goaltender in the NHL his rookie year — 1984, the same year Dyer graduated from high school. There was other talent on Barrasso's 1983 graduating team as well — future NHLers Bob Sweeney and Jeff Norton, and Alan Borbeau, who went to Harvard and played for Team USA in the 1984 Olympics.

Having such talented team-mates to practice with certainly was an asset for Dyer. Although Barrasso never spoke to her or coached her, Dyer found watching his work ethic and his dedication inspiring. "I learned a lot playing behind someone like that and watching him perform, watching him practice," Dyer said. "He was one of the most focused goalies I've ever seen. He never screwed around in practice. He always won every single sprint. He beat every forward in his goalie equipment, every single time. I almost caught him one time because he didn't see me tailing him. Then he saw me and put on the jets and I was all gone."

After graduation, Dyer expanded her experience on the ice at the New Hampton Preparatory School in New Hampton, New Hampshire, which she attended in 1985. She skated for both the boys' and the girls' teams at New Hampton, playing goal on the Varsity B boys' team and forward for the girls' team. She switched to forward because the calibre of hockey at girls' private schools was so low at that time. Participation in sports is mandatory at private schools and many of the girls on the team were on skates for the first time. Dyer was concerned that

J.D. LEVINE/NORTHEASTERN UNIVERSITY

Kelly Dyer after Northeastern University's first-ever ECAC Championship in 1988, against Providence College.

she would lose her reaction time and speed if she stayed in goal, but she wanted to remain on the team to share her hockey knowledge. Since she was still getting some time in goal with the boys' team and at Assabet, she decided to make her experience with the girls' team a fun training year. Even though she was not playing in her natural position of goal, Dyer shone, and tallied 32 goals and eight assists on the girls' team.

New Hampton boasted three boys' ice hockey teams. The varsity A team played against colleges, varsity B faced off against other prep school teams and the junior varsity matched up against public high shool teams. Although she made the varsity B team, Dyer did not see any game action. Since New Hampton was a private institution, and did offer an equivalent sport for girls, the school was not required to allow her to play during games. Dyer didn't push the issue and was happy just to have the extra practice time.

At the same time she was playing on two teams at New Hampton, Dyer managed to play 10 games for Assabet, which allowed her to compete for state and national championships. As in so many other years, Assabet dominated the state tournament. With strong players such as Kelly O'Leary and Cindy Curley, who would join Dyer on the 1990 USA women's national team, and Heather Linstad and Shelly DiFronzo, Assabet didn't allow one goal against during the entire tournament. Dyer, Linstad, DiFronzo and O'Leary all came out of Assabet at the same time, but went to different schools and ended up competing against each other at universities (except for Linstad and O'Leary, who both attended Providence College). Dyer prevailed over her former team-mates, however, when her Northeastern University team won the ECAC championship over Providence College during her junior and senior year.

Northeastern was not Dyer's first choice of colleges. The University of New Hampshire (UNH) was a powerhouse in women's hockey and Dyer wanted to be a part of the winning team. It was the only school to which she applied out of high school, and she had been speaking with coach Russ McCurdy about the women's program for two or three years. Dyer had secured on-campus housing and room-mates and nearly had her bags packed when she was told she was not accepted academically because she had not taken a language in high school. While her dreams of playing for a high-calibre women's collegiate team were delayed, a better opportunity soon unfolded. Dyer had not been courted by many other college coaches because it was clear UNH was her choice. But, on a whim,

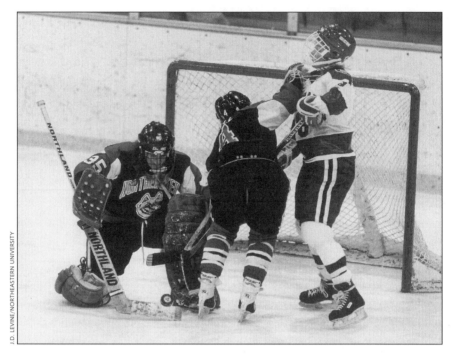

J.D. LEVINE/NORTHEASTERN UNIVERSITY

Kelly Dyer protects the Northeastern University net during the 1987-88 season.

coach Don MacLeod called her, offering her a full scholarship to Northeastern University, a five-year school with four years of classes and one year of co-op. Dyer had made her decision to go to prep school, however, and skated for the New Hampton teams, while fulfilling her language requirement.

Dyer kept in touch with McCurdy and MacLeod throughout the year. In that time, she realized she would rather play for a team that was up-and-coming instead of one that had already reached the top. "I decided it would be cool to take a team to a new height instead of be part of one that could only hold onto what it had," Dyer said. "At UNH all I could do was win [the ECAC championship], which would be okay, because you still won it. But at Northeastern it would be like breaking new ground, and it was fun."

So Dyer went to Northeastern on a full scholarship and made the Lady Huskies varsity ice hockey team. Even though the the calibre of hockey was not as high as it would have been at UNH, Dyer still had some tough competition: "I had gone from playing at Acton-Boxboro High School and all of that excitement,

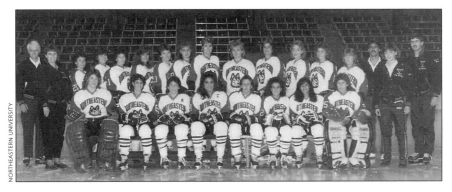

NORTHEASTERN UNIVERSITY

The 1987-88 ECAC Champion Northeastern University women's ice hockey team. Kelly Dyer is on the far left, front row.

and being the number one goalie for Assabet, to playing three games my freshman year at the university. There were three [goalies. Don MacLeod] still recruited me, but he played a senior, Patty Hunt. And there was another girl, a sophomore named T.C. Devine. It was his call. We lost that year in the ECAC semi-finals. We lost bad."

In her sophomore year, Dyer started more games but suffered a broken patella halfway through the season. Devine took over the duties in net for the remainder of the season and the ECAC Tournament. Northeastern made it to the finals, but lost to UNH. Dyer remained relatively healthy for her junior and senior years and the team went undefeated back-to-back years, compiling a 48-0-1 record. When Northeastern finally lost a game, it was to Providence College, 7-1 at home. Dyer believes the blowout was a wake-up call for the team. "I think it was good we lost that game," she said. "We came back really strong and never looked back after that. We beat Providence College both years [1988 and 1989] for the ECAC championship."

In 1990, Dyer graduated from Northeastern with a dual major in marketing and management in the school of business administration, receiving honours within the school of business. Although she attended college for five years, she was not eligible to play hockey in 1990 because she had played the maximum four years allowed according to ECAC and National Collegiate Athletic Association (NCAA) regulations. Table 7-1 summarizes Dyer's remarkable career at Northeastern.

Table 7-1

Kelly Dyer's Northeastern University Statistics

	Games Played	W-L-T	GA Avg.	Shutouts	Percentage
1985-86	6	4-2-0	1.83	1	.892
1986-87	10	8-1-1	2.00	1	.928
1987-88	21	20-0-1	2.16	3	.920
1988-89	18	15-3-0	1.89	5	.928
Totals	55	47-6-2	2.04	10	.927

Just two weeks after Northeastern won its second straight ECAC championship title, Dyer learned of tryouts for the national team. Although she knew nothing about the national team, it meant playing hockey and that was enough for Dyer. Tryouts were scheduled at arenas all over the country, including Concord, Massachusetts, the home ice of Assabet. From there a pool of players went on to Northeastern Arena for the final selection. There were about 50 women at the open tryouts, many of whom Dyer had played either with or against at Assabet. Most were from Massachusetts, but there were also players from Minnesota and Michigan, also hockey hotbeds which had faced Assabet teams at nationals. From that group emerged the first-ever US women's ice hockey national team.

Dyer attended national training sessions throughout the summer then went back to Assabet for the 1989-1990 season at the same level at which she had played as a 12-year-old. This time, however, she had a larger goal in mind — the World Championship.

For Dyer, the 1990 World Championship was an impressive event, not only because it was the highest calibre of hockey she had played at that point, but also because no one — coaches, players, governments or fans — knew what to expect. For the final game, the teams faced off in a sold-out stadium in Ottawa. There were 10,000 people on hand and 2.1 million viewers on television as the city hosted women's teams from many nations.

Dyer found the Canadians — pink jerseys and all — great hosts for the tournament. With a strong history of hockey in the country, this was no surprise. "When it comes to hockey, they just do it right," Dyer said. "I hate to say it, but I guess it's like Americans talking about baseball and our hall of fame in

Cooperstown. The Canadians have such a central focus on hockey and we have so many diversified things to focus on that it really shows. And when they put on a hockey event it's usually awesome. More credit to them. It's fun to play up there." Dyer still talks with excitement about the treatment of Team USA. "Each team had their own section of this resort hotel," she said. "Each team was provided its own private, exclusive dining room and wait staff. We had private masseuses on each floor for each country. It was like nothing any of us had ever even dreamed of before. We'd come down in the morning, and see TV cameras. Each player from each country had to do an interview for TV. If you made a great

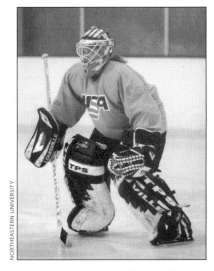

Kelly Dyer, a member of the US National Team from 1990 to 1997, practices for Team USA.

play that night, they could just pop in your interview segment on TV. We had never been exposed to that. And we had fans everywhere. We'd go out for team walks on the streets in Ottawa, and we'd have kids following us, asking us for our autographs. We'd come off of practice [with] kids begging for our sticks. We had never had a reception like that. It was amazing."

The US scored twice in the first period of the final game, but Canada came back to tie it up. When Canada scored, Dyer remembers that the roar of the crowd was so loud that it actually shook her body. She felt her upper body equipment vibrating from the impact of the applause and cheering.

Despite the fact that the US lost to Canada, Dyer played well in net. Team USA was outshot 41-10 and outscored 4-2 before Dyer was pulled to the bench so that another forward could be put on the ice. Canada dumped the puck into the empty net. Dyer was named Team USA's most valuable player for the championship game and was also named best goalie of the world tournament.

Dyer played in net for the 1992 World Championship and the 1994 World Championship. In both championships, Canada continued to dominate and the United States took home the silver.

THE DOORS OF OPPORTUNITY OPEN WIDER

Growing up, Dyer's highest aspiration was to play college hockey. In 1993, new opportunities opened up. Dyer had two Women's World Championships under her belt, and suddenly found herself in a position she had not even dreamed of — playing in a professional men's league. "[It was the summer of 1993 and] I'd just come back from a national camp in St. Cloud, Minnesota," Dyer said, "and I was only home a couple of days. I was in really good shape. I think we had triple sessions for 10 days in a row. A friend of mine, Coach Perry, called from Quincy. He had a team in the Joe Lyons Pro Draft Camp out of Quincy Arena. A league [Quincy Pro Draft League] played Sunday nights.

"Coach Perry's league goalie got hurt and he knew I was back in town. He said, 'You're in downtown Boston, can you get here at six o'clock?' I said, 'Okay, I'll play.' And I asked him, 'Am I going to get my ass kicked?' He laughed and said no. So I said what the heck. I had just come from camp, and I didn't have another camp to worry about for a while. I figured I'd heal by the next one.

"And I went and played and I played pretty well, so they asked me back for the next week. And then that next week I played against a team with white jerseys, including Chucky Hughes, a goalie for Harvard at the time. That was great because I'd always thought Chucky was a pretty fantastic goalie. Doug Keans, who used to be a goalie and goalie coach for the Boston Bruins, coached the team.

"I finished the summer season with Coach Perry's team, and then I played against Coach Keans again. They beat us two to one, but they were killing everybody.

"We didn't win the championship that summer, but I started speaking to Doug. And he said there was a new league starting up in Florida, the Sunshine Hockey League, and we just started chatting. [Keans was part owner of the Jacksonville Bullets of the Sunshine Hockey League.] I was joking around and said, 'Oh, yeah, I should go down to that camp,' and he said, seriously, 'Yeah, you should go down!' I had a pretty good job, working as an account executive for Foster Design, a marketing design firm on Newbury Street in Boston.

"I brushed it off, but then I thought about it, and said, 'All right, I'm going to do it.' Doug said he'd send the form in the mail. A couple of weeks later it came and I signed up.

"The hardest thing for me was to decide whether or not to leave my job. But my boss, Ed Foster, said, 'I'll hold your job for you for two weeks. You go try out.

If you don't make it, I'm holding your job. You come back and you can have your job back. If you make it, I don't want to lose you, but you can decide then.' So he gave me the security, knowing I had something at home still, which gave me a lot more confidence going into camp."

Dyer was also concerned about what her parents would think of her playing in a professional men's league. "My dad's an optical engineer, an electrical engineer, and he's pretty conservative," she said. "He was the second-to-last person I told. I was sort of saving it up and making sure this was what I was really going to do. He thought it was great. 'You only go around once, and you've done a lot and this is a great opportunity for you. You'll do fine with it,' he said. My mom was excited, too. She'd seen me tumbling off people, so she knew I could take care of myself. They've been supportive in everything. They were always there for the tournaments."

Dyer made the Jacksonville team and was there until Christmas, when she went to the national team camp for women in Lake Placid. She had her tickets for the next flight to Jacksonville when she called Keans to tell him her flight number. He told her to change her tickets and fly into West Palm Beach, Florida. Both of their goaltenders were injured, and they needed a goalie the next day.

Dyer was reluctant to leave Keans, but he convinced her that playing for West Palm Beach would be a great opportunity to get more playing time than she was getting in Jacksonville, where she had played in only one game. Keans assured Dyer of her position in Jacksonville after the injuries to the goaltenders had healed, if she wanted to come back. Dyer went to West Palm Beach on loan for two weeks and stayed for two and a half years.

The people of Jacksonville had thought a female goalie was fine — there was some moderate press about it, but mostly local coverage. When Dyer arrived in West Palm Beach, however, she was welcomed by four television stations, radio stations and flashing camera lights. This attention was on the heels of the international press another female hockey player, Manon Rhéaume, was receiving at the Tampa Bay Lightning training camp in the NHL. Dyer was not impressed with the reception and pushed her way through to have a word with Bill Nyrop, the coach of the West Palm Beach Blaze. Dyer made it known that she was there to play hockey, not to be a sideshow. Nyrop agreed, saying that the media coverage was normal for all new players. Dyer was skeptical but decided not to argue and just go about her business — playing hockey.

That night Dyer rotated goaltending duties with another fill-in goalie who had also played for Northeastern University. Between the two of them, they secured a win for the Blaze. Dyer was the starting goaltender the next night, and again rotated with the other goaltender, but was credited with her first professional win.

Dyer's first full win, in which she played the entire game, came her first year as a pro — 1994. Dyer played nine games in 1995. The team was 8-1 in games in which she played and she had three full wins. Her most exciting win came on March 17, 1995 — in overtime: "Usually they play us [females] when they have a big lead or they know they are going to crush a team, or there's a six-goal differential in the game, so it wasn't very challenging. It was exciting to play a game and all that but I played in 12 or so of those, and then to play an overtime game — that was a lot of fun."

The West Palm Beach Blaze won the Sunshine League championship for the two seasons that Dyer played for them, 1994 and 1995. During her second year, Dyer also started working in the executive office of the Blaze, doing extra promotion with area youths. In the summer of 1995, Nyrop, who was general manager and owner as well as coach, became ill and sold the team to Carter Allan, who renamed the team the Barracudas. Within three months the team was bankrupt. The team dropped from three-year champions to fourth place. In attendance they dropped from first to last place in the league with an average of less than 700 spectators. According to Dyer, the work ethic established by Nyrop was crumbling.

The club continued to deteriorate and Dyer began to consider other options: "The final straw was reached when a new coach came in. [Management] fired our coach Phil Berger from the Barracudas and brought in this other individual, and he made it very clear, within a few hours, that no woman would want to participate on his team. I walked off the ice and I never got back on the ice in West Palm Beach. I had told myself when I walked off, I am not ever going to step back on this ice. And I didn't."

Although the relationship with West Palm Beach Blaze came to an end, Dyer had grown substantially as a player while she was there. "I learned more about hockey in the 18 months that I played there than I had in the 10 to 15 previous years," she said. "I learned more positional play, reading the play, reacting. I've become very poised in my positioning. I always did a skate save to the left, glove save to the right. So playing where you had to play beyond yourself, whether you had to throw your head in front of the puck, you just did what you had to do to stop the puck. It took me beyond the positioning play that I used to do to more of a full-out play and it was just awesome to open up my game like that. One thing that I hadn't grown up doing was playing the puck behind the net, stopping the puck, setting it, shooting and all that. Especially with the men's game being faster, it's something I had to work on a lot, along with shooting and stickhandling.

"It was a higher level of hockey than I'd ever played, plus I had a coach who had had diverse experiences. He was an intelligent individual. He wasn't a goalie expert, but he had observed Ken Dryden [his former room-mate on the Montreal Canadiens], or my partner, Todd Bojcun, who was MVP of the league. So he'd use them for a reference. 'Watch how Todd does this. Think about these things,' Coach Nyrop would say. 'If you don't believe me, ask Todd.' My centremen used to help me out too. I'd ask our captain, Don Stone, 'What do you see when you're breaking down on me? Do you see more net — this, that, or the other thing?' They'd take the time to work with me. Actually, I went to West Palm Beach because Bojcun was hurt, and then it turned out that he needed knee surgery, so he was out for a while. So when he started his rehab, he'd come out in his skates and sweats and he'd work with me every day for the last half hour. He'd come out and say, 'Allright, Kelly, try this when the guy does that.'"

Dyer talked with a couple of different companies about a new job, but she was unwilling to go anywhere where she couldn't play hockey. There were some playing options in the Colonial Hockey League and a possibility of being traded within the Southern Hockey league (formerly the Sunshine Hockey League). In the end, Dyer was offered a postition with Louisville Hockey and a tryout in the East Coast Hockey League (ECHL) with the Louisville (Kentucky) RiverFrogs.

Dyer's first contact with Louisville Hockey, a hockey equipment manufacturer, had happened early in her career with the Blaze. Dyer had been sponsored by Louisville Hockey for about two years, wearing their equipment and endorsing their name. In the process she met pro supplier John Voss. After the injured goalies had returned to the Blaze, Nyrop had kept Dyer on as a third goalie and rotated her with the backup to starter Todd Bojcun. Another local team, Team Daytona, was touring France and Italy for two and a half weeks to play Division I and II pro teams, and they didn't have a goalie. Since she was an extra goalie for the Blaze, Daytona asked Dyer if she would go on tour with them. When she agreed, Nyrop loaned Dyer to Daytona and put her contract on pause for two and a half weeks. But there was one problem — Dyer didn't have any sticks of her own and was not provided with any through West Palm Beach or Daytona for the tour. So Dyer put in a call to Voss explaining that she couldn't afford to pay for new goalie sticks. He came up with some leftover sticks from former Olympian Ray LeBlanc.

When she returned to the US, Dyer sent Voss a thank-you note. Soon Voss was telling Graham Watson, the vice-president of business development at Louisville Hockey, about this female goalie who was playing in West Palm. Dyer had been sponsored by AeroFlex from 1990 to 1993. At the invitation of Watson, Dyer started attending a few hockey shows for Louisville, touting the benefits of Louisville hockey equipment to sports shop equipment buyers. At the shows, she was meeting more and more top executives at Louisville and becoming more and more impressed with their work standards. Dyer sensed something might be brewing when Watson invited her to an all-sports show in Atlanta, Georgia, instead of to the hockey show, which would be the following weekend. At the show, over breakfast, Dyer was informally interviewed with the vice-president of golf and the vice-president of the baseball-softball division of the Louisville Sluggers. Dyer left Atlanta on Wednesday and received a call from Watson on Thursday: "He said, 'How would you like to come back and work for Louisville and play for the RiverFrogs?' I said, 'I'll see you Monday.'"

Dyer reported to the RiverFrogs and, through special permission by ECHL commissioner Pat Kelly, was put on the roster as a third goalie. It was understood that Dyer would not get any game time unless one of the other goalies was injured. While she wasn't playing for a team full-time, it was a good situation for Dyer. She had a job developing a women's line of hockey equipment and had access to ice time every day.

THE BEST OF BOTH WORLDS

There are many proponents and opponents of women playing in men's leagues, but Dyer has taken the best of both the men's and women's leagues and strengthened her game to become the best she can be.

In Dyer's opinion, women play a smarter game of hockey — they display a more thoughtful pattern of play, similar to men's European, with a lot of passing, and, in general, they tend to play more selflessly, concentrating on making the pass instead of scoring the goal. Women's games are also played at a more consistent level compared to minor league pro men's leagues. She says of the men: "Some nights you'll see a really good game and the next night there will be 11 fights."

The tendency of women to pass has been a sticking point for many coaches of women's teams. "We had a couple of coaches screaming, 'Don't be afraid to score the goal — that's the point of the game,'" Dyer said. "Women are definitely a lot more disciplined, too, because we're so hungry for good coaches that we'll follow something that we're told to do right to the end. We had this one coach who said we weren't allowed to touch the pucks on the ice at practice. He'd dump the pucks on, but we weren't allowed to touch them until the coach said okay, pick up the puck. So we'd all skate around, stretch out, do our thing, but we wouldn't touch the puck because we weren't allowed to. Then the next coach, Olympic coach Ben Smith, comes in, dumps the pucks out on the ice, and he sees everyone skating around, but nobody's stickhandling or practicing their shot, or practicing their backhand flip or passing to each other. Coach Smith brings us all in and says, 'Excuse me. In the game I'm used to playing we use a puck. If you'd like to play the game that I'm used to playing — hockey — I suggest you pick one up.' Everyone was all excited and hollering."

Dyer also believes that the women's teams have an excellent work ethic: "I think some of the guys who have coached Team USA probably at first thought they got a demeaning assignment, but they usually end up beaming, like it was the most fulfilling experience they've ever had. The players are so motivated, they listen enthusiastically, ask good questions, will execute exactly what they're told. And they [the coaches] come back big fans of women's hockey."

Coaches assigned to Team USA were sometimes skeptical about the abilities of women hockey players at first but were usually impressed after a practice. "It's pretty remarkable to see," Dyer said. "I've even experienced it on a one-on-one basis. People whom I've played with, in a few instances they didn't really want a girl on the team, and by the end they [said], 'Whoa, a girl can play.' When I went to West Palm, Nyrop had really no intention of having a girl goalie, he just needed a goalie. I think he thought he was just going to bring me in, sell out a few games, and then get rid of me. And I stayed two and a half years. I don't know what happened."

According to Dyer, the men's game is faster and more hard-hitting than the women's. "There is also more aggression in men's hockey; however, it is the speed of the skating and the release of the shots that make it more difficult for women to play in a men's game. Girls have a tendency to receive the pass and take a look," Dyer said. "Well, as a goalie, that gives you time to get out there and set your position. Whereas a guy, he'll see the puck coming at him and he'll just shoot the hell out of it. And, for the goalie, I think that's the biggest difference in playing — the timing from male to female." In women's games, Dyer tries to offset this discrepancy by counting, not to any specific number, but just to keep a rhythm with the slower pace of women's hockey.

Dyer doesn't try to compare herself to male goalies. She stands at 5 feet 11 inches and carries 172 pounds on her sturdy frame. Although she is larger than some male professional goaltenders, she concedes that she is not as strong as they are. She has trained harder over the past few years than ever before and has nearly quadrupled her strength, but admits she probably still doesn't have the strength to play as physically as a male goaltender much smaller in weight and size. "It really makes me wonder if it has more to do with body mass or bone mass," Dyer said. "I took on this player when I was in West Palm. The puck went into the corner and I saw him coming. He's a small but scrappy guy, and I thought I'd tip him off with my left shoulder and take the puck and break it off to my wing on the other side. I had him by about a foot so I saw exactly what I wanted to do. He knew me pretty well, he probably knew what I was thinking too. He just drilled me right through the boards. Without goalie equipment I must have had 15 pounds and 2 inches on him. It just didn't matter. But he didn't score, so I guess I did win in the long run."

One of the biggest differences Dyer finds between men's and women's teams is the bonds formed between the players. Dyer felt an instant connection with every national women's team of which she has been a member. While she knew many of the women from youth hockey, the chemistry between all of them was special. "It was just amazing how well we all got along," Dyer said. "If we could win [the championships] on pure chemistry, the US would just shut everyone else out. There's really a strong feeling of being one unit."

The men's leagues are different. Dyer felt more alone in the men's pro leagues. Even though she was part of a team, at the same time she was by herself. She made a concerted effort to be very respectful of the men's space, understanding that they might not always want to have a woman hanging around. At times she longed for a female player to chat with and share her feelings with — someone who would understand better than a man. But she wasn't totally isolated. "The guys [in West Palm Beach] were like my brothers," she said. "When it was just me and Todd in net, I was there all the time so it wasn't a big deal that I was a girl. It really didn't matter. At that point they needed me as a goalie too, which was a nice situation for me. It wasn't like this person just came upon them and here she is. They needed a goalie and they shipped me down from Lake Placid. So I think the way the whole situation started worked in my favour in the long run."

There are two other women who completely understand Dyer's situation with the pro leagues. Both Manon Rhéaume, the first woman to play in the NHL, and Erin Whitten, a UNH graduate and Dyer's team-mate on the 1992, 1994 and 1995 US national team, have played for professional men's leagues. Dyer has a close bond with both women, particularly Whitten. "We've been room-mates since 1991," Dyer said. "We have a good time, and it's refreshing to be with someone who can fully understand what you're talking about.

"We have a lot of laughs. And when Manon came into town with New Jersey when I was in Orlando [playing roller hockey], there was only one extra dressing room away from the guys. She and I just dressed together, and we were laughing and laughing. Manon is really a unique individual. She's a classy lady and she's got a great way about her. And so does Erin. They are both a lot of fun."

PLAYING TIME

Being the third goaltender on a team, as Dyer was for the Blaze and the RiverFrogs, doesn't allow for much game action. It is difficult for most women to find a team that provides enough game and practice time, whether they play for a men's team or a women's team. Even though she may not have dressed for most games, Dyer believes her position as an extra goaltender benefited both her and the team: "You always sort of push the other goalies, because if one of them starts screwing up or doesn't take care of himself enough that he's going to be ready to go the next day, they know I'm going to step in.

"So I think it helps to push them a little bit, not in a bad way, just in a positive way. And it also shows them the spirit of fun. They think, 'Look at this girl, she's out here busting her ass every day, doing sprints with us ...' because they think sprints are the worst thing in the world. I love to skate. I always have. So I could probably dust them a couple of times. But you never really pass the starter goalie, you don't pass them in the sprint, it's just disrespectful. But I think it just shows everybody that I'm playing for pure fun. They might be bitching because they got short-shifted on the power play, but then they see me and say, 'Wait a minute. This girl doesn't dress, she's out there busting her butt. I'll shut up.'"

In the pros, Dyer stayed out on the ice long after the practice was over. The coach would be in his office and most of the players in the shower chatting about where they were going for lunch, but Dyer would be out on the ice with one or two players who wanted to take a few extra shots, the sound of the puck echoing throughout the empty rink. "It's a weird feeling every once in a while," Dyer said, "because I'm out there busting, and I know that inside I have a greater goal in mind. Sometimes you say to yourself, What the heck is going on? But then you've just got to stop and think of the bigger picture and what it's all about. Plus, I love to practice. I've always enjoyed playing in games, and I like practicing."

HOCKEY YEAR ROUND

Dyer is as active with hockey in the summer as she is during hockey season. In 1994 she was drafted by Las Vegas at the Roller Hockey International draft. After speaking with the owners and management of Las Vegas, however, she wasn't impressed. She shopped around for another club and ended up in Orlando, Florida. But roller hockey was not her first priority that summer. She was on a coaching tour with Rink Sport, an all-female coaching staff that travelled across the US putting on girls' hockey camps. The coaches, members from the national team and including former national team coach Karen Kay, logged miles in Alaska, Washington, California, Minnesota, Michigan and Massachusetts. The travel schedule for Dyer was grueling — one week on the road to the camps, and the next week with Orlando — but it allowed her to experience another aspect of hockey.

During the summers that followed, Dyer ran her own goalie school for girls (along with Guy Hebert from the NHL's Anaheim Mighty Ducks). She also coached with her former goaltender coaches, Joe Bertagna and Fred Quistgard, and was the junior women's national team goalie coach.

Dyer's coaching philosophy is different than most goaltender coaches in that she does not spend every practice with the players. "I don't think a goalie, especially a kid goalie, needs a full-time goalie coach," she said, "because then they become too dependent on coaches. I think you have to just somehow figure it out yourself. You still need somebody there you can trust enough to ask questions of, even stupid questions. Somebody you feel comfortable with. Of course there is no one right way to tend goal, especially with changing styles in goal. I just try to give them more tools for their toolbox.

"When I coached at Assabet, I popped in on Wednesdays and Saturdays, and I alternated age groups and different times. And that seemed to work out really well. The kids got a lot out of it, I wasn't on top of them, they had enough room to breathe. Sometimes you end up as more of a babysitter if you're there all the time — kids complaining about injuries. But if the girls know they're not going to see me again for three weeks, they get a lot more out of it and have a much greater attention span."

Coaches at each stage in Dyer's career played an important part in her development and training as a hockey player. Carl Gray at Assabet gave Dyer the fundamentals of the game and always taught her to give 100 percent: "We always had a mediocre team, but he always got the most out of us every single time. And I look at that as sort of the basis of the success that I've had." Coach MacLeod at Northeastern University continued to instil the theory of hard work and was rewarded by his team. "Northeastern had never won a championship, and he had been there 11 years," Dyer said of MacLeod. "It was fun winning for him." National team coaches Karen Kay and Ben Smith also contributed to Dyer's evolution as a player. But the coach who had the biggest impact on Dyer was Bill Nyrop, who saw her not just as a female goaltender, but rather as a professional athlete. He helped her train as a pro: to look beyond limitations in thinking about what she could do; to be very focused and put aside outside factors; to have an athlete's frame of mind.

LOOKING BACK

Dyer is grateful for the supportive coaching and the opportunities she has been afforded throughout her career. She never planned to land in the professional leagues, but capitalized on the opportunities as they were presented. Playing in minor systems could be an option for a few of the elite players in the women's system today, especially goaltenders, but Dyer warns them against jumping at it too quickly. "A lot of goalies write to me and ask me, 'What should I do?' and I tell them: 'Follow your gut feeling. Don't think you need the headlines and press clippings and get ahead of yourself to play boys' hockey. If you're being challenged, play girls' hockey. There's a certain base of friendship that's going to last a lifetime.' Cindy Curley has been my idol since I was 11 and she's still my idol today. She's also one of my best friends. It's that type of thing — that you're not going to have as much [in men's hockey]. I'll always keep in touch with Don Stone and Roman Hubalek from the Blaze, but friends like [Cindy] you don't replace.

"There was a goalie at junior development camp the summer [of 1995]. She's actually one of the most highly recruited female goalies for a university right now. She came to me and told me she thought she wanted to go try playing minor league pro instead of going to play college. I said, 'No, no, no.' If it comes about after the chance to go to the university all expenses paid, then I think it's a good opportunity. But we're [Dyer, Whitten and Rhéaume] not getting enough game time with any of the three of us to really justify giving up an opportunity to play a lot of games. College might be at a conceivably lower level, but it's the highest level of women's. I think when the girls take a look at that whole picture of life, I hope they don't get skewed or get starry-eyed about the thought of playing professional hockey."

Just the same, having seen the inside of men's hockey and the consistent training and ice time that goes along with it, Dyer wonders what type of oppportunities she might have received had her gender been different. "I feel my game has increased so much during my three years of playing minor league hockey," she said. "I would have loved to see what would have happened if I had grown up playing higher levels of men's competitive hockey when I was 15 or 16. Say if I had played in juniors, what level could I take my game to now in men's competition? But when I look at the trade-off and what that would have meant — sacrificing playing for Northeastern University — then I have to think that I'm very thankful for the opportunity I did have and I wouldn't give that up for anything. There's a certain pride in playing for your school and the team we had was unbelievable. Another thing I wonder about is training. I know how much stronger I've become in the last three years. I wonder, if I had started this when I was 17 could I conceivably hold my own in the American Hockey League?"

LOOKING TOWARDS THE FUTURE

After her year with the RiverFrogs, Dyer felt she was still on her way up in the world of hockey. There is room for growth within the professional ranks and Dyer felt she could contribute: "I definitely felt like I could be a regular player without a restriction of gender, playing in the Sunshine/Southern Hockey League. The East Coast Hockey League was definitely a step up, the guys were a little bit stronger, a little bit quicker and a lot more dedicated. A lot of the guys still had optimism and they have the vision of the NHL in their eyes. I think at least half of the guys in the Southern League pretty much realized that the dream was over, and that they were just going to play at the highest level as they could." But she knew the technical aspect of her game would have had to improve to stay competitive in the pros. Specifically her positional play with the puck still needed work: for example, setting the puck behind the net for her defencemen.

Dyer was not seeing enough action in net in the ECHL and decided to review her options once again in the fall of 1996. This time she ended up north of the border, playing for the North York (Ontario) Aeros in the Central Ontario Women's Hockey League, one of the top women's ice hockey leagues in the

Kelly Dyer retired from competitive hockey in March 1997, and devoted her time to the development of women's hockey equipment at Louisville Hockey.

world. In 1996, the Aeros won the Ontario Provincial title and were silver medallists at the Canadian Senior AAA Championship.

On March 20, 1997, Dyer retired from competitive hockey. She is now using the experiences from her successful career to help the thousands of female hockey players who will follow in her footsteps. Although Dyer will never experience the Olympics as a player, her main drive continues to be women's hockey — with Louisville Hockey. One way in which she is contributing to the sport that has given her so much is by helping to develop the first complete line of women's hockey equipment. In October 1996, with design consultation from Dyer and Cammi Granato, the first line of proportionally designed female equipment and sticks was introduced. The response to the female hockey equipment and sticks was amazing. Dyer noted, "Fitting the athletes properly to enhance their performance and give excellent protection is not revolutionary — but it is new for women's hockey."

As the product manager for female hockey at Louisville Hockey, Dyer has a new career but continues to be a pioneer in women's hockey: "I want to do what I can to further the growth and development of girls and women in sport, specifically hockey. I want to teach youngsters to believe in [Louisville Hockey's slogan]: 'Don't tell me what I can't do.'" Dyer has always followed those words herself.

8 / THE CANADIAN NATIONAL TEAM

THE 1998 OLYMPICS

Years ago, players like Marm Schmuck of the Preston Rivulettes or Bobbie Rosenfeld of the Toronto Ladies Athletic Club only dreamed of representing their country at the ice rink. Fortunately for Rosenfeld, there was track and field. She competed for Canada at the 1928 Olympics in Amsterdam, the first Summer Games that allowed women to participate. Unfortunately for Schmuck, hockey wasn't one of the sports included in the Olympics. There was no such thing as a Canadian women's national hockey team — that is, until 1990.

In Canada, some people would say that 1990 was the year of women's hockey. The first Women's World Ice Hockey Championship in Ottawa, Ontario, was held one year shy of a century since the first women's hockey game was played on the Rideau Canal near Ottawa, and women's hockey returned to its early birthplace to stage an international gala. It took a lot of preparation and involved a

Team Canada at the 1994 World Championship. *Front (from left)*: Manon Rhéaume, Geraldine Heaney, France St. Louis, Shannon Miller (Assistant Coach), Les Lawton (Head Coach), Melody Davidson (Assistant Coach), Judy Diduck, Stacey Wilson, Leslie Reddon; *Middle (from left)*: Marianne Grnak, Karen Nystrom, Nancy Drolet, Todd Jackson (equipment manager), Karen Decky (personal trainer), Dr. Maureen Grace, Cheryl Pounder, Laura Leslie, Natalie Picard; *Back (from left)*: Margot Verlaan Page, Angela James, Danielle Goyette, Hayley Wickenheiser, Jane Robinson, Cassie Campbell, Therese Brisson, Andria Hunter.

VANTAGE POINT/DAN HAMILTON – VP54290

Laura Schuler, Hayley Wickenheiser, Jayna Hefford and Cassie Campbell celebrating Canada's victory at the 1997 World Championship in Kitchener, Ontario.

touch of controversy (about Team Canada's pink uniforms), but in the end the event ushered in a new era in women's hockey. Gone were the days of just being happy to play. Now, women and girls were striving for greater achievements, including becoming world champions.

The Canadian Hockey Association (CHA) is committed to developing women's hockey in Canada. One of the objectives the CHA has set for female hockey is to promote and develop more opportunities for women and girls of all ages and skill levels to play hockey. The women's national hockey team program, which targets very skilled and talented players, is one of these opportunities.

There is no denying the dominance of the women's national team. Canada has won four consecutive World Championship titles, in 1990, 1992, 1994 and 1997. In 20 World Championship games, Team Canada buried 146 pucks behind the opposition's goalies while allowing only 24 goals to land in its own net. After the 1997 win, the team set its sights on a gold medal performance at the 1998 Winter Olympics in Japan.

Even though a program is successful, it can always be improved. Many countries, including Russia, China, Sweden and Finland, are developing their national team programs and using Canada as their benchmark. Being the leader is a challenging role. There is no one to chase. The Canadian team is the forerunner and must depend upon its own efforts to continuously challenge and improve itself.

The excitement of the first World Championship in 1990 has now become the business of the 1998 Olympics. In preparation, the national team program has emphasized two key areas: selecting the best players for the team, and running a professional program. The thrill of playing has been displaced, maybe not completely but partially, by the job of playing. Now, the players, coaches and administrators of the team face greater expectations.

KEY ISSUES AND KEY PLAYERS

Dawn McGuire played for Team Canada in the first two World Championships. McGuire fondly remembers her experiences when Team Canada competed in the first Worlds: "Playing in Ottawa became more intense and more exciting as the week moved along and you knew the next game that you played was worth a little bit more. The final game — I will never forget coming out from underneath the arena from the dressing room and stepping onto the ice. We walked out, looking out of the corner of our eyes and seeing all those people. It was the weirdest feeling. I thought, 'I don't know if I can skate.' My legs were like rubber. I remember we got to do a little warm-up and then we came back off the ice and that was probably good because it gave us an opportunity to collect our thoughts." McGuire certainly gained her composure in the tournament — she played outstanding hockey and was selected the most valuable defence for the 1990 World Championship.

McGuire was in Ontario when she joined the tryouts for the first women's national team in 1990. "The first year, the tryouts were completely open," she said. "I only remember that because of the numbers on the ice. You could hardly do a drill. You got five minutes in between drills because there were so many people." Players had to pay to attend the mini-tryout camps that were held in different provinces. Some regions held one camp while other provinces, particularly Ontario, held a series of smaller camps due to the large number of people trying out for the team. Prior to 1990, the CHA had no information about who the talented hockey players were and where they lived. Making the national team truly was an open selection process where players could simply register for a tryout camp with 50 or 60 other people skating on the ice. It was very challenging for a player to make her mark and be noticed by the evaluators.

In 1990, the final selection camp for the team was a new process for the CHA, the players and the coaches. Certain glitches emerged in terms of the format and protocol used to select the national team. Many players were not aware of the process and were overwhelmed with the experience in general. It was the first time any of these athletes had competed for stakes this high — a place on a national team. Some were concerned about the apparent lack of objectivity and the selection of players. There didn't even appear to be specific criteria for inviting players to the camp. In some instances, selection seemed to be based on whether the coaches knew who a player was rather than how talented a player might be. In other cases, selection seemed to be based on a quota system, where players were chosen to represent different regions of Canada. For example, at the 1989 CHA fall Female Council meeting, Alberta stated it was disappointed that its quota was three — this was how many players the Alberta branch could send to the final camp. After all was said and done, the 1990 Women's National Team was a strong squad, but there were probably many players who should have been on the team and were overlooked.

The selection process for the women's national team has improved dramatically since 1990. The major adjustment is that fewer provinces are running open tryouts and the CHA is basing selections, even for training camps, on player rankings. Judy Diduck, a four-time veteran with the national team, has experienced the changes in the selection process first-hand. Diduck commented, "The process they have now is much more fair. The CHA has got its act together in terms of scouting and assessing players. So there are people out there looking and keeping tabs on players — how they are playing at tournaments and throughout the year. There are profiles of potential players coming out of every province. Nowadays if you don't think you are being seen, it is probably not true."

Shirley Cameron was a teammate of Diduck and McGuire on the 1990 national squad. She was 37 years of age at the time she played for Canada and believes there were two reasons why she made the team. On one hand, she worked hard to be selected: "They had a camp in January 1990. I trained and skated every day and felt the best I had ever felt and made the camp in January." On the other hand, Cameron recognizes she was fortunate to fit the mould that the coaching staff had for the team. She continued, "But a lot of what helped me make that camp was the head coach at that time, Dave McMaster, who liked older players.

Judy Diduck fires a puck off the shin guards of Swiss player Sandra Caltaneo during 1997 World Championship round-robin play.

You just never know. If the head coach had been different at that time, maybe he wouldn't have given me the opportunity because he liked younger players."

Cameron benefited from the circumstances that surrounded the 1990 selection. She looked on the 1990 camp as a learning process for the players, coaches and the CHA: "I think they did as good a job as they could considering it was the first camp and didn't have anything to base it on. Even the coaching staff really didn't have any experience at any of these camps. It was four days, and considering it was the first one, it was done fairly well."

Cameron has noticed women's hockey change to the point where more talented players face pressures and the championship events have become a stepping stone for players striving to make the national team. Any young athlete aspiring to the Canadian women's national team is aware of scouts watching her every move. There are various events for players under 18 years of age including provincial championships, provincial winter games, the Canada Winter Games and an Under-18 National Championship which was first held in February 1993. The potential is there for the CHA to be watching a player's progress at all times. Cameron commented, "I suppose there is a lot more pressure because there are a lot more things available to young girls now than there was for me. You see it is already changing at our senior women's national championship. When I was playing at a national championship, I had one goal and one goal only — for our team to win. Now, players are going there and the good players are looking at being evaluated far beyond their own team. There is an awful lot of pressure on the player now, too. There is a double kind of pressure where they feel like every minute that they are out there on the ice they are being evaluated ... plus, they are also trying to help their club win, too."

Keeping a balance between responsibility to the team and desire to develop as an athlete is a challenge for many players in the competitive women's hockey leagues. The desire to excel as an elite athlete and to have the opportunity to play on a national team creates even more tension and pressure. Cameron coaches the Edmonton Chimos, who have represented Alberta in all but one senior women's national championship since the event was reinstated in 1982. She sees first-hand the intensity surrounding the event and the challenge for players trying to perform well for their team-mates and for the evaluators from the CHA. "I guess it's a good way for people to see how young players can play under pressure but it is an incredible amount of pressure," she said. "I try to tell the young kids that if you stay within what we want to do as a team and you play the role that you are given on our team, the people evaluating will see you do that. They will see that you have great individual talents that help contribute to the success of your team. I really try to keep players staying with our team system and remind them that people have come out of our team and made the national squad without trying to be great individuals."

When it comes to balancing all the responsibilities and handling all the pressures, Judy Diduck offers a rule of thumb for aspiring players: "My best advice to anyone thinking that way is — don't think about it. I mean, just go out and play. Twelve-, 13-, or 14-year-old girls who think they are going to make the national team have to be realistic. They need to look at the talent out there and their own talent and see the big picture."

Compared to 1990, the talent in female hockey has improved immensely. At the national team camp for the Three Nations Cup held in Ottawa, Ontario, in October 1996, two former gold medallists were among the six players cut from the team. Shannon Miller, head coach of Team Canada, commented in a press release about the camp: "I think it [cutting former medal winners] comes with

Team USA's forward Sandra Whyte takes a shot on Canada's Danielle Dubé during the 1996 Three Nations Cup.

progress. Competition for spots on the national team is getting tougher. There have been changes in the past and there will be changes in the future. As the talent pool grows, a player has to be more and more skilled to have a chance to wear the Team Canada sweater."

WHAT METHOD WORKS BEST?

Jane Robinson, who played with 1994 Team Canada and has played with the Edmonton Chimos for 14 seasons, believes the selection of national team players has to become more objective. Robinson commented, "Well, it is like anything new — it is going to be subjective. As time goes on and people are no longer in the program, they are going to turn and say, 'Okay, why didn't I make the team? What objectivity or subjectivity was used for you to decide that I wouldn't be on the team?'" No doubt, as selection for the team becomes more difficult and the calibre of players becomes higher, the coaches will be more accountable for their selections. An explanation will be required whenever a player is cut from a camp.

"It is going to put more pressure on the administration running the national team and the coaches," continued Robinson. "Yes, they had better have something that is more objective rather than subjective. They better be able to prove that a person definitely should not be on the team." With the many national level events for women and girls under the age of 18, there may be some cases where parents enter the picture and begin asking why their daughter did not make a provincial or national team. Robinson said, "The younger the girls get on the team, the more the parents are probably going to start to question why their daughter didn't make the team, or didn't make the cut, or wasn't invited to the national camp. They are going to start to look at the provincial camps and ask, 'What criteria did you use to judge my daughter? Where is the proof that she is not good enough to be on the team?'"

While recognizing the improvements in the selection of players, Judy Diduck also argues that there will always be some bias in how a team is chosen. She is careful, however, to clarify that the bias is not political or manipulative, but more a reflection of the preferences of the coaching staff: "I think the selection process has become quite fair. But there is always going to be a bias. That is just the difference of opinion between anybody. One coach is going to have her/his vision of a team and what kind of players it will take to make that team. The person next to her will have a different vision. So whatever the coaching staff vision is, is what mould you are going to have to fit into. So, in a sense, there is a bias."

There is no doubt that the scrutiny applied to decisions about who is to play will also increasingly be applied to national team staff selections, particularly coaches. Openness in decision-making has not always been part of the process. In October 1996, for example, one of the women's national team coaches, Melody Davidson, was released from the team staff at the Three Nations Cup team camp. Davidson had also been an assistant coach for the 1994 Team Canada. In a press release, Bob Nicholson, Vice-President of Hockey Operations with the CHA said, "We felt we had three excellent coaches but we weren't all going in the same direction, so we decided to go forward with two coaches." Aside from this comment, no further explanation was given for Davidson's release and amazingly, no explanation was demanded from the National Female Council of the CHA. If a coach from the senior men's national team had been released, a justification would have to be given. The same should hold true for the women's national team. The women's program should be subject to the same level of scrutiny as the men's. This kind of openness and accountability can only enhance an already impressive women's program.

Glynis Peters is a professional staff member of the CHA and since 1990 has been the manager of the women's program. To her credit, Peters has been instrumental in directing female hockey through a very volatile period of rapid growth. She has given the sport some grounding and worked hard with the volunteer National Female Council representatives to set a strategic plan for the women's program. One of her responsibilities involves managing the women's national team. Her tasks include everything from setting the apparel lists for players, to booking the accommodations and flights, to helping select national team staff members such as trainers and equipment managers. Without the vision and desire of Glynis Peters, the CHA women's program would not be as well developed as it is today.

Peters sees the women's national team as a program under continuous review and improvement. Many discussions have been held on how to prepare for the 1998 Olympics. Prior to September 1997, the program was competition driven — players were pulled together whenever there was an event such as the Pacific Rim, the Three Nations Cup or the World Championship. However, there is more and more demand for development from players. They want to be coached and taught. Elite level athletes want a chance to perform and improve. "The only way we can do that — and I think people in any sport would tell you the same thing — is to bring them together," remarked Peters. The short timeframe on which the national team functions does not allow for a learning process for the players and coaches in the program.

The key question, as Peters sees it, is exactly how to provide a learning experience for the athletes and coaches, to enable them to compete and improve. It was obvious that the event-based format was no longer acceptable. But does this mean a full-time program is needed? Peters sees two particular elements around which to build a national team program: "The players have to have some financial stability. So they have to be living somewhere decent and be eating properly. And they need competition. No one wants to just train and we have talked about how we can give them that competition."

There are a number of issues which support running the women's national team as a full-time program. There is great disparity among national team players in terms of the quality of coaching they receive with their home club teams. Even though the skill level of the players attending the national camp is more consistent, there are still tremendous differences among the players in terms of their awareness of systems and tactics. When players have experienced high quality coaching, there are differences in how the systems and tactics are taught. Coaches have different styles and their personal approaches to the game are evident in the systems they teach a team. The intensity and commitment required of players from different teams also varies. Some teams are very competitive and some have very laissez-faire atmospheres. A player may have a different role with her club team than what is asked of her when she is selected to the national team. On her club team, the player may be an offensive forward who is expected to produce a lot of goals. When she is chosen for the national squad, however, she may be expected to take the role of a defensive forward or penalty-killing specialist.

Just as the national players need time to adjust, the coaches need time to adjust the players' roles, to get everyone playing the same system the same way, and to build their own unique team atmosphere. As Peters suggested, "In order for them to make that change, they need time and we [the CHA] feel if they are going to the Olympics it should be a really good experience, a positive experience." She continued, "Now we just bring them together at the last minute and ask them to pull it off from the gut. But, how much better and more fulfilling would it be for the players to go and feel they were on solid ground? It is interesting to speculate: if Team Canada can win four gold medals from the gut, how well could they perform if they had time to iron out the kinks?"

For the women's hockey program, developing its national team is an exciting but challenging problem. The CHA men's national team program can provide a few ideas about how to design a program for the women's team. Technical and organizational expertise are needs both teams have in common. In other areas, however, the women's and men's team are not similar.

The Canadian men's national team is probably the only program of its kind in the world. Players are part of the program for different lengths of time, and most of the players join the program at different periods of time. In many cases, players are on contract from professional teams in the NHL, but they may also come from farm teams. Sometimes, a few players are added to the team for a particular event. This team prepares for international tournaments, not just for the world championships and the Olympics. For these two events, many professional players join the team at the last minute. In 1998, the Canadian men's Olympic team will most likely consist only of NHL players. Generally, there is no ongoing involvement of the players with the national team. A player may join the team for one event but not be there for the next. The program is most often used as a development step for players trying to improve their status in the NHL.

On the other hand, the women's national team is *the team* for female hockey. It is the top of the pyramid. A player cannot go any higher and may be involved with the team on a continuous basis. A player may be part of the national team program for any number of years. There are already players who have been on the women's national team for eight years, for instance Angela James, Judy Diduck, Stacey Wilson, France St. Louis and Geraldine Heaney. The competition schedule is also different from the men's. Competition is sporadic. During the early 1990s, the women's team prepared solely for the World Championships. International tournaments such as the Pacific Rim Championship and the Three Nations Cup were created in order to provide some additional competition for the women's national team.

These factors make the women's ice hockey program unique. Other women's national sports teams have very active competition schedules. The women's field hockey team can compete in the Olympics, the World Cup, the Pan American Games and the Federation of International Student Universities Games in different years and has a wide selection of annual tournaments in Europe and Australia. Not so for female ice hockey. There are no annual events for them and few major international tournaments. According to Peters, it is not only a challenge for the administrators designing the program, but also for the athletes themselves. She communicates with the players in order to find out what they want to do. "It is really hard," she said. "You are playing with peoples' lives. It seems the players are all prepared to make that sacrifice, though, and it seems they are prepared to say, 'Well, I'm just going to do whatever I need to do to get there.'"

Support for a full-time national team program varies among the team members depending on how it will impact their personal lives. Judy Diduck commented, "Well, it all depends on who you are talking to. If you are talking to the younger group, it is not really a big deal because this looks exciting in your life. Some of them are still in school so they can pursue their school and they can generally carry on expecting to be away from home. I think most of the older ones are the ones who have to uproot and it is a bigger issue. Some people are already looking into moving and preplanning to see how feasible it really is for

Team Canada captain Stacey Wilson crashes into Team China goalie Guo Hong in round-robin action at the 1997 World Championship.

them to up and move. It has never been done with the women, so we might be at each others' throats by the end of three weeks."

Many Canadian athletes are paying their own way to events and training camps. Marnie McBean, for example, is a rower who won double gold medals at the 1992 Barcelona Olympics and a gold and bronze at the Atlanta Games. She has paid her airfare to international events and even stays in youth hostels to keep costs low — all this so she can be an elite and competitive athlete. Is it fair to place the same responsibilities on hockey players who must not only be top athletes but also be able to work as a team? Glynis Peters sees the whole process of being a high-performance athlete and a member of a national team as a challenge, both on and off the playing field. "Getting to the Olympic Games is a long road. Talk to the bobsledders, the squash players, the figure skaters and the wrestlers," said Peters. "There are no two ways about it — it is not easy. If it were easy, everyone would do it. It wouldn't be such a special event."

For the athletes, the most important objective for the national team program is that it enables them to become better hockey players. For Team Canada member Danielle Dubé, the issue of where she plays during the time leading up to the Winter Games is critical for her preparation to make the Olympic team. She has played junior and semi-pro in the male hockey system. The type of competition and schedule is an important consideration for whether she joins the women's national team. "To be named to the national team ... on the men's side, you go to Spain, the Worlds, or wherever. Your schedule is set. If they had that for the women, I think that the girls would do it as a career," remarked Dubé.

It will also be increasingly important for the team to play other teams and not just practice together. The women need the opportunity to test themselves against other players, not just each other. Variety is also important. Sometimes players on teams can become a bit stir-crazy and tired of being around each other. So, if the team camp is held for blocks of time, the length of the time together is also an important consideration. Would two months be too much or not enough time? As Jane Robinson commented, "You don't want to be together too long because you can start creating small rifts or rivalries that can occur on a club team. Hopefully, people can put their differences aside. You don't want people to get tired of each other or burn out."

Glynis Peters sees the schedule as a critical issue in designing the program. "Everyone can tell you off the top of their head — of course they are going to train, and that is the whole point of them being there, they have to be on the ice. The key question is how long should the training last and what would be the effects on the players themselves and the women's hockey community in general? A lot of planning has gone into the current decision to try running the program with this format. We have talked about it ... then we talked about maybe doing some training blocks where we would bring the players in for a time in August, a block of time in September and then maybe a block of time in October," said Peters. CHA administrators make an effort to frequently consult the athletes on their views of the development of the national team program.

As a veteran member of Team Canada, Judy Diduck has been involved with every discussion between the athletes and the CHA about how to organize the program. In Spring 1997, she reflected upon the need to finally make a decision and get the national team program on track. "It is an issue and it is a very unresolved issue at this point," she said. "We just spoke about it recently at the Pacific Rim with the team. Initially, I thought yes, I want to get together everyday with these people because they are the best Canada has to offer at this given time and you just don't know how good you can get playing at that level all the time. The point that was brought up was, who do we play? That kind of triggered ... well, good point ... is that the best option?"

Glynis Peters also sees the competition issue as an important one. She said, "We have talked about the kind of competition that is needed for the players to be stretched and to be challenged. We have talked about hand-picking men's teams, midget teams. But really, hand-picking them so that they are doing things we need to play against. Picking a team that would play like Finland. Not even a team — picking players that would play like the States or a team that would play like China. Doing something like that."

Right now, the challenge for elite female hockey in Canada is developing a high-performance program within a system where there are not a lot of players. Female hockey has grown rapidly since 1990, when the first Women's World Championship was held, but grassroots participation is still nowhere near the size of boys' minor hockey. As a result, the female national team doesn't have as much talent to choose from — or at least, the talent pool isn't as deep as senior men's hockey. Also, there is a limited number of high-level women's teams. There isn't a women's team in western Canada, eastern Canada or even Quebec or Ontario which could be a practice squad for the women's national team. The closest challenger would be a B squad comprised of second-string players who didn't make the final national team roster, and that wouldn't be an effective way to train for the Olympics.

Another problem associated with the lack of depth in women's high-level hockey is the impact on club teams when their top players leave to play on the national team. In some provinces in the Maritimes and western Canada, the loss of one or two key players means the difference between performing well at the senior women's national championship, or qualifying out of the province. If the national team becomes full-time, what effect will that have on women's hockey in general? It may be right for the national team, but will it be detrimental to women's community club teams?

Shirley Cameron, coach for the Edmonton Chimos, sees the issue of the player drain as an important one for women's community teams. She remarked, "I see some of the players starting to move [to Calgary], which I am not in total agreement with because I think it is going to start to hurt your senior teams if you are taking away their elite players. An elite player leaving New Brunswick could mean the end of the success of the New Brunswick program, since many of the smaller provinces do not have the numbers. When you have someone on a national team, it gives your team credibility and confidence to compete with other provinces.

Losing key players in small markets could mean the end of their programs. Even among ourselves, if players leave our team then it is going to hurt our team." In Cameron's view, one solution might be to focus a full-time program around the premiere event — the Olympics: "In years other than the Olympics, I don't think it is a necessity, but in the Olympic years, I think they need to get together. Now whether it is for a whole year, I am not sure about that either."

Judy Diduck also feels the national team player drain would be an issue for club teams. "Speaking from the club point of view," she said, "I think it would be very detrimental to the program because you will draw all the top players off your local club teams and out of the province and that would really defeat the growth." This problem is similar to that of the most talented girls continuing in boys' minor hockey instead of joining a girls' team.

Dawn McGuire believes that female athletes should go after any high-performance opportunities that become available to them. She also recognizes the fine line between what is best for the national team versus what is best for the clubs. She commented, "Certainly, right now, the program is going to have an impact on club teams. This will be more noticeable in our smaller provinces where the numbers are both an issue and a concern. I suppose an honest view of its impact will be seen once a ruling is determined on whether the players who are drawn away from their home club teams will be allowed to retain their home province eligibility. People must understand some difficult decisions and sacrifices are going to have to be made by provincial associations and individual athletes. These decisions need to be based on what is best for the overall growth and development of our sport. The Olympic Oval program in Calgary provides a place for our elite to train and I do not think it would be fair to judge any individual who feels the program would increase her chances of the ultimate dream — to one day suit up for Team Canada! These types of programs will experience growing pains and we must be patient."

FINDING FUNDS FOR TEAM CANADA

The issue of funding is a critical point which determines the type of program that will be designed. More money means the team can be together longer. When resources are limited, options are limited to multiple mini-camps or one long team camp before a major event. Running a full-time national team program is an expensive venture. In Canada, federal funding to amateur sport has been cut back as the government has decided to reduce its support and force national sport organizations to solicit corporations for sponsorship.

When women's hockey was included as a medal event in the Winter Olympics, it allowed female hockey players to qualify for the Athlete Assistance program which is supported by the Canadian federal government and Sport Canada, the government agency which oversees all funding to amateur sport organizations. This program is based on a carding system where athletes receive monthly allowances according to their international ranking and whether they have played in a world championship. The allowance is intended to assist athletes with living expenses. The Canadian women's hockey team has a high ranking based on its reign as four-time World Champions. For the 1997-1998 season, the CHA women's program of excellence was allocated 30 athlete cards of varying levels to distribute to players. The allowance provides a monthly income of approximately $810 (for an A Card, the highest level) which is supposed to allow the athletes to work less and train more. Although these funds provide some support, they are directed towards the athletes, not the whole national team.

The CHA assumes full responsibility for finding finances for the women's national team. In the past, the CHA has found sponsors who have supported the national men's squad. As women's international competition gains momentum and more events are scheduled, however, the need to provide financial support for two programs is straining the CHA's resources. Now, with the women competing in the Olympics, the stakes are too high for the CHA to not invest more resources in the women's program.

The money can only come from two places: funds can be redirected from the men's program to the women's program, or new sources of funding have to be found, mainly from corporate sponsors. The CHA has a marketing and events division which manages areas such as corporate marketing, sponsor servicing, events, merchandising, promotions and communications. The managers working in these areas are critical to drumming up corporate interest and support for the women's program. Overall, sponsorship, licensing and event profits provide around 50 percent of the revenues for the organization. The remaining funds come from membership fees, government transfers, and other revenues such as those generated from international and interbranch permit fees.

Since 1982, sponsorship of the senior women's national championship has followed a rocky road of development. Initially, Shoppers Drug Mart, a Canadian

218

drug store chain, sponsored the event. In 1984, the company left the sponsor-ship because its marketing plan moved in another direction. When the company withdrew its support, clubs had to bear the full load of funding their trip to the championship. Each year, the tournament is hosted in a different city and costs vary depending on how far a team has to travel. The financial demands certainly had an effect on the calibre of the event. Instead of teams attending solely be-cause its players were talented and had qualified for the event by winning their provincial title, teams attended because they could afford to go. Dawn McGuire, who has attended 14 of the 16 national championships held between 1982 and 1996, commented that the high cost of competing in the mid-1980s prevented some teams from participating: "Some of the Maritime provinces dropped out of the nationals and that, I believe, was a funding issue. I think, for them, they couldn't justify spending all that money to come with a team that was possibly going to lose by a score of 10 or 12 to zero."

Ron Robison is a former CHA vice-president of business operations who now oversees corporate marketing for the CHA. According to Robison, all the high-performance programs such as the women's and men's national teams are put together in a sponsorship package with some domestic properties, including grassroots programs and national championships, to form one package that is presented to potential sponsors. This approach tries to attract corporations to the overall qualities of the CHA and generate some large sponsorship dollars, rather than getting small lump sums for various events. At this time, there are four premier sponsors with Canadian Hockey: the Royal Bank of Canada, Air Canada, Esso-Imperial Oil and Nike. Nike is involved in a grassroots hockey skills program while the other three sponsors are each associated with a national event. Air Canada is linked to the Air Canada Cup, a national midget (boys') champi-onship. Two new properties were offered to the other two sponsors. The Royal Bank became affiliated with the junior A (men's) national championship, called the Centennial Cup.

In 1995, Esso-Imperial Oil was named title sponsor for the Canadian Women's National Hockey Championship. The CHA sponsorship strategy is to bring all the properties into one package and charge sponsors a fee to join that program. Some money has been allocated to specific events. This is where the support comes into play for the Esso Canadian Women's National Hockey Championship. Teams now receive some travel subsidies and the host committees are given funds for public relations and promotion. The balance of the funding from the premiere sponsors goes into a pool of revenues, which is allocated to women's and men's domestic and international properties. Once this pool of funding is established, the Hockey Operations Division of the CHA then determines the budgets for its programs, including the women's national team.

Because of this one-package approach to sponsorship, finding an exclusive sponsor for the women's team is not necessary. Pooling the many properties of the association is more a business operation strategy. But finding sponsors for women's hockey is also a new challenge for the organization. Why have corporate sponsors been so hard to come by? Judy Diduck thinks the reason is that women's hockey is not a high profile sport: "Sponsorship means how well you do things. Nobody gives $10,000 to a local girls' league. You are lucky to get a set of jerseys from a sponsor. Unfortunately, in society's eyes, its always win, win, win ... and in our case we *have* won, won, won! And companies won't sponsor the big picture — instead they will sponsor individual athletes like Michael Jordon. He's a remarkable kind of guy but it is only making Michael Jordon richer. It is not developing basketball."

The CHA has to drum up more sponsors. According to Ron Robison, that means pooling the men's and women's properties together into the premier sponsorship program. "Whenever we present the properties, it has women's programming along with men's programming — it's all integrated into one. So, in this case, Imperial Oil indicated that in addition to sponsoring a variety of hockey programs, it wanted to emphasize an involvement in women's hockey. So the Esso Women's National [Hockey Championship] was started." But what about when an additional event is added to the picture? In particular, the women's national team or the women's under-18 national championship? All new events are added into the inventory of properties that the CHA sells to sponsors. The CHA has prepared a women's hockey sponsorship program which it is trying to sell to sponsors. Robinson said, "Our intent now is to find a title sponsor for the female hockey development program which would include the women's under-18 national championship. Right now we are focusing upon the sale of the national and international properties."

Unfortunately, many businesses aren't even aware of the scale of female hockey and, even worse, have no idea of the calibre and excitement of the game. Judy Diduck sees the women's national team as one of Canada's best-kept secrets: "A lot of companies still don't realize the character that is out there with the national team. They could be using some very quality people to promote their products. One thing I can speak for about our team is that the women are very loyal to their sponsorship. For instance, if they ask us to wear something, we will and we do. We would do everything we could to promote that product."

Danielle Dubé believes if the program had adequate funding, it could be top-rate: "I think, yes, if they put this national team together like they do the men's team — I mean, look out. If you think about it, we come together a week before a tournament and somehow become an incredible team together. If we were always together for a whole season and played like a league team, we'd play against guys' teams just to find the competition that is good enough. So, if they had the finance ... that's the problem, financial. They don't have the money to do all this ... but if they did it would be great. We would travel and tour like the guys do."

The issue of the women's national team budget has become a hot topic among some female hockey enthusiasts who argue that funding should be equal for the women's and men's programs. If funding comparisons are going to be made, it is also important to compare the popularity of the men's and women's teams. National team events are staged only when the hosting committee provides a $20,000 guarantee in revenue to the CHA. This amount of money can be raised because people are willing to pay a fair amount of money to see Team Canada play. In addition, events are only staged where organizers know they will be able to break-even financially. People are not as willing, at least not at this time, to pay the same amount of money to see the women's national team play as they are to see the men's team play. Therefore, it is much more difficult to get host committees to guarantee $20,000 in revenue to the CHA for the women's game.

One example of this problem was the 1990 Women's World Championship. The event attracted crowds and media interest but lost the CHA money. In the 1990 annual Female Council report, Frank Libera, the officer assigned to female hockey at the time, reported that $20,000 was lost on organizing the Canadian women's team and $3,000 to $5,000 was lost on staging the event itself. The 1996 Pacific Rim Tournament and Three Nations Cup also left the CHA with more expenses than revenues and for the Three Nations event, the CHA could only get a $5,000 guarantee from the host committee. At this time, the national association continues to absorb much of the cost of staging women's events, both for the team and for the tournament as well.

One big difference between the men's and the women's program is that the men have had Hockey Canada. In 1994, Hockey Canada and the Canadian Amateur Hockey Association (CAHA) merged to form the Canadian Hockey Association. From 1969, when Hockey Canada was formed to organize the national (men's) hockey team, until 1994, the men's national team has had its own marketing and sponsorship division strictly devoted to getting funds for the team. The women's national team experienced a different kind of growth since it developed within the CAHA. For many sports, high-performance budgets gradually increase. Over time, a program develops and the sport organization is able to adjust its budget. Elite, international women's hockey has not followed such a steady climb to the top. In fact, the game has experienced rapid growth, going from no world championship in 1989 to both world and Olympic events nine years later. Any financial officer for a business with that fast an increase in expenditure would find budgeting a challenge, and the CHA is no exception.

The process for setting a budget for the women's program is to decide what is the best plan for the team and set costs and revenues from there. Glynis Peters, as the manager for women's hockey, usually discusses what is needed for the women's national team with the coaches and with the CHA's vice-president of hockey operations. These people work together to compile a budget which is then sent to the Board of Directors of the CHA for review and approval. When asked if she has had any problems securing the funds for the program, Peters said, "I haven't been turned down yet."

The problem is that the plan for the women's national team changes every year. Attending a Pacific Rim Tournament in Richmond, British Columbia, is much cheaper than competing in the World Championship in Tampere, Finland. In some years, as in 1991, there are no events for the women's national team. Is it appropriate, then, to argue that the budgets for the women and the men need to be equal? Is it fair to say the women aren't getting equal opportunity because their budget isn't the same as the men? Not really. If, however, the issue is whether the women's national team program is developing and growing effectively, it is fair to expect that the CHA tries to develop a high-quality program for the women's team and provides the necessary funding. That might mean funding a second staff person to help with the women's program. It might also mean allocating more funds to the athletes to ensure they have adequate funds to live well and train with the national team. Either way, there are decisions to be made.

THE PLAN FOR OLYMPIC GOLD

For the 1997 World Championship, the usual competition-driven format was used to prepare the players for the event. In January 1997, a national development camp was held to choose the team. In March, a pre-competition camp was held. This camp was longer than previous camps and lasted 10 days. The World Championship itself took place in Kitchener, Ontario, from March 31 until April 6.

Preparing for the Olympics will involve a longer term plan. In June 1997, evaluation and identification camps were held in three different regions of Canada. Decisions about how to prepare for the 1998 Olympic Games were finalized in August 1997. All players on the women's national team were prepared to participate in a full-time program at the beginning of September 1997 and the CHA established its full-time women's national team program. This meant basing the team in Calgary, Alberta to train and prepare together. The pre-Olympic schedule for Team Canada includes exhibition games in Canada against China, Sweden and the US, a trip to Finland in November 1997 and the staging of a second Three Nations Cup in December involving Canada, the United States and Finland. The Winter Olympic Games will be held in February 1998. After the Olympics are completed, the CHA plans to continue the summer development camps with two or more regional camps scheduled for June in 1998 and 1999. For the World Championship in March 1999, Team Canada's selection camp is tentatively scheduled for October 1998.

Although this plan for the national women's team is the one currently in place for the 1998 Winter Olympics, it won't necessarily be the plan followed for future international women's events. The CHA will continue to re-evaluate the program and adjust the program to meet the needs of the athletes. As Judy Diduck remarked, "The program itself doesn't know what works best for the females yet. So, [the CHA] is still exploring and really their only model is to go from what has happened in the male program. Now, obviously, the male program has been around for a long time and it has its ups and downs. So, they can pick and choose, or at least be a little more choosy in terms of what will and won't work for the women."

Glynis Peters also feels there will be a need to review the national team program and make adjustments along the way. She does not support the idea of a set, concrete plan. She remarked, "I think we would be silly to do that. I think

CANADIAN HOCKEY ASSOCIATION

Canadian fans — "Maple Leaf Heads" — in the stands at the 1994 World Championship.

we should see how things go. After 1998 we have until 2002 to review and see what happens and get some feedback. How we do at the Olympics is important. Money is significant. Say we win the gold medal and half of our team retires and from there we have a younger team who don't have the same career demands. We are very conscious of the fact that there are people who have jobs on this team, and maybe if half of this team disappears and we have students, and a full-time sponsor comes on board, it influences what kinds of things you think you might want to do."

Whatever program is set for the Canadian women's national team, the result from playing in the Olympics should be an increased profile of women's hockey. Shirley Cameron commented: "The 1990 Worlds had such an impact, and that was on a much smaller scale than the Olympics. I can't imagine that the Olympics aren't going to do anything but just make the sport go through the roof. Even having the 1992 Senior Women's National Championship in Edmonton has created in Edmonton the Girls' Minor Hockey League, and the midget league started right after that. Everything really took off after 1992, with a combination of the 1990 Worlds and the 1992 Nationals. So, with something as high profile as the Olympics, I think that female hockey is just going to go crazy."

Dawn McGuire shares Cameron's enthusiasm over the impact of the Olympics: "I think the recognition for the players, and the number of people who are going to be exposed to the game, will make it one more sport Canadians will cheer for. Let's face it, Canada loves hockey and judging from the 1990 Worlds, the turnout at the arena and the people who watched on television, the reaction was unbelievable. So now, at the Olympic level every person in Canada rises to say 'Yeah!' whether Canada gets a gold or Canada gets a bronze. It is just one more sport where Canada is strong and is always going to be strong."

It is one thing to hope that the addition of women's hockey to the Olympics will improve awareness among Canadians that women and girls play hockey, but whether it actually translates into more opportunities and programs is a separate matter. Overall, the impact of the Olympics will depend on how the Canadian media cover the event and whether young girls become aware that they can play hockey too.

As Jane Robinson commented: "The Olympics is going to have a positive effect on the profile of women's hockey and it is going to increase the public's general knowledge depending on how it is broadcast here in Canada and how much attention it gets. Because women's hockey is in the Olympics, obviously there is more credibility for the sport than there was in the 1980s. It may encourage young girls to take up the sport and the older generation of [female] hockey players to get into coaching or administration. The Olympics will open the doors in all of these areas."

9 / PROFILE
Angela James — Team Canada

Many hockey enthusiasts would argue that Angela James is one of the most talented players in the women's game today. She is fast and powerful, she has a scoring touch ranging from a booming slapshot to around-the-crease finesse, and she has an intense aura which energizes every team-mate who comes near her. It is no surprise that James is a four-time gold medallist at the World Championships. If anyone can drive Team Canada to a gold medal in the 1998 Winter Olympics, it is James.

Angela James, often called "AJ," was born in Toronto, Ontario, on December 22, 1964. She grew up in the surrounding areas of Toronto, including North York, Markham and Thornhill, where she currently lives.

When James started playing hockey in the minor hockey system, she played with the boys a season and a half until she turned 10. Being a girl in that setting had its problems. The first was dealing with the boys themselves. "On the ice a guy would two-hand me and I would two-hand him back. I wasn't nice all the time," James said. "The second challenge was that many parents didn't want a girl to play hockey, or maybe they just didn't want a girl playing on the team with or against their son. I think the problems were with the parents. So the parents got involved and said you can't have a girl playing." Whether the resistance comes from the players or their parents or both, a lot of girls, like James, have had bad experiences playing boy's hockey. Unfortunately, unlike James, some of these girls left hockey altogether.

After her experience in boys' minor hockey, James joined Annunciation, a Catholic organization that included a girls' house league hockey program. Annunciation is now the North York Aeros, a strong women's hockey organization in the Toronto area. From this point, James followed the fast track of development: "I never played bantam. I went right from house league to ladies senior C. I played there for a year and then I went to ladies AA. Ladies AA was the top level of women's hockey in Toronto and the surrounding area in the late 1970s. Ladies C was the fourth best level at the time."

"I moved around," continued James. "I started with the Toronto Islanders when I was 15 years old. That team doesn't exist anymore. I played two seasons with them. From there I went to Burlington for three years, then to Agincourt for a year and then to Brampton for a year. After that I went to Mississauga for three years and then I went to the Toronto Aeros for three years, and now I am with my current team, the Toronto Red Wings. For the 1996-97 season the team was renamed the Newtonbrook Panthers. Moving from team to team wasn't for the purpose of playing with the best team. It was simply a matter of necessity or enjoyment. I moved to where my friends were or where they were going," James said. "I moved if I didn't agree with some of the coaching philosophies. I moved if a team folded. And I moved because of areas or locations. Different things."

Moving to many different teams over the past 17 years shows how much James wanted to play the game. She likes to play for many different reasons: "I like getting sweaty and I like working out. Most important is the team atmosphere — friends. It is a fast game and there are so many things nowadays that you can do with the game. But I guess overall, it's just to have fun and get out and exercise."

BRANCHING OUT

During the mid-1980s, James played both community and college hockey. While enrolled in the Recreation Facilities Management Course at Seneca College in North York, Ontario, James played both women's hockey and softball. She was an all-star softball player from 1983 until 1985, a period when the Seneca team won a silver and two gold medals in the Ontario Colleges Athletic Association (OCAA) championships. However, it was in hockey she made her mark. During the same three-year period, James played defence for the Seneca Scouts. The team won a silver and two gold medals and was considered stronger than some of the university teams in the Ontario Women's Interuniversity Athletic Association (OWIAA) league. Even as defence, she was high scorer for the league all three years. Her talent in both hockey and softball resulted in James receiving the Seneca College Athlete of the Year award in 1984 and 1985.

In Canada, colleges and universities have separate athletic associations and leagues. The OCAA women's hockey league, in which Seneca competed, folded in 1989. At the time, the OWIAA would not allow the remaining OCAA women's college teams to join its women's hockey league. As a result, when the college league folded, James and many other players had to find somewhere else to play.

Since the mid-1980s, the OWIAA had undergone some very low and high times. At the time the OCAA women's league folded, there were only five universities competing in women's hockey in Ontario. By the early 1990s, the OWIAA was reduced to four teams when McMaster University withdrew its women's hockey program. That was a dangerous time for the OWIAA because if one more team was lost, the whole league would be forced to disband. Fortunately, by the 1996-1997 season, the league rebounded with the addition of squads from the University of Guelph, Sir Wilfred Laurier University in Waterloo, and the University of Windsor, for a total of seven varsity teams.

James began to officiate when she was a teenager. She would often call a few games in between her college and women's club team schedules. She first became accredited in 1980 and is currently a Level IV official. Although James never played in the Ontario university league, she has refereed a number of games. In her opinion, the calibre of the league is difficult to assess because of the mixture of talent playing on the teams. Some teams have athletes who have come from ringette and transferred into hockey because there aren't any ringette programs in university athletics. These players have strong skating skills but need to develop puck control and tactical skills. On the other hand, there are ladies AAA-calibre players who are attending university and playing on the varsity team. These athletes are very skilled and even play on ladies AAA community teams or, in some cases, the national team.

Nonetheless, the OWIAA league plays a very important role as a development forum for female hockey players. The league is experiencing a resurgence and the number of players trying out for each team has increased consistently over the past number of years. "I think it is important for the universities to have their hockey," remarked James. "It is a game that has been in their schools for years, both for women and for men. I believe the league has come a long way because there are some new teams in there now." While the calibre of this league is improving, many players remain in the community leagues where they can be identified for the national team program. Until players feel confident they will be seen in the university system, they will be hesitant to play on those teams. In James' opinion, the Ontario university league is not as strong as it could be because the universities don't offer athletic scholarships. Many young players are opting to play at US colleges, where they can receive scholarship funds, rather than remain in Canada.

When the OCAA league folded, James directed her attention solely to the Ladies AAA League, the top women's league in the Toronto area. Even though she had dominated the OCAA league, her talent really began to shine in the Ladies AAA League where the skill level was high amongst all the players. As a power forward who primarily plays centre, she was the highest scorer in the Central Ontario Women's Hockey League (COWHL) from 1989-1990 to 1995-1996 and has won the COWHL most valuable player award six times. James has competed in the Canadian senior women's national championships for 12 of the past 14 years. During that time, she has established herself as one of the most talented women hockey players in the country by winning eight most valuable player honours at the senior national championships.

With eight Team Canada players coming from the COWHL, it can be considered the strongest women's league in Canada. Some may argue that other leagues, particularly in Quebec, rival the calibre of the COWHL. Although there are many strong players from Quebec, such as Nancy Drolet, France St. Louis, and Danielle Goyette, all of whom have played on the national team, the COWHL has the depth of talent to make a well-rounded league. The competition continues to get stronger within the league and there is growing parity among the teams. The calibre of the league has also improved to the point where the games are very entertaining. "I think the competition is much better: Everyone is pretty much on an even keel," said James.

To James, however, the COWHL needs to encourage growth and try to increase acceptance of the game. As she remarked, "We have had the same person in our executive forever. So we've had this one person calling the show for our league, and that person looks at the league only as a place in which to play. Now we have expanded. We play two 15-minute periods and a 20-minute period [in a game] now and we have a flood between, and we charge at the door. So, from that end of things it has picked up. Otherwise, it's the same old thing."

Aside from playing and officiating, James is also a coach and hockey entrepreneur. She has her Intermediate Level coaching certification and coached a competitive atom (ages nine and 10 years) girls' team, the Scarborough Sharks, in 1992-1993. In 1994-1995, she also coached a women's senior A team three categories below the level she plays.

James is also the Senior Recreation Coordinator at Seneca College. One of her job responsibilities includes directing the Seneca College Women's Hockey

School. Based in part on this experience as well as her desire to teach the game of hockey, she owns the Breakaway Adult Hockey School and runs a hockey camp for young girls. She has very definite opinions about how, and when, a hockey school should be held: "I don't agree with hockey schools in the middle of the summer. I think it is a waste of time. I don't mean that because that is how I do mine, but I just think that if you go to a hockey school in the middle of July for a week or two, it's not ongoing and there are problems. I run two hockey schools. I run a school for little girls at the end of August and I run an adults' school for eight weeks. To me, going out on the ice every week, or twice a week, seems a little more logical than a week in the middle of July."

VANTAGE POINT/DAN HAMILTON — VPS4572

Four-time Team Canada member Angela James at the 1997 World Championship.

While summer hockey schools are a touchy topic among some hockey volunteers who believe the players need a break from the long season, hockey schools in general are a booming business, especially in female hockey. As women's and girls' hockey becomes more competitive and as the opportunity to play on provincial and national teams increases, so does the demand for proper instruction, and James always supports that. As she remarked, "I think that as long as the female hockey schools have good instructors and are run properly, which the ones I am familiar with are, then I think the schools are a great idea."

ONWARD AND UPWARD

James has been a member of the Canadian women's national team since the first World Championship in 1990. It has been an interesting ride, with some ups and downs. She found the selection process for that first national team far from objective. Time was tight and the Canadian Hockey Association (CHA) had to move quickly to prepare a team for the Championship. Unfortunately, the CHA entered the process fairly blind. In men's hockey, there was a strong scouting and player identification system, but there was no information on the female hockey talent in the country which the CHA could use to invite players to the tryouts.

The 1990 coaching staff included Dave McMaster, head coach for the women's varsity team at the University of Toronto, Rick Polutnik, Technical Director for the Alberta Amateur Hockey Association and coach of the Edmonton Chimos, and Lucie Valois, who was the female Hockey Director in the Quebec women's hockey scene. It was a hit-and-miss style for inviting players to the final tryout camp. Maybe you were invited because someone put in a good word. Maybe you were invited because there was a policy to have different regions of the country represented. Maybe you were invited because one of the coaches knew you.

James was cut at the final camp. Luckily for her, there was quite an uproar within female hockey circles about the selections and some players were given a second chance, including James. In the end she made the national team, won the gold medal with Team Canada and was selected to the tournament all-star team. Imagine what might have happened if the informal selection process had left James off the 1990 national team roster! "Well, in 1990, it was a funny year. Nobody knew anything," reflected James. "There were all the rumours and assumptions about people but nobody knew anything. Nobody knew who the players were and I fell right into that category because I got cut that year. I didn't know what was going on and I still don't know what happened. Politics, a lack of information and a lack of evaluation."

Since then James has been selected to all but one national team, including the 1992, 1994 and 1997 World Championship teams, the 1996 Pacific Rim team and the 1996 Three Nations Cup team. She was not named to the 1995 Pacific Rim team because it was a development opportunity for up-and-coming rather than established players. During the past six years, she has seen a significant number of changes in the women's national team program. For one thing, promising players are no longer identified according to the whimsical likes and dislikes of one individual. And there is a better idea of where the good players can be found. As James commented, "I think the coaching staff and the CHA have a good feel for who is out there. I think there might be one or two players who are talented that they don't know about. But for the most part, the program has got a good grip on the athletes and where they are at, whether it be psychologically, physically or emotionally."

Angela James with the gold medallists Team Canada at the 1992 World Championship. *Front (from left)*: Manon Rhéaume, Geraldine Heaney, Heather Ginzel, Shannon Miller (Assistant Coach), Rick Polutnik (Head Coach), Pierre Charette (Assistant Coach), Nathalie Rivard, France St-Louis, Marie-Claude Roy; *Middle (from left)*: Nathalie Picard, Dawn McGuire, H. Coombs (Team Doctor), Glynis Peters (Program Manager), R. Antworth (Equipment Manager, T. Sutherland (Personal Trainer), B. Nicholson (CAHA), Stacey Wilson, Sue Scherer; *Back (from left)*: Margot Verlaan, Karen Nystrom, Andria Hunter, Diane Michaud, Nancy Drolet, Danielle Goyet, France Montour, Laura Schuler, Angela James, Judy Diduck.

Shannon Miller has been involved with the national team since 1992, first as an assistant coach and now as the head coach. According to James, having some consistency within the national team coaching staff is important for player selection. "It is really nice to have Shannon, who has been there for a number of years. I think you need that," remarked James. "Shannon has some insights and has seen different things. When you are in constant change with coaching staff it makes it difficult. The CHA has also become more professional in how it conducts the national women's program. I think they inform you more and you know what is coming up," said James. "Before it was all a big secret and all this hush-hush. But now, you can talk to the coaching staff and even the CHA. They hand you a five-year plan and you know what to expect."

To James, the greatest challenge facing the women's national team is deciding how to organize the program. Until the 1996 Three Nations Cup, the team was put together only days before an event. Unlike the men's senior national team, which is based full-time in Calgary, Alberta, the women's team is event-driven — that is, the players come together only when there is a major competition. This is an outdated practice compared to other countries. In the United States, the women's national team had monthly training throughout 1996. China and Russia ran full-time programs where players lived and trained together. James found Canada's lack of centralization frustrating. In 1996, she said, "We are falling behind and it is because we are not centralizing. The US are together right now. I'm sure the Finns are together, and China. What is Canada doing?"

The main reason that the women's program is undergoing an overhaul is that there's a significant rise in the stakes — the Olympics. Other countries are trying to close in on Canada's hockey reign. For example, Team USA was together for three weeks prior to the Three Nations Cup in October 1996 and had been training as a group before that time, while Team Canada invited 33 athletes to a five-day selection camp and ended up carrying 27 players for the event. "It was a different atmosphere for a lot of people because we carried 27 players ... so it wasn't a feeling that we were together," James commented. "It was the first time that everyone has experienced that. It was like competing for our jobs." James believes that coming together at the last minute, as they did in 1996, and playing on heart and desire will no longer be enough.

Other countries, such as Finland, who won the bronze medal behind Canada and the United States at the first four World Championships, are also becoming more competitive, although James was not impressed by Finland's performance at the 1996 Three Nations Cup: "I was really surprised at Finland. I found them not as quick. They weren't even close to the United States. They don't have the size and they aren't as strong. With the increasing competition at the international level, physical size is of growing importance. At the 1990 World Championship for instance, Susanna Yuen, from Winnipeg, Manitoba, was a tiny forward for Team Canada, but she was also aggressive and finished seventh in overall scoring at the event. It is very difficult for a player with that size and style to make the team today."

Canada and the United States have faced each other in the gold medal game of every major senior women's international hockey event since 1990, except the Women's European Championship where North American teams do not participate. The frequency of the match-ups, combined with the pressures to win gold at the 1998 Olympics, has lead to a strong rivalry between the two countries.

Although James respects the US team, she has a very definite opinion of its style. "To me, the US players are like robots," she said. "They seem like they are all the same size, although there are a few that are bigger than the others. It's all the same style. You can tell they have been together a lot because they are constantly doing the same thing. But for a lot of those girls to break out of their shells and go and do their own thing — it seems like there is no room for them to do that. I would say they are fairly aggressive. They move the puck well, they skate well and they have some very talented hockey players on their team. It is just, for some reason, they are pulled back. I don't know what it is."

The rivalry between the teams is extending beyond the international forum into regular season play. Many American players, who have played their maximum number of years according to National Collegiate Athletic Association (NCAA) rules, are moving to Canada to play for Canadian universities or community club teams. Two American players, Sue Merz and Jeanine Sobek, were on James' club team, the Newtonbrook Panthers. Kelly Dyer, the former goalie for Team USA, played with the North York Aeros in Toronto during the same season. Cammi Granato, four-time member of Team USA and a prolific scorer, played for Concordia University in Montreal, Quebec. In fact, to some extent each country is developing the other's talent. For example, Canadians Laura Schuler and Vicki Sunohara, also team-mates of James, played in the US college system. The question is, which forum — the Canadian women's community clubs or the US college team — is the strongest system for developing players?

The United States has beaten Canada only twice. The first defeat was during round-robin play at the 1995 Pacific Rim Tournament and the second loss was during round-robin play at the 1996 Three Nations Cup. James believes the two countries are very close in calibre. "To be quite honest," she said, "every game that we play the Americans, not just the 1-0 final at the Three Nations Cup, has been close — except when we played them in Finland and beat them 8-0. Other than that, they have always been close and have always been leading us. We always come back and beat them."

After the Three Nations Cup gold medal game, the Canadians enjoyed the victory and were accused by some American players of over-celebrating. "So what?" laughed James. "We won and if someone's emotions are higher than the next, for whatever reasons, what are we supposed to say? You are in a competition. You are playing for your country and you just beat the United States of America!"

DEALING WITH NATIONAL TEAM EXPECTATIONS

As Team Canada's undefeated streak in international competition continues, the pressure also increases. With each victory comes higher expectations. The hopes and aspirations of a country seem to rest on each player's back. But James keeps such pressure in perspective. Her performance is set according to her own expectations, which in all likelihood are far greater than the expectations of anyone else. She sees her role with the national team from the perspective of a veteran who has played in four World Championships. She keeps tries to focus on the task. "I have been pretty fortunate because I have had to deal with the international scene for a number of years now," she said. "So for myself it is pretty easy. I know what to expect because I have gone through it. So it isn't a surprise. I am not a real excitable person as it is ... I try not to let my emotions get the best of me."

Focusing on the task may be the reason why James performs so well in clutch situations for Team Canada. She was selected to the all-star team at the 1990 and 1992 World Championships and was named the best forward for the gold medal game at the 1994 World Championship. A veteran member of Team Canada, James is one of the most solid performers at the international level. Her unique mindset gives her an edge over other players. Have the demands and pressures of being a national team player changed over the past six years? "Pressures? No, it is easier," she replied. "It is like a pressure point. When you apply pressure, it kind of goes out. So [it's] the same thing. I think, with the coaching staff being more experienced, and the players being more experienced, that the pressure isn't there, but I think the intensity is always there. That is important — to have the intensity and the drive. Without them, nothing else will work." The opportunity to compete in the Olympics is just another task James has set for herself.

It's hard to predict what the impact of having women's hockey as an official event in the 1998 Olympics will be on the overall profile of female hockey. No doubt, the media coverage will increase awareness of the sport. Young girls will see the players on the national team and look to them as role models. Not every young girl will make the national team, but if one girl plays hockey in order to compete in the Olympics or if another girl plays hockey simply because she sees women's hockey on TV and becomes interested in the game, James thinks the result will be the same — more girls will play. "The Olympics are the Olympics.

I think we could be playing tiddly-winks and be known," she remarked.

Even though women's hockey will be at the Olympics, there are still a lot of challenges facing the CHA and its member branches when it comes to developing female hockey throughout Canada. James suggested some areas have already seen improvement: "Women's hockey is big in southern Ontario now. It is really big in the grassroots, which it needs to be. I think that the more people see the senior women's hockey on the TV and the more they hear about the scholarships to different schools, the more parents will start thinking they want their kids involved." According to

Geraldine Heaney and Angela James celebrating with the Championship Plate at the 1994 World Championship.

her, the main challenge for the CHA is to develop other areas of the country so that they have the same level of participation that exists in southern Ontario.

James sees Canada's chances for an Olympic gold medal in very practical terms. "I think the key is that we have to get to the Olympics first of all through the 1997 World Championship," she said. "Then you have six teams in the Olympics, so you have a 50-50 chance of getting a medal — whether it is a bronze, silver or gold. Everybody wants a gold." If winning gold is the goal, then it is obvious to her that the CHA needs to provide the support to develop the national team. Remarked James, "We are not being developed outside of the national program in order to play in it. So, from this point of view, there isn't a whole lot of opportunity out there for developing my skills as a hockey player." The CHA's job, primarily through Glynis Peters, the manager of the women's program, will be to provide those opportunities.

JAMES' VIEW OF WOMEN'S HOCKEY

As someone who officiates, coaches and organizes hockey schools, James has many interesting opinions about the state of female hockey, what it has accomplished to this time and where it needs to go in order to grow and improve.

Angela James and Team Canada celebrate winning gold at the 1994 World Championship.

For James, hockey is above all just a game which women or men can play. "I go out and play with the guys and they play just as well as the girls, sometimes worse and sometimes better," she said. "And the girls play just as well as the guys, sometimes worse and sometimes better." While she would like to look at the game of hockey this simply, she realizes that there are still many problems. What, for instance, happens to the eight-year-old girl living in a rural area, who is not exceptionally skilled and just wants to play hockey? Are the attitudes open enough to see her as just another player? Maybe, maybe not. James does see some hope. Reflecting upon one weekend where she refereed many hockey games, she said, "When I was at the rinks, the little boys were running around playing in the back and I was laughing because I was sitting there thinking, years ago, it was always the little girls running around." She continued, "Before, the mother would bring the daughter to the game and the father would take the son to his game. But now, the mother and father are bringing their daughter to the game. So, I don't think it is distinct that way anymore. I think it is natural, more natural."

There is tremendous debate among female hockey volunteers about whether women's and girls' hockey should be called distinct or whether it should just be part of the big hockey picture. James sees certain differences between women's and men's hockey: "Major differences would be physical strength, right away. As far as the actual game, not much of a difference. In terms of the strategy, plays and systems, there is no difference. In terms of physical strength and the ability to pass from one side of the rink to the other side of the ice, there is a difference." But does it matter if the women's and men's games are different? Is this diversity positive for the game of hockey, providing more styles and facets of the game to enjoy? "I don't think in terms of the values of the women's and men's game," James said. "How guys are going to treat a situation is different from how girls are going to treat a situation. I don't know this in terms of the young kids and how they treat the situations, but I look after the men's college program here at Seneca College. I really don't see a huge difference. They come to the game prepared, they get dressed, they get prepped, they get pre-ice. You know, it's almost exactly the same."

One other discussion that emerges alongside the growth of women's hockey is the idea of a women's professional hockey league. Some players already play in professional men's hockey, including Manon Rhéaume from Lac Beauport, Quebec, and Erin Whitten from Glen Falls, New York. Danielle Dubé, from Vancouver, British Columbia, plays professional men's roller hockey. Each of these players are goaltenders, as no woman playing forward nor defence has ever signed a contract to play men's professional hockey. James believes many female hockey players would enjoy an opportunity to play women's professional hockey regardless of the salary levels. She doesn't see professional hockey as a likely option for her future, however. "It would definitely depend upon a few things. I am 31 years old now and I have been working for 10 years and I am not about to give up my career," she explained. "To just go off and leave everything for the sake of playing hockey — it isn't necessarily my dream. Right now, my dream is to take some time off in 1997 and train and shoot for the Olympics. My dream is not centred around the professional hockey league."

10 / THE WOMEN'S GAME
Distinctions and Opportunities

THE DIFFERENCE

One of the largest debates in women's hockey today is whether the women's game is different from the men's. Many fans who watch a lot of women's and men's hockey certainly have their opinions, but some of the most qualified people to discuss the issue are the women who have played with and against boys' and men's teams.

When asked about this topic, some national team players from both the US and Canada were emphatic that the men's and women's game should not be considered separate entities. American Maria Dennis said, "Everything's the same [except checking] and whether you like men's hockey, girls' hockey — hockey is hockey and it will never change. And if you love the sport, if you go watch any kind of game — a women's game or a men's game, it doesn't matter — if you love pure hockey, you'll get pure hockey if you go to one of the games. When I was at the 1994 World Championship at Lake Placid as an observer, I watched the gold medal game between the US team and the Canadian team. The rink behind me had a men's tournament in it and these guys came in. They were done with their game and they put their bags down beside me and they were watching and they were watching and they were watching and after 10 minutes, one guy finally said to his friend, 'Oh, my God, they're women.' It took them 10 minutes because the game was so fast and hard-hitting. It was a wonderful game. It was very physical and the principles were executed very well."

Canadian Dawn McGuire agreed: "[Maybe] we play two different styles of the game but no different than men's and women's basketball, men's and women's lacrosse. There is the physical aspect that changes the nature of the game a bit. But it is still lacrosse, it is still basketball, it is still hockey, it is still field hockey, whatever the sport is."

"It is like female and male tennis — they are both tennis. You don't compare the two. They are each a sport within themselves," Canadian Shirley Cameron said. "I think it is all hockey, but when it is showcased, like it has been, say, with

TSN [a Canadian sport channel] covering the 1990 Worlds and now the coverage of the [Canadian senior] nationals ... one thing that is always commented on is how the women play as aggressively, but the fair play is also there. Once the play is over then that's it, and people just go to their respective benches or the face-off circle. So I think that once we start to showcase the game more and more, people will see that."

On the other hand, Karen Kay, coach of the 1994 and 1995 US national team, sees a big difference in the game, especially at the coaching level. "As much as everyone wants to say 'it's hockey, it's the same thing,' it's not," she said. "There are just different parts of the game that are more important in ours and different in the men's. It doesn't mean you really teach the game any differently but you have to respect the differences in the game and in the personalities. No matter what level you're coaching and no matter how competitive the women are, they still have a different attitude about things than the men do and different things are important to them ... I think a male has to have experience coaching women because it's definitely different. I think with the women you spend a lot more time trying to build up their confidence because a lot of them aren't as confident as they should be. You spend a lot more time doing that than you do [when] coaching the boys or coaching the men. There are a lot of differences."

Most players concede that there are obvious differences in the game, such as the physical presence that drives many girls from boys' teams when they become teenagers. There is no denying that male and female bodies develop differently and men gain more strength than women. Shirley Cameron said, "The biggest difference I see in female hockey over male hockey is the physical part. Women will play and be very competitive and go hard at each other and the whistle blows and that's the end of things. In the male side, there is a lot more of the aggressive pushing and shoving and stuff like that. Maybe the female game will go there, down the road, but I just don't see that happening now."

Having played in a semi-professional men's league, American Kelly Dyer has seen the ultimate form of aggression — fighting. "In women's hockey, in 20 years of playing, I've only seen maybe three fights," she said. "I'm not really a fan of fighting, but I do understand it as a tool in the game, especially in the men's game as far as intimidation and dominance and strength. It's just a factor of the game."

There was a time when women's hockey allowed intentional bodychecking, but in the mid-1980s, the Canadian National Female Hockey Council voted to remove checking from female hockey. The main reason for this change was that the game was becoming dangerous. At that time, many women's teams had a wide range of ages — some players were teenagers and others were in their forties. There weren't enough players to form separate teams for different ages, so bodychecking was removed to balance the playing field. Canadian referee Karen Kost remembers what it was like for some of the younger players to take the hits: "We got to the point where the moms and dads didn't want their daughters playing in a sport where they were going to get hurt. It was probably the best rule that ever came out. It gave participants the ability to concentrate on their skating, shooting and stickhandling skills." The United States has never allowed bodychecking in female hockey, but there is still plenty of body contact in the women's game, whether it is played by Canada or the United States.

In the 1970s, when girls' programs were beginning to develop in the US and Canada, the differences in the women's game were what drove the skilled female players to the boys' or men's programs. For the most part, people thought that girls' and women's hockey wasn't as good as boys' and men's hockey. Many parents kept their daughters in boys' hockey because they thought it was more challenging — that their daughters would become better players playing with and against boys.

Given the calibre of female hockey in the past, Canadian Danielle Dubé felt her best option to become a skilled goalie was to stay in the boys' system and face the hard shots. "I have never played a full season in a girls' league," she said. "Female hockey in British Columbia is growing a lot. Actually, before this Pacific Rim [1996], I have never really had anything to do with [female hockey]. Since the Pacific Rim was here, I started doing some stuff to promote it. It's growing. There are a lot of young girls coming up, but the senior women's level — if I played [just] that I don't think that I would be fully prepared to go back and play with the national team. So as a goaltender ... playing with the men is what helps me the most and is probably what got me to where I am now."

Some players think what makes the women's game different is what makes it more attractive to fans. "It is naturally distinct because males are naturally different," Canadian Judy Diduck said. "No matter where you go, the press always seem to ask the same thing. They always want to compare the female and male game. There really is nothing to compare. They are playing the same game, but we play it differently and in some eyes it is better hockey."

Canadian Jane Robinson agrees with Diduck that the media plays an important role in promoting women's hockey. "The media can argue that women's hockey is the same or different and influence people's attitudes. They are two different games. Physically, they have to be," Robinson said. Because it is relatively new to the media, and to the general population, it is only natural to compare the two. Those who are more versed in the sport see two different games, with perhaps more finesse in the female game.

Some suggest that values are different between men and women, as is the spirit in which they approach the game. Karen Kost, a top-level official who has refereed at European and Women's World Championships, sees a difference in how women play hockey. "I enjoy officiating the women's game for its sportsmanship qualities and the men's game for the challenges that it provides," she said. "I am a high achiever and in this respect I enjoy the men's game. But, on the flip side, I enjoy the women's game because it is more sportsmanship oriented. Even though they are aggressive and they want to win as badly as the guys, they don't come out to win at all costs. In other words, fighting and berating the opponent is not their style. I just think that is the female makeup. They very rarely argue a call and if they do, it is with dignity and sportsmanship. Some of this might change in the future as the women's game grows and becomes more competitive at the national and world levels."

Danielle Dubé echoed Kost's comments: "I think the atmosphere of the game is the same. In the dressing room is where I think it is different. The girls seem to gel better as a team. Everything is so — this is with Team Canada — so Canada-oriented. Everything is so passionate. What we do in the dressing room helps us so much on the ice. Sometimes I wonder if the men's national teams go through these same things. I have played men's hockey at a high level but it's always been just like a team game, not like Team Canada. It would be interesting to see what the guys from Team Canada go through."

People often refer to women's hockey as a pure form of the sport. The players are motivated by the sheer excitement of playing the game and of one day representing their country in the Olympics. There is no professional league to aspire to. Judy Diduck noted, "I think females use their heads more efficiently. They are not so worried about killing somebody because they have to get to the NHL. There is no NHL for girls except in the rare occasional situation. I think girls play more for the enjoyment of the game rather than a professional focus."

Another side to this argument suggests that women's hockey emphasizes the strategic parts of the game. American Cammi Granato found that with the women she could take time to develop the play more than with the men. "With the boys I was too anxious to get rid of the puck and anxious to shoot the puck. I didn't realize I had that extra time," she said. "In the women's game you had a lot more time to calm down and take the extra step."

The mental side of the women's game is certainly approached differently than in the men's game. The women's games are won with tactics, not brawn, since fighting and bodychecking are not allowed. The game can certainly be physical, however, as Danielle Dubé commented: "Women's hockey has a more European style. It's a smarter game, a passing game. You don't get the big shots as much as you do with the guys and you don't get the big hits, because there is no hitting. So it is a smarter game where you get a European style with passes, the pretty plays. Because I played with guys for so long, I prefer it because my style is set to that style. I like getting set, I like having the big shots to start off the game. What I find hard in women's hockey is the scramble in front of the net. You can have everyone with their head down swinging at this puck, whereas in men's hockey whoever puts their head down is going to get run over. So I had to get used to different things. I played a really stand-up style. When I play with females I have to play more butterfly kind of style because of the scrambling in front as well as the passes across."

Canadian Dawn McGuire believes women's hockey is the way hockey should be played. "I think the women play a much smarter game. I think we play more the way the game should be played," she said. "Especially now that there is no contact. It's a quicker game because there is no checking. It allows the game to beplayed at a higher pace."

JACKIE ISAAC'S STORY

Whether or not women think their game is distinct from the men's, there are several areas where women still struggle just to play the game, or have to play on men's teams in order to see action on the ice. Many girls and women find ways to succeed in these situations. Their determination and attitude is proof that women can play the game, in many cases in harmony with men. Jackie Isaacs of Cincinnati, Ohio is one of those women. Here is her story, as told to Joanna Avery.

"My hockey career did not start until I was 31 years old. I had been a hockey fan since the days of the WHL Cincinnati Stingers. After a few years of not having a pro hockey team in this city, I got re-interested when we became home to the IHL's Cincinnati Cyclones. Although I was taught to skate at the age of five and was a fairly adept skater, I had never played organized hockey. After attending a few Cyclones games, I wanted to play myself. Everybody, including my husband, thought I was nuts. I started doing research and found a learn-to-play-hockey clinic. That was all it took for me. I set my goal to be the best female hockey player to have picked up the game after the age of 30!

"I am a firm believer in setting goals for yourself. I was fortunate in that former New York Islander and Cincinnati Cyclone, Doug Melnyk, saw my talent and determination and took me under his wing for instruction. Since then, I have been instructed by many people, from former ECHL players to Russian Red Army players and everything in between. I average 15 to 20 hours a week on the ice. One of my pro friends swears I get more ice time than he's gotten in his whole career. I knew that I had a lot of catching up to do and I've been told that I seem to have 10 to 15 years experience in only three. I know that I am *extremely* lucky because of the access I have to the ice. We have two rinks within a mile of each other and one is a multi-million dollar facility built for the Cyclones with dual rinks. After spending weekday mornings weight training, I'm off to the ice. I take to the ice immediately following the Cyclones practice and they check on my progress, give me pointers and support. There is additional hockey time at night when a lot more people gather and play high-level pickup games and I use that time to get my "game" together.

"Since 1995, I have played for the Roadmen in the USA Hockey-sponsored league. I am the only woman on the team. After an uninspired first season, we went on to win the league championship in our second. My team-mates are like brothers to me and have pulled for me 100 percent. Through playing I have met 200 to 300 men and I have yet to experience any overt sexism. Last season alone, I was asked to join four other men's teams. I think the men welcome me because of the attitude that I have. I never came into it with the attitude, 'Here I am, you better make room, like it or not.' I gave them respect and in turn and in time, I got respect back. Some women seem to never want to ask a man how to do anything, but when I see someone with a backhand or slapshot I admire, I compliment them on it and ask if they can help me. Through this, I not only gain a new buddy, the guy will show me exactly what he's doing and keep on helping me until I get it right. In the end, we both win. In addition, I found that my style has commanded a lot of respect. I'm the first one to go in corners and fight in the crease. My style has been likened to Dino Cicarelli's in that I'm feisty and strong for someone so small.

"This whole experience has been like a dream. I have made many friends and I've been interviewed for the news and filmed for a magazine show in Lexington, Kentucky. One of the neatest things that has happened to me was one afternoon while I was playing a pick-up game. I started hearing loud cheers from the stands. I looked up and there was a group of elementary school age kids and all the girls were hooting and hollering every time I touched the puck. It was one of those days where the competition was not all that keen and I scored four or five goals. When the game was over, I was mobbed by fifth-grade girls. They followed me to my locker room asking me questions like, 'Do you play for the Cyclones?' and 'My brother said girls can't play hockey, wait 'til I tell him about you!' It was very satisfying.

"I've always realized that I'm being watched by people who have never seen a woman play and I have gone out of my way to act appropriately and respectful. I've gotten a lot of stares from people but I feel it's only because women hockey players are still out of the ordinary to most people."

A WOMEN'S NHL?

If there are differences between women's and men's hockey, could you market these unique characteristics — could you sell a different product?

Longtime hockey journalist Shirley Fischler would say yes. She said, "It would be great if they marketed it as a women's game because it is different. There's no checking and it might be a good selling point for the women's game. I'd rather see it done that way instead of blending it in with men's hockey."

Over the past decade, so many new programs have been created for female hockey that the players are now looking to the future with dreams of even more opportunities. Now that there are Olympics, and world championships, what else is there to add to the sport? Maybe a professional league.

There is certainly interest from the players. "When I started playing, you played just because you loved the game," Dawn McGuire said. "Now there is more out there for females, but I think when women first started playing, certainly from my age group anyhow, they were playing because they loved the sport. There was nowhere for them to go. When I played, there was Provincials but that was it. So I think when I started I was playing just because I wanted to play the game. Now, like I said, there is more for the people to play for Worlds and Nationals and everything. I think a lot of boys are probably playing with the big dream of making NHL and making it a career. It isn't there yet for women but certainly that possibility gets stronger and stronger every year. There have already been rumours of some professional [league]. You know the situation is possibly happening. At least the interest is out there for it."

Maybe a women's professional league wouldn't have high salaries, but many players believe that the women would most likely play anyway. Why? "I think, for themselves," commented Canadian Angela James. "I think there would be a lot of people who would play for $25,000. That would be a lot of money for a lot of people. But aside from the money aspect of things — just going in and being a part of that. I think that would be history in the making and I think people would jump on it."

Player interest has been established. But can a professional women's ice hockey league survive? Perhaps part of the answer can be determined by looking at the professional women's basketball leagues that emerged in the US after the 1996 Olympics in Atlanta. The US team had just come off a gold medal win in which they easily defeated the competition and established themselves as the best women hoopsters in the game. Naturally a professional women's league was not dreamed up overnight, but took years of research and hard work by many individuals. On October 18, 1996, the American Basketball League debuted with eight teams.

It was not the first time women's basketball had introduced its own professional league. Four previous leagues had tried and failed, the most recent just five years earlier. There were a variety of reasons why the leagues failed, but all experienced poor attendance and a lack of sufficient funding. The 1996 entry stands the best chance of succeeding for three reasons: attendance at women's college basketball games is rising; women's basketball was in the national spotlight for over a month during the Olympics and was well-received; and a television contract has been signed with a US cable station, SportsChannel.

Basketball currently has something that hockey does not — a tremendous number of girls who play the sport, which in itself will ultimately lead to a larger audience. According to the 1995-1996 US National Federation of State High School Associations Survey, 445,869 girls played basketball — the most playing any girls' sport. This number also represented 45 percent of the total number of high school basketball players. There were under 2,000 girls playing hockey in high school that same year. Nearly every high school in the US offers basketball to girls. Only one state recognizes girls' high school ice hockey, and a handful of other states sport a dozen or fewer girls' hockey teams. The numbers are somewhat misleading, though, since most girls who play hockey at the high school level play on a community youth team — about 5,000 of them in 1995-1996. But the base of both players and fans for girls' ice hockey cannot begin to compare with the participation numbers for basketball. The numbers for college participation and support are similar. The 1995 National Collegiate Athletic Association women's college basketball championship game was televised on ESPN, the largest cable sports network in the United States, and was the second-highest-rated college basketball game, men's or women's, in two years. No women's hockey game has been able to approach that.

Obviously more than numbers are needed to make a professional women's league successful. The sport needs good athletes. Women's ice hockey certainly has many good athletes, but drawing them out of women's programs raises some concern among Canadian players and organizers of women's senior leagues.

Such a league would also need public acceptance and interest, which continues to rise, but is certainly not at the same level as for basketball. Proper funding and sponsors are also needed — difficult to obtain in any sport. The assistance of some major equipment suppliers and other major sponsors is critical to the success of a women's ice hockey league. Advertisers, however, still try to reach their female audience with daytime or prime-time television, not sports. Media coverage will continue to spark interest in new fans and sponsors, but is very difficult to acquire and sustain. When the ABL started, newspapers nationwide — for example, *USA Today* and *The New York Times* — covered the story. After the season began, the stories trailed off to a few times a month and were generally restricted to newspapers in cities with women's teams.

A national television contract is also a determining factor in the success of a professional league. In Canada, the NHL has had national coverage through *Hockey Night in Canada*, which began on radio in 1931 and on television in 1954. Over the years, however, the NHL has had trouble landing a national television contract in the US. The NHL received sporadic national television coverage in the US, but it was not until the early 1990s that a season-long national television sponsorship was established with sports cable networks ESPN and ESPN-2. Coverage for a women's league will be even harder to find.

The timing for a professional league will be optimal after women's hockey debuts at the Olympics. If Canada and the United States do well and bring home medals, interest and participation in women's hockey will surely take off. The US women's soccer national team provides a model to emulate. The national team kicked off a victory tour in the spring of 1997, to be followed by an all-star tour in the fall. The all-star tour will consist of four teams coming together for a week of clinics, autograph sessions and media interviews, followed by semi-finals and finals matches on the weekend. In the spring of 1998, eight to 10 teams will play in cities across the country, then break for camps and national team duties before the best players regroup for another tour. A similar schedule will unfold until a professional women's soccer league opens in the year 2000. It is hoped that the tour will increase visibility and produce interest in women's soccer, establishing a fan base, and more importantly, enticing sponsors for a pro league. Organizers of a professional women's ice hockey league might want to consider a similar path — as many people still don't even know that women play hockey. By scheduling a national tour after the Olympics, an accurate measure of fans could be made and built upon, instead of creating teams in six or eight cities and hoping there might be enough interest in those cities to sustain a professional team.

Establishing a fan base is a challenge for a professional women's hockey league. Besides the NHL, there are other professional and semi-professional hockey leagues in the US and Canada with which the women must compete. Attendance is often low at American Hockey League, East Coast Hockey League, Colonial Hockey League, Central Hockey League, Southern Hockey League and Western Hockey League games. Support of a women's league by the NHL would be a boost and attract much-needed corporate sponsorship. Many believe that if the women could attract fans for just one game, they might win over quite a few people with their style of skating and their finesse — qualities often not present in the men's game. "I honestly think if you could just get people to come see one game, they'd come back again," American Karyn Bye said. "A lot of people don't realize the high calibre of women's ice hockey. Yes, we're a little bit slower than men, and physiologically there's nothing we can do about that. But as far as our skills — our passing, our shooting and the play-making out there is comparable to what the men do."

American Ellen Weinberg disagrees that forming a professional women's league is a good idea. "I don't ever think you are going to make money on it," she said. "I think it's going to be really tough to get spectators, other than those who are interested in seeing up-and-coming players. And I think that's what the ABL is getting: a family crowd with young girls that want to come watch their idols play."

Whether a professional league develops or not, the women can certainly market their product as unique. In an article in the Worcester (Massachusetts) *Telegram & Gazette*, USA Olympic softball coach Ralph Raymond said, "I preach to women: 'Don't try to compete with men. Play your own game, improve your own game, and sell your own game.'" That is exactly what women's hockey, or any sport, needs to do to gain the respect and support of American audiences. True, hockey is hockey, but the way the women interpret the game is different. Instead of using power and physical presence to win a game, the women use skating and brain power. That is not to say that all men's hockey games fall into the stereotype of bench-clearing brawls between players missing vast quantities of teeth — and brains. It means that the women have something more to offer — hockey the way it should be — graceful, precise and fast.

AFTER THE PLAYING DAYS ARE OVER

With more opportunities for girls and women to play hockey, both on the local and international level, more opportunities within hockey open up for women off the ice.

Coaching is the most natural step for many players to take after their playing career ends. Youth and minor hockey programs are volunteer, but they are a good way to gain experience in coaching. It is essential to have women involved at this level to help the grassroots programs grow, especially in those areas where hockey is just developing. One such woman has been particularly active in the Pacific Northwest region of the USA. Cindy Daley is the first head coach for the Northwest Admirals, the girls' midget rep team in the Seattle Junior Hockey Association (SJHA). As a youngster in the early 1970s, she played with the boys initially until she was forced off the team by parents who wouldn't stand for a girl showing up their sons. At the age of 11 she played on a women's team and played with them through high school. After graduation she looked for the best place to play hockey and chose to move to Canada to play women's AAA hockey, the best in the world at that time. She became one of the leaders and helped her team go to the national championships, but as an American, she was not allowed by the coach to play for her Canadian team at those events.

Daley eventually stopped playing in Canada and returned to the United States. In the late 1980s she helped establish the Seattle Wings, the only women's hockey team in the Pacific Northwest. She played on this team for approximately five years and then coached the Tier Two team, which had also been developed. She coached adult teams and individual players for a few years and then began coaching youth hockey as a career. In 1993, she joined the SJHA and coached the girls' squirt team (there were only three girls' teams and more than 30 boys' teams). She then became the head coach of the midget girls' house team which she helped get into the Lower Mainland Female Hockey League (LMFHL) for the first time. In 1996, after a successful year of the team winning more than half the games it played in the LMFHL, she worked with the association to make the team an official rep (travelling) team with the financial backing that the boys' rep team received. The team was placed in the LMFHL AA Division along with another midget girls' house team which was created to compete in the AA Division. In the 1996-1997 season, the rep team took first place in the LMFHL in the regular season and in the playoffs. It was the first time a US team won the title in the Canadian league for the girls' and/or women's levels. Also for the first time, the team competed in tournaments across the US — California, Minnesota and Connecticut.

Along with her achievements as a coach, Daley helped the growth of girls' hockey in the SJHA by submitting a five-year plan for the girls' program. She has also gained exposure for the association and the girls on the team. In 1997, Daley and her coaching staff aided in the players' efforts to play for Division I colleges and universities. For the first time in SJHA history, two senior players were recruited by schools with women's varsity ice hockey programs.

One of the few chances women currently have at obtaining a coaching job is at colleges and universities. Women who were among the first female hockey coaches are already being offered better opportunities. Laura Halldorson was one of the first women college coaches when she began coaching at Colby College in Maine in 1989. She began coaching at the high school level, then became an

COURTESY ZOE HARRIS

Cindy Dayley, the first head coach of the Northwest Admirals, has helped girls' hockey in Seattle, Washington gain national recognition.

assistant coach at Princeton after she had enjoyed a successful career there. She stayed at Colby for eight seasons before moving on to coach the first varsity women's ice hockey team at the University of Minnesota in 1996. It is the first Division I school in the Midwest and the first school in the Big 10 Athletic Conference to offer women's hockey. Halldorson is also on the cutting edge in one other area. She is the first female coach of a women's hockey team to be paid on par with a male coach of a men's team. When Halldorson began coaching the first women's varsity ice hockey team, her salary was comparable to a male coaching the same calibre of hockey.

Another coach who is well established in the US system is Karen Kay. Kay grew up in Marlboro, Massachusetts. She was the only one in her family interested in playing hockey. Her parents were fans of the Boston Bruins. After watching Bobby Orr and Phil Esposito, Kay wanted to give hockey a try, and when she was nine, she began playing for the local boys' team. By the time she was 14, there were enough girls interested in hockey in the area to form a girls' team, but the team played in a boys' league.

In 1981, Kay entered Providence College on a partial hockey scholarship. A shoulder injury ended her playing career in 1985, just before her senior year. She stayed active with the team and was the student assistant coach that year and also began coaching youth hockey at Assabet Valley. Kay described these years: "When I left Providence my senior year as a student assistant coach, there really weren't any full-time opportunities at the college level for women. You'd get paid $2,000 to $3,000 in order to coach, so you had to have something else. So, I coached in Assabet Valley for about 13 years." The coaching position at Assabet was volunteer, but Kay said it helped her to become a full-time coach: "But I had been fortunate because it had been a good program for a long time and I started coaching 12-and-under and then coached 14 and then 15 and then 17. Then I coached the 20-and-overs. So, it was a great experience. It's a big part of why I've been successful because I've always been careful about how I chose my experiences. In order to do well, you have to be good at what you do, but you need good players and you need a good organization and all the way through I've been able to do that." While at Assabet, Kay also coached the Massachusetts State Select Team, a group of 19-and-under or 17-and-under girls, and took them to Europe to play internationally at the end of the year.

It was partly because of her international experience that Kay was selected as an assistant coach for the US national team at the 1990 World Championship. That experience helped her coaching career tremendously: "I look back and there's a few [experiences] that really stick out, and that was one of them — being an assistant coach and in a very fortunate position at that age [27], getting that experience ... even though I had paid my dues." Kay went through the selection process for head coach of Team USA in 1992 and was among the final four candidates. "I applied to go through and learn from the process and it was one of those situations where I knew I wasn't going to get the job," she said. "Coach McCurdy was here at the University of New Hampshire (UNH) prior to me and had been coaching a long time. Everybody knew he was going to get the opportunity. But I thought it would be good to go through the process — learn how to present myself and do all that — and I did." Although she wasn't on the coaching staff in 1992, Kay worked with USA Hockey through all their training camps and tryouts for the team. Since Kay already had some international experience, and since there was an effort to give as many women as possible international opportunities, Margaret Degidio, head coach of Brown, was sent to Finland.

Kay had other opportunities in 1992, when she was selected as the head coach for women's ice hockey at UNH. It was the first time that coaching was her full-time job. While at UNH, Kay gained respect in the women's hockey circuit. "I think that at UNH the tradition of the program before I got here, and the success that I had ... now we've been able to build on that along with the growth of the sport. And having the support of the Athletic Department has been unbelievable," she said. "The opportunities are increasing and we're at a point right now where we're up to 11 scholarships and when I came we had none my first two years here. They used to have them and they got cut and when I came they didn't have them. Now, just in that short amount of time, we're from zero to 11. Probably in the next year or two we'll be able to get up to 18 and be fully funded just like the men's team."

Kay respects the differences between the men's hockey program and doesn't demand equal portions of the athletic budget. She concedes that the women's program doesn't need as much money as the men's and only asks that her program get the equipment and budget that it needs to run a successful program. Kay believes one of the biggest factors that makes the women's program a success is the support it gets from the men's program and the entire staff at UNH. "We take great pains here and our support staff does, to treat — even though we don't [sell out] the building — to treat the women's game exactly as we would a men's game," she said. "It sounds like a little thing, but I'm a big believer in: you have to treat it that way if you want it to get that way. That's the philosophy that we've used. We use the same off-ice officials that staff the men's games. We're trying to do all the little things like that in order to get it to a point where it will be like that. We're trying to treat it that way. I think that we're extremely fortunate. I don't think there are too many places still where the men's program is as supportive as ours is of us. It's not just good for the relationship but it's a great recruiting tool because people are immediately impressed by the fact that here we are down here together, and our locker rooms are the same and the facility treats us the same. That goes a long way with the women's sports. And I think that someone's got to step forward and do that and we're doing it."

Kay is continually striving to improve the quality of the women's game on the college level. "There are a lot of women's college programs that still maybe only have 15, 18, players, so everybody plays every game, everybody dresses," Kay noted. "For the past couple of years here we've got 29 or 30, so people sit just

Karen Kay became the first female head coach of a national team in 1994 when she led Team USA to a silver medal at the World Championship.

like you would with the men's program. I think it's an important part. There are other college coaches that say, 'Why do you guys have 30 players? We've only got 20. Isn't that a hassle?' It is. It's a lot more difficult to coach when you've got 30 instead of 18 and everyone's happy because everyone dresses. But, if you want to teach them anything, this is how a Division I program is supposed to be run. And, that's what you should be shooting for. Then, the players are more competitive. Then, the girls learn how to be competitive everyday at practice not just when they go out for those 30 games. So, that's another area where we've been trying to say, 'That's the way it should be in a Division I school.' Anybody can play 30 games. That's not where you're going to get to the next level. It's going to be what you're practicing against everyday, so that's what we really try to work off of here when we're recruiting to the kids and to the parents."

Kay continued, "The game is getting a lot more competitive at this level now and our season is so long. The kids start training off the ice the day after Labour Day when they get here to start school and we go until March 15. Then we usually take about two weeks off. Then we come back and do a lot of physical testing off the ice for the last six weeks of school. Then they have a program they do all summer, a condition program. So, it's gotten to be such a long season and the game's gone to a different level at the college level that we get a lot more kids hurt. It's getting to be a lot more like the men's game where every game you come out and somebody's got a little something wrong with them. So, you're constantly shuffling line-up and you didn't see that before in the women's game."

Kay fought the battle for respect as a player growing up in a boys' league, but she says it's even more difficult to prove to people that women can be good coaches. According to her, female coaches and referees also have another responsibility, which is to provide role models to the players on the bench and the young girls in the stand. Kay hopes she is proving to them that they don't have to associate hockey with men in terms of coaching and refereeing. In 1994 she became the first female head coach of Team USA. She was also a final candidate for the position of head coach for the 1997 national team and the Olympic team — a position which went to Ben Smith. While Kay respects the experience Smith brought to the position, with previous men's Olympic teams to his credit, her goal is to coach an Olympic team. She believes that with her foresight and dedication to coaching she will succeed. "There aren't that many quality women coaches right now at a high level," she said. "It's very competitive and you're always in a position where you've got to do ten times as much as the guy next to you even at the coaching level right now in order to succeed. That can get frustrating at times, just like it has been for women in other sports. But, if you're real good at what you do and it's your passion and you want to pursue it then you're going to keep working at it. I think now I face just as many challenges coaching as I did playing, as far as competing with the men goes. And, that experience playing in the beginning where I only had that kind of opportunity is helping me now. It's made me a better coach."

Kay sees more opportunities for women coaches in the future. "A lot of these players who are going to be on the '98 team, it will probably be their last hurrah as players, and I think there's quite a few of them that want to get into coaching," she said. "Now, with all their experiences, they'll do a quality job and that's what we need. But, it's a little hard being in this position … at the same time you feel that responsibility, because you've had all these experiences that no other woman has had. As much as you might get discouraged at times, you need to keep going because you're the one who's already fought through all that. And if you don't keep going, who is going to get the opportunity?"

Many colleges and universities in the US are trying to hire female coaches for the women's sports programs. In 1972, 90 percent of women's teams were coached by women. By 1996, that number had dropped to about 48 percent. This statistic is misleading, however, because the number of women participating in intercollegiate sports during that period increased more than 800 percent. In hockey the pool from which to choose coaches is limited. The addition of World Championship teams, Olympic teams and other international events have extended the number of years women can play competitively, thus keeping would-be coaches out on the ice a bit longer. After the first Olympics, some players may retire and join the coaching ranks. It is likely they will find coaching positions without much effort, as many US colleges and universities are expected to upgrade or add women's hockey programs. As it stands, many of the teams on the East Coast are coached by women. The top three women's hockey programs — University of New Hampshire, Providence College and Brown University — are all coached by women. Over the next five to 10 years, the number of women coaching women's hockey will undoubtedly increase substantially.

Three former US national team members have already gone on to coach. After 1990, Julie Andeberhan made a tough decision and quit hockey at the elite level. She had just experienced the first Women's World Championship in Ottawa and had come away with a silver medal. She decided to move on with her life, got married and moved to California, where her husband was working. Within a few months she started coaching a soccer team and then landed the head coaching job at California State University at Hayward. Andeberhan had been coaching since her senior year in high school when she began working summer camps as a coach. She knew then that she wanted to get involved in coaching. "I really enjoy the teaching aspect of it," she said, "and I really enjoy helping people maximize their potential." Andeberhan is now the Head Women's Ice Hockey Coach at Cornell University.

Because of the number of colleges and universities offering women's hockey, the American Women's Hockey Association (AWHA) was formed in the early 1990s. It is made up of active members — coaches of varsity and club college teams — and allied members — private school and high school coaches, and anyone who wants more information about women's hockey. In all, there are nearly 100 members. The AWHA was established to oversee things at the college level and keep communication lines open between the different programs.

Recently, the AWHA has become more active, and members have met in the fall and the spring each year. Some coaches have also gone to the men's coaching convention in Florida in the spring. The AWHA has begun to actively solicit members, particularly allied membership. It offers a directory of women's ice hockey coaches at colleges and universities, and publishes three newsletters a year to keep members informed on what's happening with women's ice hockey. Founding members hope that allied members will use the AWHA as a tool to learn about women's ice hockey programs at colleges. For its active members, the association discusses how the women's leagues should be structured and the issues they face as coaches, such as officiating and the length of the games. The AWHA also hosts a seniors' banquet for all the college seniors and presents an award to one senior voted as most valuable player by all the coaches.

In Canada, coaching a university team is an option for many women, but in the past there have been few varsity teams. While Ontario and Quebec have had university leagues since the 1970s, there has been little activity in the Maritimes or western Canada. In December 1996, however, the Canadian Interuniversity Athletic Union announced that it would stage its first national championship in women's hockey. This will likely inspire more universities to begin women's varsity ice hockey programs. An invitational tournament held at the University of Alberta in January 1997 included six universities from the western provinces: the University of Alberta, the University of Calgary, the University of Lethbridge, the University of British Columbia, the University of Saskatchewan and the University of Manitoba.

Coaching opportunities are also available with Canadian women's national and provincial teams. The 1990 Team Canada coaching staff included two men and a woman. Dave McMaster, the head coach, coached at the University of Toronto at the time. His two assistants were Rick Polutnik, a women's club team coach in Red Deer, Alberta, and Lucie Valois, an active member of the women's hockey community in Quebec. By 1995, the women's national team was coached by three women. Shannon Miller from Calgary, Alberta was the head coach. Her assistants were Melody Davidson from Castor, Alberta, and Karen Hughes, who had replaced Dave McMaster as the University of Toronto coach. Miller was also the head coach for the women's national team that competed at the 1997 World Championship. Miller has gained a tremendous amount of international experience through her involvement with the women's coaching pool of the Canadian

259

Team Canada Head Coach Shannon Miller (left) and Assistant Coach Danielle Sauvageau on the bench during the 1996 Three Nations Cup.

Hockey Association (CHA). Assistant coach Danielle Sauvageau from Quebec also came from the CHA's women's coaching pool. The other assistant coach, Ray Bennett from Alberta, was involved with the women's national program for the first time.

The addition of the Canada Winter Games and the national under-18 championships has also created new coaching positions with provincial select teams. At the 1995 Canada Games in Grand Prairie, Alberta, at least three teams had former national team players on their coaching staff — New Brunswick had Stacey Wilson, Diane Michaud was with Quebec and Alberta's coaching staff included Shirley Cameron.

A handful of women have found success outside the women's game. Coaching skating is one of the few professions in which women have been able to break through to the NHL. Barbara Williams, for example, was the first official female skating coach in the NHL when she instructed the New York Islanders in 1977. Williams had been a champion figure skater. She also coached the New Jersey Devils and four farm teams. Audrey Bakewell has also instructed the pros, including the Edmonton Oilers, the New York Rangers and Calgary Flames, and runs her own power skating schools and summer hockey camps in western Canada, Europe and in the US.

In 1992, at the age of 26, Deborah Wright became the first female scout for an NHL team when she was hired by the San Jose Sharks. Wright began scouting as a hobby. At age 18 she began regularly attending junior hockey games in Ottawa, Ontario, and was interested in the wide range of performances by the players. She began tracking statistics and made notes during the games. She got her first scouting job two years later at a tournament in Hull, Quebec. An official from the Trois-Rivières (Quebec) junior club noticed her working in the stands and offered her a part-time position on the staff. She scoured the Quebec midget and junior leagues for talent. Then Pierre Dorion of the NHL's Central Scouting Bureau advised Wright of the part-time scouting position in San Jose. Her sharp eye for technical ability and skill, and her ability to sense the proper hockey attitude has helped Wright make it to the big leagues.

ADMINISTRATIVE OPPORTUNITIES

There are very few paid administrative positions in women's hockey organizations. The CHA established a full-time administrative position for the women's program in August 1990. Glynis Peters has held the position since that time and holds the title of Manager — Women's Program. She is the only person working exclusively on the women's hockey program in the national office. At the provincial level, nearly all administrative positions in female hockey are volunteer. Two exceptions exist. The Ontario Women's Hockey Association (OWHA) has a paid administrative coordinator position. The OWHA is currently overhauling its structure and hopes to develop some management roles, including the current administrative coordinator and a new development coordinator. The Quebec Ice Hockey Federation does not have an exclusive position for female hockey, although one of its professional staff members oversees some activities in female hockey.

In 1993, three women held powerful positions in Canadian junior hockey. Chris Segiun was chairperson for the Ontario Hockey Federation's 37 junior clubs and in 1996 she became the first female board president. Pat Parker was president of the Central Ontario Junior Hockey League, which had 10 clubs, and had been involved in hockey on a volunteer basis for over 20 years. Pat Adams was president of the Maritime Junior A League and its seven teams. She had previously presided over the Nova Scotia Senior Hockey League and the Maritime Senior Hockey League after getting her start as a hockey secretary.

Susie Mathieu is another example of opportunities available for women in hockey administration. Mathieu was the tournament organizer of the 1996 World Cup. In 1976 she made arrangements for the US hockey team to play in the World Championship in Vienna, Austria. She had worked in public relations for the St. Louis Blues of the NHL for 19 years at a time when women simply did not hold that type of position. But Mathieu proved she was more than capable. She got bodies in the seats despite some shaky times, through five ownership changes and, during the 1980s, a potential move to Saskatoon. In 1986, Mathieu received her "big break" when new Blues owner Mike Shanahan asked her to develop a marketing and promotions department. Mathieu became the department's first vice-president. As World Cup tournament organizer, Mathieu was responsible for setting up the arenas in which the games were played, arranging licensing agreements for merchandise, and working with the NHL and its players.

Another career in hockey administration might be an athletic director, who oversees all of the sports at a high school or college. While the position isn't apparently based on gender, but rather on leadership, it has still been a tough field to crack for women. In 1996, of 305 Division I colleges in the US, only 17 had female athletic directors. Pat Richardson became the first woman to direct a high school athletic program in Massachusetts when she took the reigns of Assabet Valley Regional Vocational School in Marlborough in September 1973. At that time, there was still some criticism about whether or not it was appropriate for a woman to have access to a men's or boys' locker room. Most of the concern came from male coaches or other athletic directors. Students seemed to be unaffected by her gender. In 1983, San Diego State was one of the first schools to hire a female athletic director, but in more than 10 years since, the numbers have been slow to rise. In August 1988, Phyllis Hedges became the first woman to serve as president of any national co-ed sports organization when she accepted the position with the National Association of Intercollegiate Athletics. Just two and a half years later, the National Collegiate Athletic Association (NCAA) acquired its first female president, Judy Sweet. A few months later, Barbara Hedges became the first athletic director of an NCAA Division I school with football at the University of Washington.

WEARING THE STRIPES

Refereeing is another option for women who love hockey. Women have been calling penalties and off-sides since the 1970s. As the popularity of hockey increases and the number of players and teams multiply, the need for officials increases as well. Nineteen thousand officials registered with USA Hockey in 1997, an increase of more than 100 percent over the past 10 years. The number of female officials registered — approximately 450 — is low in comparison, but it is encouraging that 300 of the women are 17 and under. In recent years, USA Hockey has made a commitment to developing qualified female officials for international events, such as the Olympics, particularly those involving women's teams. In the summer of 1994, the first-ever development camp was conducted for female officials. One of the purposes of the program was to identify female officials for advancement in the system and for potential use in international games. The International Ice Hockey Federation (IIHF) has also asked member countries and federations to start developing more women's officials for competition. The US currently has up to 10 candidates who could step into that type of competition. USA Hockey has also made a financial commitment towards using a large number of women's officials in the women's national championships. The goal is to work towards making female referees competitive at any level.

In 1994, American Heather McDaniel became the first female to ever referee a professional hockey game when she called a game in the Central Hockey League, a men's semi-professional league in and around Ohio. McDaniel was 22 and had been a hockey referee for six years. Now a Level 4 referee, the highest USA Hockey rating, she became interested in officiating after a fall ended her figure-skating career. In an interview with Kevin Paul Dupont of *The Boston Globe* in 1994, Bryan Lewis, head of officiating for the NHL, said he doesn't think the goal of having female referees in the NHL is far-fetched. Like men, women can be strong skaters, quick decision-makers and cool under pressure — all trademarks of a good referee.

For over 20 years, many Canadian leagues have favoured using female referees — within limits. In the 1970s, Administrative Director Tom Hogan of the Metropolitan Toronto Hockey League (MTHL) said he was more than willing to allow women to officiate games involving players up to 12 years old in the lower A and AA levels. Hogan and others, however, questioned whether a woman could keep up with the skating of a 16-year-old or whether she would be capable of handling the fighting that took place in the MTHL. At the time, Dave McMaster, coach of the University of Toronto Lady Blues, had been using female referees for five years. The school traditionally used male MTHL referees, but the officiating was particularly horrid one night, prompting McMaster to give women a chance. He then began alternating between male and female referees.

In Canada, improving officiating of female hockey games is an important issue. In 1973, the CHA founded the National Referee Certification Program to train and certify officials, but these referees generally gained experience in men's

and boys' hockey. As a result, female hockey volunteers spent a lot of time trying to help officials understand the difference between the men's checking game
and the women's "non-checking with contact" game. In many cases, referees
were expected to call women's games without any previous experience with the
game. The CHA addressed the issue by producing a video to be shown at officiating clinics. The video teaches referees how to call the female game by allowing
contact but not full bodychecking.

The 1996-1997 CHA registration report listed 31,090 officials who were certified throughout all levels of accreditation. Only 520, or 1.7 percent, of these registrants, however, were female and 86 percent of the women referees were only
certified at Level I or Level II. No doubt, increasing the number of female officials is critical.

Major efforts have also been made to develop women as officials. For the 1991
and 1995 Canada Winter Games, all officials for women's hockey were women
from across Canada. The CHA is continuing to develop women officials for national and international events. The IIHF assigns all officials for international
hockey championships. Generally, they inform different countries of how many
officials they need for an event and the countries will submit lists which rank
their officials from the top down. There is a conscious effort in Canada to develop women as officials for women's international hockey. In July 1996, the IIHF
held a major training camp in Spain for the top 21 female officials from around
the world.

Karen Kost was one of those who attended. She had invested a lot of time and
energy into becoming a skilled official and felt she deserved the opportunity to
represent Canada at the camp. Kost has become a highly skilled and knowledge-
able referee and at the moment is the most qualified female official in Canada.
The Canadian officiating program includes six levels. The top referees are capable of doing international and national junior and senior men's hockey. Kost is
at Level V and is able to do international senior women's hockey. She became
an official in 1980 and has never returned to the game as a player. In fact, her
experiences with a women's team ultimately stirred her refereeing interest: "I
started playing when I moved to Calgary, for the Calgary Adanac team. There
was a point in time when I was the second leading scorer on the team. I was on
the bench when I remember missing a shift and then a second shift and the next
thing I knew I wasn't playing in the game at all. It was hard to figure out, since it

was the western Canada championship, the Western Shield. I was so terribly disturbed, I took my gloves and helmet off and said if this is the way it is going to be then I will enjoy the game from another perspective. So I stood on the end of the bench and started talking to the linesman. He suggested that I should try my hand at officiating. Sure enough, we met at the Mount Royal College in Calgary in September of 1980. We went to class together where I was introduced to others and I haven't looked back since."

Kost's officiating career has taken her to different parts of the world, places she never would have seen if it weren't for hockey. As a Level V, she has gained lots of international experience. "The first World Championship that I was chosen for was in Finland in 1992 as a linesman," she said. "That was an absolutely awesome experience. It was the first time I had seen an international ice surface. I was fortunate to be chosen to do the bronze medal game between Finland and Sweden. The game went into double overtime and then a shoot-out decided the winner. It was great! My second experience was as a referee at the 1994 World Championship in Lake Placid, New York. I learned a tremendous amount from that experience. My next assignment took me to the Women's European Championship in Yaraslovl, Russia. That was in 1996."

Kost believes that being an official is a long learning process. "There is a learning curve that all hockey officials must go through," she said. "Young officials should try not to move up the ranks too quickly. It is important to obtain a sound grounding in the basics of hockey officiating, because everything builds and manifests itself from that point. As officials, we never stop learning. I think back to when I was in Lake Placid, and I learned so much from that experience as a referee. When I went to Russia, I felt much more comfortable and I think it showed, because I had the best tournament I ever had. It's all based on experience and learning from others."

Kost has found that the routine for officials selected for an international event is just as strict as for the players on the teams. "There is usually someone from the IIHF supervising the officials ... as we had in Russia," she said. "Each morning we were on the ice at 7:00 a.m. for our training sessions. After our workout, we would return to the hotel, shower, have breakfast together and then attend our daily meeting at 10:00 a.m. The officials also received a lot of feedback on their performance, both from the IIHF representative and from coaches. The supervisor might come into the dressing room between periods if there was something important to discuss, otherwise he would sit down with you after the game to discuss a particular situation or call," said Kost. "It was absolutely incredible because, what that does is it brings consistency among all tournament officials and that is what you want to achieve as an officiating team in a tournament."

Kost has also found that when an official first goes to a tournament, all she or he can count on is the first one or two assignments. The games assigned later in the tournament depend upon performance. "The teams know that the officials are from different countries and the first one or two games are needed to build the necessary consistency for the

COURTESY MICHAEL DESJARDINS

Top-level official Karen Kost keeping her eye on the action at the 1997 Esso National Hockey Championship.

remaining games," she said. As a measure of her outstanding skill and experience, Kost was assigned the gold medal game at the 1996 European Championship.

Along with officiating women's hockey, Kost has been assigned boys' midget AAA and junior B games in Edmonton, Alberta, where she lives. She believes this mix of both men's and women's competitive hockey helps her improve her skills as an official. In fact, Kost's work in male hockey is not common for a woman. "I have worked my way up like any guy has done," she commented. "I think from that perspective you get respect. Plus, on top of that, once you go through the program for a number of years and you get experience and opportunities as I have, they expect you to give something back into the program. I believe that goes without saying. So I have done that and I'm still doing that. I am in my seventh year as an instructor [of officiating clinics] in the Canadian Hockey Officiating Program. Also, I have been Referee-in-Chief for the Alberta Winter Games in Lethbridge [in 1996]."

SPORTS REPORTING

Since newspapers have mostly focused on men's teams, there have been few opportunities for women sports reporters to cover women's sports. Some women have tried to cover the men's professional games, but with limited success.

In Canada, historically there have been several women journalists who not only wrote about sports, but wrote about women's sports. Many began writing as early as the 1920s and some lasted through the late 1960s. These journalists wrote daily and weekly columns exclusively devoted to women's sport. They brought news about hockey, softball, basketball, golf, track and field, speed skating, cycling, swimming, diving and many other sports, and played a critical developmental role at the time by improving the profile of women's sports in general. One of these journalists, Phyllis Griffiths, wrote for the *Toronto Telegram* from 1928 to 1949. She was an active basketball player in the Toronto Ladies League and through her column, The Girl and the Game, she raised questions and issues about all women's sports in general. Alexandrine Gibb also wrote of women's sports in Toronto in the 1930s and 1940s. Her column, "In the No Man's Land of Sport," appeared in the *Toronto Daily Star*. Bobbie Rosenfeld was a star hockey player in the 1920s and 1930s. In 1937, after arthritis ended her career, she became a sports journalist for the Toronto *Globe and Mail*. Her column started as the "Feminine Sports Reel" then later became the "Sports Reel" until the end of her career in 1957.

Women in other parts of Canada were a part of the female sports reporting scene as well. In Montreal, Quebec, Myrtle Cook's column, "In the Women's Sports Light," was a regular feature in the *Montreal Star* for approximately 40 years, from the late 1920s to 1968. Women's sports in the western part of the country received coverage as well. From 1937 to 1942, in Manitoba, Lillian "Jimmie" Coo wrote "Cherchez la Femme" in the *Winnipeg Free Press*. From 1943 to 1945, in British Columbia, Anne Stott and Ruth Wilson wrote "Femmes in Sport" and "Femmes and Foibles in Sport," for the *Vancouver Sun*. In Alberta, Patricia Page's contribution to the *Edmonton Journal*'s "Feminine Flashes" ran from 1935 to 1940. This tradition of women writing about women's sports continues in Canada with, for example, Wendy Long writing for the *Vancouver Sun* and Lois Kalchman writing for the *Toronto Star*, along with many other women writing about both men's and women's sports.

In the US, hockey journalist Shirley Fischler estimates that there are approximately 20 female hockey writers covering the NHL. Fischler has been writing about hockey in the United States since 1970. She is managing editor of *The Fischler Report* and also contributes to *Rinkside Magazine*. She has been instrumental in the advancement of female journalists in the hockey industry. She started writing as a freelance reporter for the *Toronto Star*. Her first article about hockey focused on hockey wives and was in the woman's section of the newspaper. In 1970-1971, while writing for the *Kingston/Whig Standard* in Kingston, Ontario, she was denied access to the Madison Square Garden press box. She sued the New York Rangers and Madison Square Garden and gained access by the end of the season. Despite the conflict, Fischler had fallen in love with the game: "I wanted to stay connected to the game professionally. I didn't just want to be a spectator." Despite the advances she made, more than 15 years later women were still discriminated against. Women were banned from men's locker rooms as late as 1986, when Helene Elliott, a reporter for *Newsday* on Long Island, was prohibited from the Toronto Maple Leaf dressing room. Elliott had been a sports reporter for five years. She continued to have difficulty with most teams in the NHL, but was eventually accepted.

For the 1973-1974 season, Fischler became the colour commentator for the New England Whalers (of the now defunct World Hockey Association). The only other female colour commentator for a professional men's hockey team has been Sherry Ross, who provided the colour for the New Jersey Devils in the early 1990s.

Other women broadcasters have been successful in semi-professional hockey leagues. In 1977, Bev Lockhart was one of the pioneers of women's sportscasting when she took the microphone as play-by-play announcer for the Swift Current Broncos of the Saskatchewan Junior Hockey League for radio station CKSW. The first radio broadcasting of women's ice hockey was announced by a man. The game was between the Goodlands Starettes and an all-star team selected from teams in Elkhorn, Pierson, Souris and Brandon, Manitoba, and it was broadcast on November 22, 1975, on CJRB Radio in Boissevain, Manitoba.

Mrs. Harry Johnson was certainly among the earliest US women sportscasters. In the late 1930s and early 1940s, she provided colour commentary for her husband, who was a sports announcer for the Central States Broadcasting in Omaha, Nebraska. By the 1960s, women began to surface in greater numbers on the sportscasting scene. In the mid-1960s, Jane Chastain became the first woman to work for CBS, a national network. On the other hand, Jeannie Morris had proven journalistic skills which did not protect her against the discrimination she encountered. In the early 1970s, she was assigned to cover a Minnesota Vikings vs. Chicago Bears game at the Metropolitan Stadium in Minnesota. Morris was banned from the press box because of her gender and was forced to report on the game from the seats outside in the snow. When she finally was allowed into the press box later in the year, she still had to travel outside to use the public women's washroom in the halls of the stadium.

Also in the early 1970s, women began announcing sports scores on the eleven o'clock local news. ABC hired Ellie Riger as the first female sports producer. More women were hired in the 1970s, including Plyllis George, a former Miss America, and Jayne Kennedy. Unfortunately, neither woman had any journalistic training and were hired just to add a feminine dimension to sports. That trend gradually changed and in 1976 Lesley Visser became the first female beat reporter for the NFL. But it was Gayle Gardner who helped make sportscasting for women a viable profession. She was the first female sports anchor to appear on a major network, and it wasn't just a pretty face that got her there. To attain the position, Gardner put in many hours of hard work and never gave up.

Sports announcing was a more difficult nut to crack, simply because there were fewer jobs. Several women, including Suzyn Waldman, made their mark. Waldman was the first female radio beat reporter for the New York Yankees and the New York Knicks. She was also the first woman announcer on a nationally televised baseball game, and the first woman to do play-by-play for the Yankees. Gayle Sierens broke the NFL barriers when she announced a game in 1987.

Television has always lagged behind radio and print when offering sports anchoring or reporting jobs to women. Cable sports network ESPN was the first network to hire women for anchor positions. In 1989, Cable News Network (CNN) hired Hannah Storm as a sports anchor, and CBS offered three sports positions to women — Lesley Visser on *NFL Today*, Mary Carillo on tennis and Andrea Joyce on *College Football Report*.

Sports broadcasting has skyrocketed in the last 10 years and could provide exciting opportunities for women. In 1994, for instance, Nanci Donnellan became the first female to have her own nationally syndicated sports show as the "Fabulous Sports Babe" on ESPN radio. By 1996, she was broadcasting in more than 170 markets.

Whether or not players and fans believe that the women's game is distinct from the men's, one fact remains certain — women are gradually gaining more opportunities to play, coach, referee, administer, broadcast and report on hockey. Women bring another perspective to the sport, both in playing and in watching it. There is still much ground to cover, but the women are getting there one smooth stride at a time.

EPILOGUE

The national women's hockey teams of both the United States and Canada will be competing in the 1998 Winter Olympics. The US team is in full swing. By the fall of 1997, the players had been together for a year, training and competing in a full-time program. Come the new year, they will have travelled to Canada, China and Finland for international exhibitions and tournaments, and of course, they will have played at the 1997 World Championship in Kitchener, Ontario. On the other hand, members of Team Canada have trained individually for most of 1997. They had a training camp in January to select the team to compete at the World Championship in March. The decision to centralize for Olympic preparation was under discussion at the beginning of the year, but it was not until September 1997 that the team began training together in Calgary.

Which team will be better prepared for Olympic competition — Canada or the United States? Given the amount of time that USA Hockey's players and coaches have devoted to training and competing, they seem to be the obvious choice. But the results of the 1997 Women's World Championship in March show the race will be very close. Canada and the US battled in overtime until Canada finally prevailed on Nancy Drolet's third goal of the game to win 4-3. The intensity and physical play only served to enhance the rivalry between the two countries. The US team played physical and disciplined hockey. Whenever Canada tried to pull ahead, the Americans kept the game close by answering quickly with their own goal. By the time the Olympics roll around, however, the Americans might be *too* ready. Perhaps the Canadians, with their train-at-home, train-together strategy will have the edge. It is hard to say. There is no doubt that both countries want gold and have their plans in place. And there is no doubt that once both teams get to Nagano, the games will be great to watch!

What effect will the Olympics have on girls' and women's hockey? Many predict that in the US, female hockey will take off at both the grassroots and the college levels. Colleges that currently have club teams will turn varsity. More teams and conferences will be added and within a few years the women will be vying for a National Collegiate Athletic Association championship. Likewise, in Canada, more girls will be attracted to the game. Local minor hockey associations will begin to manage and promote girls' teams and leagues. More universities will start women's varsity programs in order to capture the Canadian Interuniversity Athletic Union title. Provincial branches will continue to develop elite youth hockey and the players from these events will flow into the ever increasing talent pool for the national women's team.

With the growing interest in women's sports, whether it be basketball, soccer or hockey, it would seem natural that more women would coach, manage or referee the growing number of teams, or cover, announce and produce the shows that spotlight female athletes. Whether or not that scenario unfolds remains to be seen, but one fact is certain: The opportunities for women beyond the game are just starting to unfold. Many of the players who have experienced the growth of the game — through girls' grassroots hockey to outstanding US college and Canadian senior women's teams to international tournaments — are just now retiring. Whether they choose coaching, refereeing, sports journalism or another avenue, these women will have a wealth of knowledge to share with future generations of the game to raise the sport to even higher levels.

The growth has already started, it seems. In their promotional material, the Canadian Hockey Association predicts that 150,000 women and girls will be playing hockey in Canada by the year 2000. As of 1997, total female registration in the country was 27,305. The many girls who play on boys' teams are not included in that number. If they were estimated at 1,000 players for each province, the national total would rise to just less than 38,000 players. Will this increase to 150,000 in four years? Maybe. From 1990, when the first World Championship was held, to 1997, the rate of growth for female hockey in Canada has been 235 percent. Compressed into three years, from 1997 until 2000, at this rate the projected number of women and girls playing hockey in Canada would be around 100,000. A similar projection for the US would take the total registration there to approximately 74,000 women and girls playing hockey by the year 2000.

This is certainly a pretty picture.

But when you consider that, historically, the impact of the state, provincial, national and international programs has been somewhat lacklustre, perhaps the expectations around the Olympics are over-rated. Will the excitement of the Olympics entice more girls to join?

Senior and junior national and, in Canada, provincial, team programs focus on girls who are already playing hockey. In fact, they focus on girls who are not just players but good players. For real growth to occur, new players have to join. The Olympics has to pique girls' interest in hockey, and USA Hockey and the CHA have to provide a place for them to play. The grassroots needs to be developed. Can current facilities support the growth? In the US and Canada, there is already a problem with overpopulation in grassroots hockey — too many teams wanting to play and not enough rinks or hours in the day to accomodate them.

Unfortunately, with the Olympic surge, elite hockey is becoming the focus. It is important to remember that girls want to join hockey just to play on a team, not necessarily to play on an Olympic team. As this book has shown, even elite players recognize the importance of getting everyone to play, not just the best players. Former Team USA player Kelly Dyer has had parents approach her and brag about their child's prospects for Olympic glory. Dyer commented, "I've had mothers come up to me about their nine-year-old daughters and say, 'She's going to be on the Olympic team.' I said, 'Good, why don't you let her be 10 first?' I think it's very important to work hard, but to always have fun."

In our discussions with players, coaches and administrators, the importance of girls being able to play hockey with other girls was constantly mentioned. Mentioned just as often, however, was that the important thing is to get the girls playing — period. In Ontario, there has been a 30-year struggle to ensure that girls play on girls' teams. In Massachusetts, the popularity of Bobby Orr and the Boston Bruins made the state a hotbed for female hockey, resulting in plenty of girls' teams. Both Ontario and Massachusetts started to promote female hockey in the 1970s, when fighting for separate teams apart from the boys seemed the best way to make progress. The reality of the matter in the 1990s is that in many areas, boys and girls play together. Resources are tight, ice time is limited and girls' minor hockey numbers are only just starting to grow. In the meantime, girls just have to find a way to play. In many places across the US and Canada, this means female hockey volunteers continuing to cooperate with existing youth hockey associations to develop co-ed minor hockey. While this gets girls started in hockey, the ultimate goal is to develop girls' hockey programs.

The creation of national, world and Olympic events in women's hockey is an exciting yet risky venture. Exciting because women are able to expand their game to higher levels. Risky because of the danger that high performance will become the focus and grassroots development ignored. Balancing elite performance with development of the game is the greatest challenge in female hockey today.

FURTHER RESOURCES

BOOKS

Etue, E. and M. Williams. *On The Edge: Women Making Hockey History*. Second Story Press, Toronto, 1996.

Guttmann, A. *Women's Sports: A History*. Columbia University Press, New York, 1991.

Lenskyj, H. *Out of Bounds, Women, Sport & Sexuality*. The Women's Press, 1986.

McFarlane, B. *Proud Past, Bright Future: One Hundred Years of Canadian Women's Hockey*. Stoddart Publishing, Toronto, 1994.

Nelson, M. Burton. *Are We Winning Yet?* Random House, 1991.

Rhéaume, M. with C. Gilbert. *Manon: Alone In Front Of The Net*. HarperCollins Publishers Ltd., Toronto, 1993.

Stewart, B. *She Shoots...She Scores! A Complete Guide to Women's Hockey*. Doubleday Canada Limited, Toronto, 1993.

MAGAZINES

Women's Hockey, a publication of *Hockey Player Magazine* and the journal of women's ice and roller hockey in North America. Editorial and Administrative offices: 1715 W. Grand River, Okemos, MI 48864. Telephone: (517) 347-1172.

INTERNET SOURCES

Canadian Hockey Association website: http://www.canadianhockey.ca

Andria Hunter's women's hockey website: http://www.cs.toronto.edu/~andria

USA Hockey website: http://www.usahockey.com

Subscribers to the women-in-hockey mailing list: women-in-hockey@plaidworks.com

OTHER PRINT SOURCES

Coach puts job on line for girl. *Globe & Mail*, February 18, 1981.

Blauvelt, Harry. Women slowly crack athletic director ranks. *USA Today*, October 2, 1996.

Bonanno, Rocky. Making changes in locker rooms. *Newsday*, October 23, 1994.

Bonfiglio, Jeremy. Women's and girls' hockey. *American Hockey Magazine*, September, 1996.

Canadian Hockey Association:

   Minutes from various Plenary, Minor Council, Centre of Excellence, Research and Development Council and Female Council meetings between 1988 and 1997.

   Registration reports between 1982 and 1997.

   CHA Promotional material for Women's Hockey Program.

Canadian Provincial and City Archives:

   Claresholm Museum.

   City of Cambridge Archives.

City of Edmonton Archives.

City of Toronto Archives.

Fernie Historical Society.

Red Deer and District Museum and Archives.

University of Alberta Archives.

Cobb, Nathan. Just who is the Fabulous Sports Babe? *The Boston Globe*, January 11, 1996.

Dupont, Kevin Paul. Woman ref ready for first pro call. *The Boston Globe*, October 30, 1994.

Enright, Greg. Hockey powerhouse. *Toronto Star*, August 18, 1996.

Gearan, John. Women sitting pretty. *Telegram & Gazette*, August 14, 1996.

Hockey Hall of Fame Archives, Toronto, Ontario

Heckman, Diane. Women & athletics: A twenty year retrospective on Title IX. *Miami Entertainment and Sports Law Review I*, 1992.

Hunsaker, Lee. Just the beginning. *American Hockey Magazine*, Spring 1987.

Kalchman, Lois. No girls, hockey league told. *Toronto Star*, October 18, 1984.

Kalchman, Lois. Controller seeks end to hockey ban on females. *Toronto Star*, November 3, 1984.

Kalchman, Lois. Etobicoke to defy warning by MTHL about playing girls. *Toronto Star*, November 7, 1984.

Kalchman, Lois. Let girls play, MTHL told. *Toronto Star*, May 21, 1985.

Kalchman, Lois. Girls heading south — to play. *Toronto Star*, December 9, 1985.

Kalchman, Lois. Women take on key junior hockey roles. *Toronto Star*, December 5, 1993.

Mando, Rosann. Midwest college club league established. WOMEN'S HOCKEY, January/February 1997.

Marmo, Tony: Personal Collection

NCAA Gender Equity Study Summary of Results, April 1997.

Ormsby, Mary. Female scout will be at ease with these Sharks. *Toronto Star*, July 25, 1992.

Smith, Rick. Metrowest hockey's global ambassadors. *The Middlesex News*, July 21, 1996.

Stevens, Julie. (1992) The development and structure of women's hockey in Canada. Master's Thesis. Queen's University, Kingston, Ontario.

Stiles, Janet. Pat Richardson: First woman to direct high school athletic program in Mass. *Beacon Sports Light*, November 23, 1973.

University of Minnesota Archives.

USA Hockey, Colorado Springs, Colorado.

Villalobos, Michael P. The Civil Right Restoration Act of 1987. *Marquett Sports Law Journal*, 1990.

Westlaw - Legal Research CD-Rom Library.

Wilde, T. Jesse. Gender equity in athletics: Coming of age in the '90s. *Marquette Sports Law Journal*, Spring 1994.

Women in Sportscasting: A Brief History. *Insider Newsletter*, American Sportscasters Association, August 1996.

Women's World Ice Hockey Championships: Official programs from 1990, 1992, 1994, and 1997.

Women's Hockey magazine.

Young Prochnow, Bettina. You've Come A Long Way Baby! *Hockey Player*, January 1995.

MAJOR HOCKEY ORGANIZATIONS IN NORTH AMERICA

CANADA

National Hockey Organization:
Canadian Hockey Association, National Office
Suite 607, 1600 James Naismith Drive
Gloucester, Ontario K1B 5N4
Tel: (613) 748-5613   Fax: (613) 748-5709

Canadian Hockey Association, Calgary Office
2424 University Drive NW
Calgary, Alberta T2N 3Y9
Tel: (403) 777-3636   Fax: (403) 777-3635

Regional Hockey Centres:
British Columbia Centre of Excellence
800 Griffiths Way
Vancouver, British Columbia V6B 6G1
Tel: (604) 899-7770   Fax: (604) 899-7771

Western Centre of Excellence
Canadian Airlines Saddledome
P.O. Box 1060, Station M
Calgary, Alberta T2P 2K8
Tel: (403) 777-3642   Fax: (403) 777-3641

Toronto Centre of Excellence
30 Yonge Street
Toronto, Ontario M5E 1X8
Tel: (416) 360-8432   Fax: (416) 360-1316

Quebec Centre of Excellence
1275 St-Antoine Ouest
Montreal, PQ H3C 5H8
Tel: (514) 925-2241   Fax: (514) 925-2243

Atlantic Centre of Excellence
Building B, Hilyard Place
580 Main Street, Suite 206
Saint John, New Brunswick E2K 1J5
Tel: (506) 652-8494   Fax: (506) 652-6641

Provincial Hockey Associations:
British Columbia Amateur Hockey Association
6671 Oldfield Road
Saanichton, British Columbia V8M 2A1
Tel: (250) 652-2978   Fax: (250) 652-4536

Hockey Alberta
#1-7875-48th Avenue
Red Deer, Alberta T4P 2K1
Tel: (403) 342-6777   Fax: (403) 346-4277

Northwest Territories Amateur Hockey Assoc.
P.O. Box 93
Fort Simpson, Northwest Territories X0E 0N0

Saskatchewan Amateur Hockey Association
1844 Victoria Avenue, East
Regina, Saskatchewan S4N 7K3
Tel: (306) 789-5101   Fax: (306) 789-6112

Ontario Women's Hockey Association
1100 Central Parkway West, Unit 30
Mississauga, Ontario L5C 4E5
Tal: (905) 275-8866   Fax: (905) 275-2001

Hockey Manitoba
200 Main Street
Winnipeg, Manitoba R3C 4M2
Tel: (204) 925-5759   Fax: (204) 925-5761

Fédération Québecoise de Hockey sur Glace
4545 av Pierre-de-Coubertin
C.P. 1000, Succursale M
Montreal, Quebec H1V 3R2
Tel: (514) 252-3079   Fax: (514) 252-3158

New Brunswick Amateur Hockey Association
P.O. Box 456, 165 Regent Street, Suite 4
Fredericton, New Brunswick E3B 4Z9
Tel: (506) 453-0862   Fax: (506) 453-0868

Nova Scotia Hockey Association
6080 Young Street, Suite 910
Halifax, Nova Scotia B3K 2A2
Tel: (902) 454-9400   Fax: (902) 454-3883

Prince Edward Island Hockey Association
68 University Avenue
Charlottetown, Prince Edward Island C1A 6B5
Tel: (902) 566-5171   Fax: (902) 894-8412

Newfoundland Amateur Hockey
15A High Street, P.O. Box 176
Grand Falls/Windsor, Newfoundland A2A 2J4
Tel: (709) 489-5512   Fax: (709) 489-2273

Independent Hockey Program:
Olympic Oval High Performance Female
Hockey Program
2500 University Drive NW
Calgary, Alberta T2N 1N4
Tel: (403) 220-7954   Fax: (403) 284-4815

Women's Sports Organization
Canadian Association for the Advancement of
Women in Sport and Physical Activity (CAAWS)
1600 James Naismith Drive
Gloucester, Ontario K1B 5N4
Tel: (613) 748-5793   Fax: (613) 748-5775

UNITED STATES

National Hockey Organization:
USA Hockey, Inc.
4965 N. 30th Street
Colorado Springs, CO 80919
Tel: 800-566-3288

Karen Lundgren
Girls/Women Section Director
15868 Silver Lake Lane
Addison, MI 49220
Tel: (517) 547-6565   Fax: (517) 547-3066

District Registrars:
(Please note: Each district in the US has a
registrar. Contact USA Hockey for more
information on names and addresses.)

Atlantic: Delaware, Eastern Pennsylvania, New
Jersey
Joan Schofield
3 Pendleton Drive
Cherry Hill, NJ 08003
Tel: (609) 424-8343   Fax: (609) 751-8968

Central: Illinois, Iowa, Kansas, Missouri,
Nebraska, Wisconsin
Bill Peluse
509 Wingfoot Drive
North Aurora, IL 60542
Tel: (630) 406-6011   Work: (630) 879-6200
Fax: (630) 879-9111

Massachusetts
Ron DiFilippo
83 Maple Street
Wenham, MA 01984
Tel: (508) 774-2813   Work: (617) 969-2501
Fax: (508) 750-6107

Michigan
Ralph Bammert
234 Tamarack Street
Laurium, MI 49913
Tel: (906) 337-2370   Fax: (906) 337-2370

Mid-American: Indiana, Kentucky, Ohio,
Western Pennsylvania, West Virginia
Roger Sharrer
3142 Vernon Avenue
Pittsburgh, PA 15227-4229
Tel: (412) 884-3452
Hockey Office: (412) 884-2922
Fax: (412) 884-3272

Minkota: Minnesota, North Dakota, South
Dakota
Gerry Brown
3327 Yosemite Avenue South
St. Louis Park, MN 55416
Tel: (612) 929-5565   Fax: (612) 929-5565

New England: Connecticut, Maine, New
Hampshire, Rhode Island, Vermont
Wayne Letourneau
58 Meridan Street
Burlington, VT 05401
Tel: (802) 658-6473 / (802) 769-4681
Fax: (802) 769-4760

New York
Tom Korpolinski
P.O. Box 587
Coudersport, NY 16915
Tel: (814) 274-1723   Work: (814) 272-9021
Fax: (814) 274-1723

Pacific: Alaska, Hawaii, California, Nevada,
Oregon, Washington
Frank Lang
5703 Sun Ridge Court
Castro Valley, CA 94552
Tel: (510) 728-0133   Fax: (510) 728-0133

Rocky Mountain: Arizona, Colorado, Montana,
New Mexico, Oklahoma, Idaho, Texas, Utah,
Wyoming
Bruce Karinen
6379 Senoma Drive
Salt Lake City, UT 84121-2264
Tel: (801) 278-8865   Fax: (801) 278-6914

Southeastern: Alabama, Arkansas, District of
Columbia, Florida, Georgia, Louisiana,
Maryland, Mississippi, North Carolina, South
Carolina, Tennessee, Virginia
John Crerar
12800 Cherrywood Lane
Bowie, MD 20715
Tel: (301) 352-2342   Fax: (401) 721-6804

College Programs:
Eastern College Athletic Conference
P.O. Box 3
Centerville, MA 02362
Tel: (508) 771-5060   Fax: (508) 771-9481

INDEX

JOANNA AVERY is a journalist and communications manager. As a member of the American Sportscasters Association, she has covered the Boston Bruins and a variety of AHL teams. More recently, she has turned her attention to the growing American fascination with women's hockey. She lives in Westboro, Massachusetts.

JULIE STEVENS is a PhD student specializing in organizational analysis and sport in the Faculty of Physical Education and Recreation at the University of Alberta in Edmonton. She was the top female athlete in team sport at Queens University, where she wrote her MA thesis on women's hockey.

Polestar Book Publishers takes pride in creating books that enrich our understanding of the world and introduce discriminating readers to exciting writers. These independant voices illuminate our history, stretch the imagination and engage our sympathies. Here are some of our best-selling sports titles.

Behind the Mask: The Ian Young Goaltending Method, Book One
Beyond the Mask: The Ian Young Goaltending Method, Book Two
IAN YOUNG AND CHRISTOPHER GUDGEON
Drills, practice techniques, equipment considerations and more are part of this unique goaltending series.
$18.95 Can/$14.95 US

Celebrating Excellence: Canadian Women Athletes
WENDY LONG
A collection of biographical essays and photos that showcases more than 200 athletes who have achieved excellence.
$29.95 Can/$24.95 US

Get the Edge: Audrey Bakewell's Power Skating
AUDREY BAKEWELL
Skating specialist Audrey Bakewell provides basic and advanced drills for power skating, a skill fundamental to the game of hockey.
$18.95 Can/$16.95 US

Lords of the Rink
IAN YOUNG AND TERRY WALKER
Here is every goaltenders handbook, including physical and psychological techniques, and many game-action photos. The final book in the Ian Young goaltending trilogy.
$18.95 Can/$14.95 US

Our Game: A Collection of All-Star Hockey Fiction
DOUG BEARDSLEY, editor
From the Forum to the backyard rink, this collection of 30 stories illuminates the essence of the hockey soul.
$18.95 Can/$16.95 US

Thru the Smoky End Boards: Canadian Poetry About Sports and Games
KEVIN BROOKS AND SEAN BROOKS, editors
The glory of sport is celebrated in this anthology of poems from more than 70 poets.
$16.95 Can/$14.95 US

Polestar titles are available from your local bookseller. For a copy of our catalogue, contact:
POLESTAR BOOK PUBLISHERS, *publicity office*
103-1014 Homer Street
Vancouver, BC
Canada V6B 2W9
(604) 488-0830; fax (604) 669-8250